DELIBERATE PRACTICE IN
PSYCHEDELIC-ASSISTED THERAPY

Essentials of Deliberate Practice Series
Tony Rousmaniere and Alexandre Vaz, Series Editors

Deliberate Practice in Child and Adolescent Psychotherapy
Jordan Bate, Tracy A. Prout, Tony Rousmaniere, and Alexandre Vaz

Deliberate Practice in Cognitive Behavioral Therapy
James F. Boswell and Michael J. Constantino

Deliberate Practice in Dialectical Behavior Therapy
Tali Boritz, Shelley McMain, Alexandre Vaz, and Tony Rousmaniere

Deliberate Practice in Emotion-Focused Therapy
Rhonda N. Goldman, Alexandre Vaz, and Tony Rousmaniere

Deliberate Practice in Motivational Interviewing
Jennifer K. Manuel, Denise Ernst, Alexandre Vaz, and Tony Rousmaniere

Deliberate Practice in Multicultural Therapy
Jordan Harris, Joel Jin, Sophia Hoffman, Selina Phan, Tracy A. Prout, Tony Rousmaniere, and Alexandre Vaz

Deliberate Practice in Psychedelic-Assisted Therapy
Shannon Dames, Andrew Penn, Monnica Williams, Joseph A. Zamaria, Tony Rousmaniere, and Alexandre Vaz

Deliberate Practice in Psychodynamic Psychotherapy
Hanna Levenson, Volney Gay, and Jeffrey L. Binder

Deliberate Practice in Rational Emotive Behavior Therapy
Mark D. Terjesen, Kristene A. Doyle, Raymond A. DiGiuseppe, Alexandre Vaz, and Tony Rousmaniere

Deliberate Practice in Schema Therapy
Wendy T. Behary, Joan M. Farrell, Alexandre Vaz, and Tony Rousmaniere

Deliberate Practice in Systemic Family Therapy
Adrian J. Blow, Ryan B. Seedall, Debra L. Miller, Tony Rousmaniere, and Alexandre Vaz

ESSENTIALS OF DELIBERATE PRACTICE SERIES

TONY ROUSMANIERE AND ALEXANDRE VAZ, SERIES EDITORS

DELIBERATE PRACTICE IN PSYCHEDELIC-ASSISTED THERAPY

SHANNON DAMES

ANDREW PENN

MONNICA WILLIAMS

JOSEPH A. ZAMARIA

TONY ROUSMANIERE

ALEXANDRE VAZ

AMERICAN PSYCHOLOGICAL ASSOCIATION

Published by
American Psychological Association
750 First Street, NE
Washington, DC 20002
https://www.apa.org

Order Department
https://www.apa.org/pubs/books
order@apa.org

Typeset in Cera Pro by Circle Graphics, Inc., Reisterstown, MD

Printer: Sheridan Books, Chelsea, MI
Cover Designer: Mark Karis

Library of Congress Cataloging-in-Publication Data

Names: Dames, Shannon, author.
Title: Deliberate practice in psychedelic-assisted therapy / authored by
   Shannon Dames, Andrew Penn, Monnica Williams, Joseph A. Zamaria,
   Tony Rousmaniere, and Alexandre Vaz.
Description: Washington, DC : American Psychological Association, [2024] |
   Series: Essentials of deliberate practice | Includes bibliographical
   references and index.
Identifiers: LCCN 2023041033 (print) | LCCN 2023041034 (ebook) |
   ISBN 9781433841712 (paperback) | ISBN 9781433841729 (ebook)
Subjects: LCSH: Hallucinogenic drugs–Therapeutic use. | BISAC: PSYCHOLOGY /
   Education & Training | PSYCHOLOGY / Psychopathology / Post-Traumatic
   Stress Disorder (PTSD)
Classification: LCC RC483.5.H3 D36 2024 (print) | LCC RC483.5.H3 (ebook) |
   DDC 615.7/883–dc23/eng/20240104
LC record available at https://lccn.loc.gov/2023041033
LC ebook record available at https://lccn.loc.gov/2023041034

https://doi.org/10.1037/0000399-000

Printed in the United States of America

10 9 8 7 6 5 4 3 2 1

We dedicate this book to two groups of practitioners who built the foundation on which our knowledge stands.

First, this book is dedicated to practitioners in Indigenous cultures who use psychedelic medicines in a ceremonial context for healing, community, and spiritual purposes. The modern use of psychedelics has benefited from the wisdom and lessons learned by Indigenous traditions through ceremonial use of psychedelics over thousands of generations, and practitioners owe them a debt of gratitude.

We also dedicate this book to the 20th- and 21st-century practitioners in Western cultures who championed the ethical, compassionate, and conscientious use of psychedelics for healing, spiritual growth, creativity, and insight. They risked their careers and personal freedom to serve their clients, despite the prohibition of legal services and widespread misinformation from the "war on drugs." Without their courage and dedication, the current rising wave of psychedelic research and advocacy would not be possible. We stand on your shoulders.

Contents

Series Preface

Tony Rousmaniere and Alexandre Vaz

We are pleased to introduce the Essentials of Deliberate Practice series of training books. We are developing this book series to address a specific need that we see in many psychology training programs. The issue can be illustrated by the training experiences of Mary, a hypothetical second-year graduate school trainee. Mary has learned a lot about mental health theory, research, and psychotherapy techniques. Mary is a dedicated student; she has read dozens of textbooks, written excellent papers about psychotherapy, and receives near-perfect scores on her course exams. However, when Mary sits with her clients at her practicum site, she often has trouble performing the therapy skills that she can write and talk about so clearly. Furthermore, Mary has noticed herself getting anxious when her clients express strong reactions, such as getting very emotional, hopeless, or skeptical about therapy. Sometimes this anxiety is strong enough to make Mary freeze at key moments, limiting her ability to help those clients.

During her weekly individual and group supervision, Mary's supervisor gives her advice informed by empirically supported therapies and common factor methods. The supervisor often supplements that advice by leading Mary through role-plays, recommending additional reading, or providing examples from her own work with clients. Mary, a dedicated supervisee who shares tapes of her sessions with her supervisor, is open about her challenges, carefully writes down her supervisor's advice, and reads the suggested readings. However, when Mary sits back down with her clients, she often finds that her new knowledge seems to have flown out of her head, and she is unable to enact her supervisor's advice. Mary finds this problem to be particularly acute with the clients who are emotionally evocative.

Mary's supervisor, who has received formal training in supervision, uses supervisory best practices, including the use of video to review supervisees' work. She would rate Mary's overall competence level as consistent with expectations for a trainee at Mary's developmental level. But even though Mary's overall progress is positive, she experiences some recurring problems in her work. This is true even though the supervisor is confident that she and Mary have identified the changes that Mary should make in her work.

The problem with which Mary and her supervisor are wrestling—the disconnect between her knowledge about psychotherapy and her ability to reliably perform psychotherapy—is the focus of this book series. We started this series because most therapists experience this disconnect, to one degree or another, whether they are beginning trainees or highly experienced clinicians. In truth, we are all Mary.

To address this problem, we are focusing this series on the use of deliberate practice, a method of training specifically designed for improving reliable performance of complex skills in challenging work environments (Rousmaniere, 2016, 2019; Rousmaniere et al., 2017). Deliberate practice entails experiential, repeated training with a particular skill until it becomes automatic. In the context of psychotherapy, this involves two trainees role-playing as a client and a therapist, switching roles every so often, under the guidance of a supervisor. The trainee playing the therapist reacts to client statements, ranging in difficulty from beginner to intermediate to advanced, with improvised responses that reflect fundamental therapeutic skills.

To create these books, we approached leading trainers and researchers of major therapy models with these simple instructions: Identify 10 to 12 essential skills for your therapy model where trainees often experience a disconnect between cognitive knowledge and performance ability—in other words, skills that trainees could write a good paper about but often have challenges performing, especially with challenging clients. We then collaborated with the authors to create deliberate practice exercises specifically designed to improve reliable performance of these skills and overall responsive treatment (Hatcher, 2015; Stiles et al., 1998; Stiles & Horvath, 2017). Finally, we rigorously tested these exercises with trainees and trainers at multiple sites around the world and refined them based on extensive feedback.

Each book in this series focuses on a specific therapy model, but readers will notice that most exercises in these books touch on common factor variables and facilitative interpersonal skills that researchers have identified as having the most impact on client outcome, such as empathy, verbal fluency, emotional expression, persuasiveness, and problem focus (e.g., Anderson et al., 2009; Norcross et al., 2019). Thus, the exercises in every book should help with a broad range of clients. Despite the specific theoretical model(s) from which therapists work, most therapists place a strong emphasis on pantheoretical elements of the therapeutic relationship, many of which have robust empirical support as correlates or mechanisms of client improvement (e.g., Norcross et al., 2019). We also recognize that therapy models have already-established training programs with rich histories, so we present deliberate practice not as a replacement but as an adaptable, transtheoretical training method that can be integrated into these existing programs to improve skill retention and help ensure basic competency.

About This Book

The 11th book in the Essentials of Deliberate Practice series is on psychedelic-assisted therapy (PAT). PAT training combines the study of theory, hands-on experiential learning, expert supervision, personal experience with psychedelic medicines, and the development of self-awareness. Experiential training involves trainees taking the role of both client and therapist, while the "client" works on personal material. Trainees often find the experiential component to be particularly potent and humbling because the therapeutic approach is experienced in a bottom-up, hands-on manner from the inside out.

Deliberate practice is intended as an additional piece designed to enhance this rich training tradition. Practice of skills set forth in this book can allow trainees to have the skills at their fingertips. Ideally, deliberate practice can help therapists integrate the core skills into their repertoire, allowing them to access needed skills in a flexible and authentic manner in response to the client context. The skills set forth in this book are the basic skills for PAT; they are not intended to be holistic or comprehensive. Deliberate practice is not intended to be the only training format through which PAT skills are acquired. It is vital for PAT practitioners to embrace a lifelong commitment to learning, personal growth, and receiving feedback from elders. Mentorship holds significant importance when working with psychedelic medicines, where unpredictability and ambiguity often arise. Enjoy your learning—enjoy the process!

Thank you for including us in your journey toward psychotherapy expertise. Now let's get to practice!

Acknowledgments

We acknowledge and honor the debt of gratitude we owe to the Indigenous peoples whose ancestral wisdom and cultural practices form the bedrock of psychedelic-assisted therapy. Their knowledge and respect for these substances have guided their communities with wisdom and reverence, offering an understanding of the interconnectedness of all beings and the vital role of these plants and substances in human experience. We recognize that the contemporary psychedelic renaissance owes its existence to the tireless efforts of Indigenous communities, who have not only preserved these ancient traditions but have also fought tirelessly against cultural erasure and exploitation. Their struggles have been instrumental in reclaiming the rightful place of these sacred substances within the broader consciousness of humanity. We extend our heartfelt appreciation to these communities for their resilience, knowledge, and generosity in sharing their wisdom and practices with the wider world. May we approach this work with humility, actively seeking to dismantle colonial legacies and foster true reciprocity in our relationships.

Our author team represents various universities and psychedelic care settings from the United States and Canada. The knowledge we share was first shared with us, forged through relationships with esteemed mentors and fellow travelers in the field. It is within the interplay of connection, the dynamic exchange of ideas, and the collective exploration of meaning that we transform what is merely "memorized" to what is truly "known." In particular, we extend heartfelt appreciation to Elder Geraldine Manson (C'Tasia) and Dr. Pamela Kryskow for their enduring wisdom, compassion, and unwavering integrity. They serve as constant reminders of what it means to walk a trustworthy path. We are deeply grateful for their selfless dedication as mentors in the psychedelic-assisted therapy field, generously offering countless volunteer hours to support and guide others on their journey. We also acknowledge Charles Raison, Clay Jackson, Noel Gardner, Rakesh Jain, and Saundra Jain for always creating a ready intellectual salon and for being wise elders, as well as Kate and Cyrus for reminding us that where you find love, you find your home.

We are grateful to Karin Gagnon for providing editorial advice and historical context for this book. We acknowledge Rodney Goodyear for his significant contribution to starting and organizing this book series. We are grateful to Susan Reynolds, David Becker, Elizabeth Budd, Joe Albrecht, and Emily Ekle at American Psychological Association (APA) Books for providing expert guidance and insightful editing that has significantly improved the quality and accessibility of this book. We would also like to acknowledge the International Deliberate Practice Society and its members for their many contributions and support for our work. We are deeply grateful to the late K. Anders Ericsson, the inventor of the concept of deliberate practice. Without his pioneering work on the development of expertise, this book series would not have been possible.

The exercise format in this book series has undergone extensive testing at training programs around the world. More than 130 testers (trainees, therapists, and supervisors) from 16 countries contributed to testing the exercises. We thank all the students, supervisors, and faculty who tested the exercises in this book. We especially want to thank Vancouver Island University's Psychedelic-Assisted Therapy Post-Graduate Certificate trainees, who tried out the responses as a component of the development process, with a special callout to Wes Taylor for providing consistent feedback along the way.

Overview and Instructions

In Part I, we provide an overview of deliberate practice, including how it can be integrated into clinical training programs for psychedelic-assisted therapy (PAT), and instructions for performing the deliberate practice exercises in Part II. **We encourage both trainers and trainees to read both Chapters 1 and 2 before performing the deliberate practice exercises for the first time.**

Chapter 1 provides a foundation for the rest of the book by introducing important concepts related to deliberate practice and its role in psychotherapy training more broadly and PAT training more specifically. We review the cultural and theoretical foundations of PAT, the arc of PAT training, the scope of the exercises in this book, and the role of deliberate practice in PAT training. We also individually review the 12 skills from these exercises.

Chapter 2 lays out the basic, most essential instructions for performing the PAT deliberate practice exercises in Part II. They are designed to be quick and simple and provide you with just enough information to get started without being overwhelmed by too much information. Chapter 3 in Part III provides more in-depth guidance, which we encourage you to read once you are comfortable with the basic instructions in Chapter 2.

Introduction and Overview of Deliberate Practice and Psychedelic-Assisted Therapy

Welcome to the world of psychedelic-assisted therapy (PAT). The goal of this book is to help therapists acquire and refine the fundamental skills necessary to be effective in helping clients with PAT. Psychedelics have been used by Indigenous and religious traditions around the world for millennia (e.g., Grof, 2019; McKenna, 1993; Schultz et al., 2011). For example, there is evidence to suggest that the use of psychedelics was an instrumental part of early Buddhist, Christian, Greek, and Hindu traditions (e.g., Crowley & Shulgin, 2019; Muraresku, 2020). More recently, the modern field of PAT has been influenced by three large bodies of knowledge. The first, and oldest, are Indigenous cultures that use psychedelic medicines in a ceremonial context for healing, community, and spiritual purposes (e.g., Grof, 2019; R. Harris, 2017; Metzner, 2015). The second body of knowledge that influenced PAT comes from practitioners, mostly in the United States and Europe between the 1950s and 1990s, including psychotherapists, physicians, religious clergy, and anthropologists (e.g., Fadiman, 2011; Harner, 1990; Richards, 2015; Shulgin & Shulgin, 1990, 2002; H. Smith, 1964; Stolaroff, 1994, 2020). Third, and most recently, PAT has been informed by a wave of clinical research performed since the mid-1990s (e.g., Mithoefer et al., 2016; Nutt & Carhart-Harris, 2021). For example, since 1996, more than 50 randomized clinical trials and nine meta-analyses have been published on clinical applications of psilocybin (Oregon Psilocybin Evidence Review Writing Group, 2021; Rush et al., 2022).

Due to the multifaceted roots of PAT, we aspire to cultivate a "relationally informed" approach to learning and teaching that views knowledge as more than an object to be used but rather as a dynamic relationship to be fostered. We aim to honor the interconnectedness of knowledge and the cultural roots and communities from which it emerges. Without a relational approach to knowledge application, there is a risk of cultural appropriation, where knowledge is taken out of its relational and cultural context for personal gain (Celidwen et al., 2023). Seeking consent from Indigenous cultures when integrating their teachings into our practice is an act of honoring the knowledge sharer, who is also the knowledge keeper. By seeking permission, we

https://doi.org/10.1037/0000399-001

Deliberate Practice in Psychedelic-Assisted Therapy, by S. Dames, A. Penn, M. Williams, J. A. Zamaria, T. Rousmaniere, and A. Vaz

demonstrate acknowledgment and respect for the original holders of that knowledge (e.g., Celidwen et al., 2023).

It is vital for PAT practitioners to embrace a lifelong commitment to learning and personal growth. This commitment is reinforced by practicing research-informed approaches and receiving the invaluable support of mentorship. Mentorship holds significant importance when working with psychedelic medicines, where unpredictability and ambiguity often arise (e.g., Shulgin & Shulgin, 1990, 2002). In most Indigenous cultures, individuals aspiring to facilitate medicine-assisted healing undergo extensive training, supervision, and mentorship spanning many years to attain competency (e.g., Metzner, 2015). Likewise, learning to provide PAT requires developing personal and professional awareness, regulation skills, intuitive capacities, empathic development, somatic approaches, a multicultural orientation, and the confidence to navigate a wide range of challenging situations (e.g., Stolaroff, 2020). It is crucial for Western-trained practitioners to approach this training with humility and recognize themselves as novices in this field for a significant period of time. Completing a training program does not equate to practice competency or readiness. Instead, these activities provide an introduction to the field, a foundation in core skills that are critical for safety, and a path for ongoing skill development to gain proficiency over time. Experiential training also provides an opportunity to explore one's reactions to the strong emotional content often present in PAT (Shulgin, 2019), which can help practitioners develop the "person of the therapist" and inner skills of psychotherapy (e.g., Aponte & Kissil, 2016; Rousmaniere, 2019). To set realistic expectations and support trainees in continuous learning and skill development, we strongly recommend the creation of a comprehensive plan for continuous education and mentorship as an integral component of their PAT training.

Overview of the Deliberate Practice Exercises

The main focus of the book is a series of 14 exercises for PAT skills. The first 12 exercises each represent an essential PAT skill. The last two exercises are more comprehensive, consisting of an annotated transcript and improvised mock therapy sessions that teach practitioners how to integrate all these skills into more expansive clinical scenarios. Table 1.1 presents the 12 skills that are covered in these exercises.

Throughout all the exercises, trainees work in pairs under the guidance of a supervisor and role-play as a client and a therapist, switching back and forth between the

TABLE 1.1. The 12 Psychedelic-Assisted Therapy Skills Presented in the Deliberate Practice Exercises

Beginner Skills	Intermediate Skills	Advanced Skills
1. Redirecting to the body	5. Boundaries and informed consent	9. Navigating strong emotions
2. Compassionately witnessing strong emotions	6. Responding to relational ruptures	10. Making sense of the experience: integration I
3. Exploring intentions and expectations	7. Working with the client's internal conflict	11. Working with disappointment: integration II
4. Cultural considerations: racially and ethnically diverse communities	8. Addressing transference	12. Embodying insights: integration III

two roles. Each of the 12 skill-focused exercises consists of multiple client statements grouped by difficulty—beginner, intermediate, and advanced—that calls for a specific skill. For each skill, trainees are asked to read through and absorb the description of the skill, its criteria, and some examples of it. The trainee playing the client then reads the statements, which present potentially challenging conversations and situations that can emerge in the process of PAT. The trainee playing the therapist then responds in a way that demonstrates the appropriate skill. Trainee therapists will have the option of practicing a response using the one supplied in the exercise or immediately improvising and supplying their own.

After each client statement and therapist response couplet is practiced several times, the trainees will stop to receive feedback from the supervisor. Guided by the supervisor, the trainees are instructed to try statement–response couplets several times, working their way down the list. In consultation with the supervisor, trainees will go through the exercises, starting with the least challenging and moving through to more advanced levels. The dyad (client–therapist) or the triad (supervisor–client–therapist) will have the opportunity to discuss whether exercises present too much or too little challenge and adjust up or down depending on the assessment.

Trainees, potentially in consultation with supervisors, can decide which skills they wish to work on and for how long. On the basis of our testing experience, we have found that practice sessions last about 1 to 1.25 hours to receive maximum benefit. After this, trainees become saturated and need a break.

Ideally, PAT learners will both gain confidence and achieve competence by practicing these exercises. Competence is defined here as the ability to perform a PAT skill in a manner that is flexible and responsive to the client. Skills have been chosen that are considered essential to PAT and that practitioners often find challenging to implement.

The skills identified in this book are not comprehensive in the sense of representing all one needs to learn to become a competent PAT clinician. Some will present particular challenges for trainees. A short history of PAT and a brief description of the deliberate practice methodology is provided to explain how we have arrived at the union between them.

The Goals of This Book

The primary goal of this book is to provide an introduction to core PAT skills. The expression of that skill or competency may look somewhat different across clients or even within session with the same client.

The PAT deliberate practice exercises are designed to achieve the following:

1. Help PAT therapists develop the ability to apply the skills in a range of clinical situations.

2. Provide PAT therapists with an opportunity to observe and explore their emotional reactions to the strong emotional content often present in PAT.

3. Move the skills into procedural memory, so that PAT therapists can access them even when they are tired, stressed, overwhelmed, or discouraged.

4. Provide PAT therapists in training with an opportunity to exercise each particular skill using a style and language that is congruent with who they are.

5. Provide the opportunity to use the PAT skills in response to varying client statements and affect. This is designed to build confidence to adopt skills in a broad range of circumstances within different client contexts.

6. Provide PAT therapists in training with many opportunities to fail and then correct their failed response based on feedback. This helps build confidence and persistence.

Finally, this book aims to help trainees discover their own personal learning style so that they can continue their professional development long after their formal training is concluded.

Who Can Benefit From This Book?

This book is designed to be used in multiple contexts, including graduate-level courses, supervision, postgraduate training, and continuing education programs. It assumes the following:

1. The trainer is knowledgeable about and competent in PAT.

2. The trainer can provide good demonstrations of how to use PAT skills across a range of therapeutic situations, via role-play and/or video, or that the trainer has access to examples of PAT being demonstrated by others through video examples.

3. The trainer can provide feedback to students regarding how to craft or improve their application of PAT skills.

4. Trainees will have accompanying reading, such as books and articles, that explain the theory, research, and rationale of PAT and each particular skill. Recommended reading for each skill is provided in the sample syllabus (Appendix C).

The deliberate practice exercise format covered in this book series was piloted in training sites from 16 countries across four continents (North America, South America, Europe, and Asia). This book is designed for trainers and trainees from different cultural backgrounds worldwide.

This book is also designed for those who are training at all career stages, from beginning trainees, including those who have never worked with real clients, to seasoned therapists. All exercises feature guidance for assessing and adjusting the difficulty to target precisely the needs of each individual learner. The term "trainee" in this book is used broadly, referring to anyone in the field of professional mental health who is endeavoring to acquire PAT psychotherapy skills.

Deliberate Practice in Psychotherapy Training

How does one become an expert in their professional field? What is trainable, and what is simply beyond our reach, due to innate or uncontrollable factors? Questions such as these touch on our fascination with expert performers and their development. A mixture of awe, admiration, and even confusion surround people such as the artists Mozart, Mary Cassat, Leonardo da Vinci, or more contemporary top performers such as the painter Frida Kahlo, basketball legend Michael Jordan, and chess virtuoso Garry Kasparov. What accounts for their consistently superior professional results? Evidence suggests that the amount of time spent on a particular type of training is a key factor in developing expertise in virtually all domains (Ericsson & Pool, 2016). "Deliberate practice" is an evidence-based method that can improve performance in an effective and reliable manner.

The concept of deliberate practice has its origins in a classic study by K. Anders Ericsson and colleagues (1993). They found that the amount of time practicing a skill and the quality of the time spent doing so were key factors predicting mastery and acquisition. They identified five key activities in learning and mastering skills: (a) observing one's own work, (b) getting expert feedback, (c) setting small incremental learning goals just beyond the performer's ability, (d) engaging in repetitive behavioral rehearsal of specific skills, and (e) continuously assessing performance. Ericsson and his colleagues termed this process deliberate practice, a cyclical process that is illustrated in Figure 1.1.

Research has shown that lengthy engagement in deliberate practice is associated with expert performance across a variety of professional fields, such as medicine, sports, music, chess, computer programming, and mathematics (Ericsson et al., 2018). People may associate deliberate practice with the widely known "10,000-hour rule" popularized by Malcolm Gladwell in his 2008 book *Outliers*, although the actual number of hours required for expertise varies by field and by individual (Ericsson & Pool, 2016). This, however, perpetuated two misunderstandings.

The first is that this is the number of deliberate practice hours that everyone needs to attain expertise, no matter the domain. In fact, there can be considerable variability in how many hours are required.

The second misunderstanding is that engagement in 10,000 hours of work performance will lead one to become an expert in that domain. This misunderstanding holds considerable significance for the field of psychotherapy, where hours of work experience with clients has traditionally been used as a measure of proficiency (Rousmaniere, 2016). Research suggests that the amount of experience alone does not predict therapist effectiveness (Goldberg et al., 2016). It may be that the quality of deliberate practice is a key factor.

Psychotherapy scholars, recognizing the value of deliberate practice in other fields, have called for deliberate practice to be incorporated into training for mental health professionals (e.g., Bailey & Ogles, 2019; Hill et al., 2020; Rousmaniere et al., 2017; Taylor & Neimeyer, 2017; Tracey et al., 2015). There are, however, good reasons to question

FIGURE 1.1. Cycle of Deliberate Practice

Note. From *Deliberate Practice in Emotion-Focused Therapy* (p. 7), by R. N. Goldman, A. Vaz, and T. Rousmaniere, 2021, American Psychological Association (https://doi.org/10.1037/0000227-000). Copyright 2021 by the American Psychological Association.

analogies made between psychotherapy and other professional fields, like sports or music, because by comparison psychotherapy is so complex and free form. Sports have clearly defined goals, and classical music follows a written score. In contrast, the goals of psychotherapy shift with the unique presentation of each client at each session. Therapists do not have the luxury of following a score.

Instead, good psychotherapy is more like improvisational jazz (Noa Kageyama, cited in Rousmaniere, 2016). In jazz improvisations, a complex mixture of group collaboration, creativity, and interaction are coconstructed among band members. Like psychotherapy, no two jazz improvisations are identical. However, improvisations are not a random collection of notes. They are grounded in a comprehensive theoretical understanding and technical proficiency that is only developed through continuous deliberate practice. For example, prominent jazz instructor Jerry Coker (1990) listed 18 skill areas that students must master, each of which has multiple discrete skills including tone quality, intervals, chord arpeggios, scales, patterns, and licks. In this sense, more creative and artful improvisations are actually a reflection of a previous commitment to repetitive skill practice and acquisition. As legendary jazz musician Miles Davis put it, "You have to play a long time to be able to play like yourself" (Cook, 2005, p. 112).

The main idea that we would like to stress here is that we want deliberate practice to help PAT therapists become themselves. The idea is to learn the skills so that you have them on hand when you want them. Practice the skills to make them your own. Incorporate those aspects that feel right for you. Ongoing and effortful deliberate practice should not be an impediment to flexibility and creativity. Ideally, it should enhance it. We recognize and celebrate that psychotherapy is an ever-shifting encounter and by no means want it to become or feel formulaic. Strong PAT therapists mix an eloquent integration of previously acquired skills with properly attuned flexibility. The core PAT responses provided are meant as templates or possibilities, rather than "answers." Please interpret and apply them as you see fit, in a way that makes sense to you. We encourage flexible and improvisational play!

Simulation-Based Mastery Learning

Deliberate practice uses simulation-based mastery learning (Ericsson, 2004; McGaghie et al., 2014). That is, the stimulus material for training consists of "contrived social situations that mimic problems, events, or conditions that arise in professional encounters" (McGaghie et al., 2014, p. 375). A key component of this approach is that the stimuli being used in training are sufficiently similar to real-world experiences, so that they provoke similar reactions. This facilitates *state-dependent learning*, in which professionals acquire skills in the same psychological environment where they will have to perform the skills (R. P. Fisher & Craik, 1977). For example, pilots train with flight simulators that present mechanical failures and dangerous weather conditions, and surgeons practice with surgical simulators that present medical complications. Training in simulations with challenging stimuli increases professionals' capacity to perform effectively under stress. For the psychotherapy training exercises in this book, the "simulators" are typical client statements that might actually be presented in the course of therapy sessions and call upon the use of the particular skill.

Declarative Versus Procedural Knowledge

Declarative knowledge is what a person can understand, write, or speak about. It often refers to factual information that can be consciously recalled through memory and often acquired relatively quickly. In contrast, procedural learning is implicit in memory; it "usually requires *repetition of an activity*, and associated learning is demonstrated through *improved task performance*" (Koziol & Budding, 2012, p. 2694, emphasis added). *Procedural knowledge* is what a person can perform, especially under stress (Squire, 2004). There can be a wide difference between their declarative and procedural knowledge. For example, an "armchair quarterback" is a person who understands and talks about athletics well but would have trouble performing it at a professional level. Likewise, most dance, music, or theater critics have a very high ability to write about their subjects but would be flummoxed if asked to perform them.

The sweet spot for deliberate practice is the gap between declarative knowledge, which tends to be limited to what we can memorize, and requires conscious effort to practically apply, and procedural knowledge, which reflects embodied ways of knowing, enabling ease of application. As we develop expertise, we develop more embodied knowledge. In other words, effortful practice should target those skills that the trainee could write a good paper about but would have trouble actually performing with a real client. We start with declarative knowledge, learning skills theoretically and observing others perform them. Once learned, with the help of deliberate practice, we work toward the development of procedural learning, with the aim of therapists having "automatic" access to each of the skills that they can pull on when necessary. This automatic access neutralizes the effort and nerves associated with completing unfamiliar tasks in the PAT session, enabling us to direct our attention to the relational process.

Psychedelic-Assisted Therapy

PAT is showing great promise in the treatment of mental health issues and in the promotion of wellness (e.g., Nutt & Carhart-Harris, 2021; Rush et al., 2022). The focus of this book is clinical training in PAT. However, clinical practice with psychedelic medicines currently takes place in the context of a shifting legal landscape and considerable public misinformation regarding psychedelics (e.g., Hart, 2022; Nutt, 2022). It is important for therapists to understand this context because clients will often present with related questions or concerns. Thus, in the following section, we present a brief review of this area.

From the 1950s to 1970s, early research on the use of psychedelics suggested that they had potential to benefit clinical treatment, personal growth, and human flourishing (e.g., Grof, 2019). This promising area of clinical research was shut down in the late 1960s when President Richard Nixon adopted the "war on drugs" as part of his political reelection strategy.[1] Popular media ran numerous reports about salacious psychedelic scandals, many of which have been proven false or exaggerated (Nutt, 2022; for a review, see Schlag et al., 2022). In 1971, Nixon declared drug abuse "public enemy number one" and established the agency that later became the Drug Enforcement

---

1. In a 1994 interview with journalist Dan Baum (2016), John Ehrlichman, who served as President Richard Nixon's assistant for domestic affairs, made the following remarks: "The Nixon campaign in 1968, and the Nixon White House after that, had two enemies: the antiwar left and Black people. You understand what I'm saying? We knew we couldn't make it illegal to be either against the war or Blacks, but by getting the public to associate the hippies with marijuana and Blacks with heroin and then criminalizing both heavily, we could disrupt those communities. We could arrest their leaders, raid their homes, break up their meetings, and vilify them night after night on the evening news. Did we know we were lying about the drugs? Of course, we did."

Administration (DEA). Almost all clinical research in psychedelics was shut down due to DEA regulations and stigma regarding psychedelics, partially a result of misinformation disseminated from Western governments (Hart, 2022; Nutt, 2022). However, this early period should not be romanticized because there were also a number of harmful psychedelic research studies and abusive treatments that were occurring at this time, underscoring the need for better approaches and ethical standards (e.g., Strauss et al., 2021).

In the mid-1990s, a new wave of clinical research on psychedelics began (e.g., Nutt & Carhart-Harris, 2021). At the time of this writing, at least eight major hospitals and research universities have created departments specifically dedicated to the study of psychedelic medicines, including Imperial College of London, Johns Hopkins, Massachusetts General Hospital, Mount Sinai, New York University, University of Wisconsin–Madison, and University of California–Los Angeles (e.g., Zarley, 2019). In the past 2 decades, researchers at these institutions have published a large body of peer-reviewed research demonstrating that psychedelic medicines can be effective (e.g., Rush et al., 2022) and safe when performed in the right context and with the appropriate training (e.g., Breeksema et al., 2022; Schlag et al., 2022). On the basis of the results of randomized, controlled trials, the U.S. Food and Drug Administration (FDA; n.d.) has declared both psilocybin and MDMA to be "breakthrough therapies," described as "a significantly improved safety profile compared with available therapy (e.g., less dose-limiting toxicity for an oncology agent), with evidence of similar efficacy." Psychedelic experiences have been found to increase well-being (e.g., Mans et al., 2021), and study participants commonly rate their psychedelic-healing experiences, despite often being challenging, as some of the most profoundly important experiences in their lives (e.g., Griffiths et al., 2006).

Despite this rise in clinical research, legal prohibition has made PAT hard to access, especially for Black and Indigenous peoples, people of color, low-income, and rural communities (e.g., Rea & Wallace, 2021; D. T. Smith et al., 2022). Veteran-advocacy groups that connect military veterans with PAT services to treat posttraumatic stress disorder must send their clients on expensive trips out of the country to receive treatment (e.g., https://heroicheartsproject.org/; https://vetsolutions.org/). Likewise, both media and government sources continue to disseminate misinformation about psychedelics. For example, as of this writing, the DEA lists psilocybin, LSD, and MDMA as "Schedule 1" drugs, which is defined as having "no currently accepted medical use" (U.S. DEA, n.d.), despite all the prior cited research. Marks (2021) noted, "Psilocybin has now been administered to more research subjects than some FDA-approved psychiatric medications." The DEA's stance on psychedelics is particularly puzzling given that highly addictive drugs that have caused widespread human suffering have been allowed to flourish, such as alcohol and opioids (Nutt, 2022).

How PAT Works

PAT works by reorienting the patient away from unhelpful patterns and toward a more functional framework of awareness (Schenberg, 2018; Watts & Luoma, 2020). The PAT treatment model is based on an integration of Indigenous traditions with multiple models of psychotherapy, including transpersonal, humanistic, experiential, cognitive behavior, and somatic therapies. It is considerably different from traditional therapy because it involves a medicinal adjunct that enables the client to enter a nonordinary state of consciousness. Grof (2000) termed psychedelics a "non-specific amplifier," meaning that clients often experience an amplification of whatever they are experiencing, whether it comes from their conscious thought, unconscious processes, or external environment. The way that psychedelic medicines open and engage with the unconscious is sometimes referred to as supporting clients' "inner healing intelligence"—the innate orientation that people have toward healing and wellness that is thought to, at times, become impeded by current or past circumstances and events (e.g., Gorman et al., 2021; Horton, et al., 2021). The concept of the inner healer is often invoked within the context of neuroplasticity research, which explores the brain's ability to reorganize itself and form new neural connections throughout life (e.g., Carhart-Harris et al., 2018). In PAT, psychedelic medicines can induce altered states of consciousness that may promote introspection, emotional release, and heightened receptivity to therapeutic insights (Schenberg, 2018). The inner healer concept suggests that the therapeutic benefits observed in psychedelic experiences are not solely due to the pharmacological effects of the substances but also to the inherent healing potential of the individual's mind and brain (Nichols et al., 2017). Psychedelic experiences may facilitate neuroplasticity by disrupting rigid patterns of thought and behavior, allowing for new perspectives, emotional processing, and the integration of previously inaccessible or repressed memories (Carhart-Harris & Nutt, 2017).

One of the major ways that PAT is different from traditional psychotherapy is the stance of the therapist. In PAT, the main role of the therapist is to facilitate the positive conditions necessary to let the psychedelic medicine and the client's inner healing intelligence do the work. Facilitative conditions for PAT include the clients internal psychological state and intentions, as well as the external environment in which PAT is performed (termed "set and setting"; Grof, 2019) and individual factors, including biology (Fogg et al., 2021).

This novel approach requires a different type of training and personal development from that required for traditional forms of therapy. Psychedelic medicines make clients especially vulnerable and permeable to outside influences. In PAT, the quality of practitioner presence has as much or more impact on the client as the therapist's actions (Grof, 2019). Because psychedelics put clients in an open and vulnerable state, PAT practitioners must be emotionally secure, be able to self-regulate, stay centered, behave ethically, and always be conscious of their disposition (Shulgin & Shulgin, 2002). When the therapist can be aware of their projections, remain self-regulated, be compassionate to themself and others, and be grounded in their body, the client's inner healing intelligence can do its work most effectively (Shulgin, 2019).

Practitioners providing PAT require a certain degree of confidence in nonordinary states of consciousness to provide PAT proficiently (e.g., Nielson & Guss, 2018). This confidence can be gained by experiencing nonordinary states themselves and by observing others in these states. The more secure the practitioner feels in their ability to understand and move through challenging PAT experiences intuitively, the more likely they are to promote a similar sense of confidence and security in their patient's ability to navigate such challenges. These benefits flow into all forms of safety, including psychological, cultural, and spiritual safety (Winkler et al., 2016). Thus, practitioners having personal experience using psychedelics is thought to promote more positive treatment outcomes (Mangini, 1998; Oram, 2014; Winkler & Csémy, 2014).

The Person of the Therapist in PAT

The exercises in this book are centered on the core elements of psychedelic therapy, encouraging somatic awareness, cultural safety, the capacity to leverage relational ruptures to facilitate healing, and the integration of insights into one's way of knowing, being, and doing. These exercises are not meant to promote a rigid way of "doing" PAT. Rather, they are meant to demonstrate the variety of ways a PAT session can unfold, reducing the risk of surprise. The experiential nature of deliberate practice is designed to uncover gaps in therapists' intuitive processes, identify therapists' blind spots, and to shine a light on areas of therapists' psychological and emotional selves that need to be tended to. Many of the exercise scenarios were designed to elicit strong emotions. Just like any journey from novice to expert (Benner, 1984), it is normal for students to feel activated by the scenarios and for exercises to feel effortful and awkward at first. Navigating one's emotions and insecurities in a safe practice environment mitigates the risk of therapeutic errors with real clients. It also reduces the risk of problematic countertransference emerging in therapy sessions. Conversely, if PAT therapists lack awareness of the vulnerabilities they bring into the therapy session and the ability to regulate themselves when activated, they cannot provide a secure and predictable therapeutic environment (e.g., Grof, 2019; Shulgin, 2019). The importance of therapists developing psychological and emotional self-awareness, often termed "the person of the therapist," has been endorsed by leaders of virtually every psychotherapy model, from psychoanalysis to client-centered therapy to systemic therapy to third-wave cognitive-behavioral models (Aponte & Kissil, 2016; McConnaughy, 1987; Rousmaniere, 2016, 2019). The potential for psychedelics to open and reveal the unconscious makes therapist personal development especially important for the safe and effective application of PAT. Ann Shulgin (2019), a widely respected pioneer in PAT, used Carl Jung's (1979) term *shadow work* to describe the process of self-exploration that is essential for all PAT therapists. In a speech near the end of her life, Shulgin (2019) emphasized the importance of therapists doing their own shadow work as a necessary precondition for providing PAT:

> No matter what motivates you to nibble mushrooms or drink ayahuasca tea, sooner or later you are going to have an encounter with the dragons and the demons in your soul. The Buddhists teach that when your body has died, your soul will meet what they call the guardians at the gate. And that what you must do is not run away. Or try to escape them. But look them in the face and acknowledge them as aspects of yourself. . . .
>
> Do your own Shadow work first. You can't do [PAT], and you certainly shouldn't try, if you haven't done the work . . . on your own Shadow. It could be very harmful to the patient because you have to know the territory. And when you ask [the patient] to trust you and what you say, you need to mean it. And he can't trust what you say, if you don't know what he's going through yourself. (paras. 4, 48)

Multidisciplinary Teams in PAT

Psychedelic therapy recognizes the holistic nature of healing, encompassing mental, emotional, spiritual, and physical-energetic aspects of human experience (Grof, 2019). To ensure effective and culturally sensitive practice, it is helpful for practitioners to be connected to multidisciplinary teams that embrace diverse ways of knowing. This includes moving beyond the confines of the Western-dominant biomedical paradigm and involving professionals from various disciplines and cultural backgrounds. Traditional therapists may need to expand their knowledge of pharmacology, and medical professionals should receive training in spiritual care to address the full spectrum of clients' needs. Cultural themes often surface during psychedelic experiences, and integrating these themes is crucial for successful healing (M. L. Williams et al., 2021; M. T. Williams et al., 2021).

Therefore, clinicians must prioritize cultural understanding as a foundational element of safety and efficacy in psychedelic therapy. Understanding the unique challenges faced by individuals who have experienced racism is vital to prevent inadvertent harm.

Client Safety and Risks in PAT

All therapies have the potential for negative effects (Mohr, 1995). The average deterioration rate across all models of psychotherapy has been estimated at 5% to 10% (see Lambert & Ogles, 2004). Like many strong medicines, psychedelics pose risks to some clients (for reviews, see Breeksema et al., 2022; Schlag et al., 2022). However, it can be challenging for clients to gain accurate information on the risks of psychedelics due to decades of sensationalized and inaccurate reporting from media and government sources (Nutt, 2022). For example, previous reports of psychedelics being neurotoxic and addictive have been largely disproven (e.g., Malcolm & Thomas, 2022; Nichols, 2016).

The most common risk from psychedelics that has been best supported by high-quality research is the risk of having an extremely adverse, difficult, or challenging experience (e.g., Breeksema et al., 2022; Schlag et al., 2022). One mixed-method study (Evans et al., 2023) collected quantitative and qualitative data from 608 participants who reported extended difficulties after psychedelic experiences and found the most common forms of extended difficulty were feelings of anxiety and fear, existential struggle, social disconnection, depersonalization, and derealization. For approximately one third of the participants, problems persisted for more than a year, and for one sixth, they endured for more than 3 years (Evans et al., 2023).

These risks are complicated by the finding that clients frequently report that their challenging experiences with psychedelics are also valuable. Schlag and colleagues (2022) summarized this finding:

> In Carbonaro et al.'s (2016) survey, 39% of the respondents rated their "worst bad trip" as one of the five most challenging experiences of their lifetime—yet the degree of difficulty was positively associated with enduring increases in well-being. Griffiths et al. (2006) found that in a controlled study of healthy volunteers, high doses of psilocybin created extreme fear in 30% of participants, yet 80% of these participants also reported subsequent improvements in well-being. Similarly, in healthy volunteers administered high doses of LSD of 100 and 200 µg in a controlled setting, fear (with ratings >50% on a visual analogue scale) is reported in approximately 20% and 30% of participants, respectively. Notably, more than 90% of the participants report good drug effects (>50%) in the same session (Holze et al., 2021; Schmid et al., 2015). (p. 5)

Other risks from psychedelics include uncomfortable or alarming physical symptoms (e.g., headache or migraine, nausea, fatigue, jaw clenching, perspiration), visual experiences long after the drug experience is over ("flashbacks"), harmful interactions with other psychiatric medication, and the risk of psychedelics triggering psychotic episodes (e.g., Breeksema et al., 2022; Dos Santos et al., 2017; Schlag et al., 2022; Tapia et al., 2021). Therapists can address many of these risks through careful screening for client suitability before proceeding with PAT. Before providing PAT, therapists must obtain thorough training in methods to protect client welfare, including client screening, appropriate boundaries, the safe and consensual use of touch, protecting client's confidentiality, preventing adverse cultural experiences, effective use of preparation and integration sessions to ensure client well-being, procedures for helping clients who are feeling overwhelmed, ensuring client safety after psychedelic medicine sessions, and other topics.

PAT Skills in Deliberate Practice

The skills in this book can be seen as the basic building blocks to be integrated into the therapist's repertoire and thus adopted for moment-by-moment use when needed. They guide the cultivation of trust, the fostering of presence, the ability to tolerate and leverage intense emotions, the engagement and validation of clients, the navigation of cultural opportunities and tensions, the skillful use of self-disclosure, the exploration and deepening of emotions, the work with intentions and disappointments, the management of expectations, the establishment of boundaries and agreements, the provision of ongoing informed consent, the awareness and navigation of transference, the skillful work with conflicting parts, the addressing of ruptures, and the facilitation of repair. These skills embody a relational approach and serve as the essential components of PAT. They embody a fundamental complementarity between ways of being and ways of doing, making this approach to therapy both rich and challenging.

Categorizing PAT Skills

To form a solid, safe therapeutic relationship and facilitate meaningful change, the PAT therapist must develop four broad skill categories:

1. A somatic and empathic attuning with the client to fortify the therapeutic alliance.
2. Preparing the client and the therapeutic alliance for the PAT session.
3. Navigating challenges and leveraging opportunities in PAT sessions.
4. Promoting integration of insights from the PAT session into one's daily life.

Table 1.2 organizes the skills in this book into these four categories, but bear in mind that these skills overlap in their application across these four categories. Grounded in therapeutic presence and facilitated by empathic and somatic attunement, all these skills are used throughout therapy, both within and outside of specific tasks.

The PAT Skills Presented in Exercises 1 Through 12

The exercises are presented in a linear order that privileges the importance of building a strong therapeutic alliance and a culture of trust between the therapist and the client. Exercise 1, "Redirecting to the Body," teaches skills to attend to bodily sensations and emotions that can shift us from fixating on solutions of the mind to learning to trust

TABLE 1.2. Four Categories of Psychedelic-Assisted Therapy Skills

Somatic Approaches	Preparation	Psychedelic Treatment	Integration
1. Redirecting to the body 2. Compassionately witnessing strong emotions	3. Exploring intentions and expectations 4. Cultural considerations: racially and ethnically diverse communities 5. Boundaries and informed consent 6. Responding to relational ruptures	7. Working with the client's internal conflict 8. Addressing transference 9. Navigating strong emotions	10. Making sense of the experience: integration I 11. Working with disappointment: integration II 12. Embodying insights: integration III

Note. The somatic approaches ground the entire therapeutic encounter and therefore apply to all exercises in this book.

the healing intelligence of the body. Exercise 2, "Compassionately Witnessing Strong Emotions," teaches how to mirror unconditional positive regard through an embodied, felt sense connection with another. This skill promotes a greater ability for the client to notice and work with the emotional content and core experience that is coming up in the body, while sharing that felt experience with the therapist. Exercise 3, "Exploring Intentions and Expectations," teaches how to explore client's intentions and expectations in preparation sessions and at the beginning of each psychedelic medicine session. Exercise 4, "Cultural Considerations: Racially and Ethnically Diverse Communities," teaches how to identify blind spots, discomforts, and triggers that can lead to unconscious projections and feel into ways to respond that feel authentic and demonstrate humility. Exercise 5, "Boundaries and Informed Consent," teaches how to clarify and maintain boundaries during psychedelic medicine sessions. Exercise 6, "Responding to Relational Ruptures," helps readers learn how to create safety within the therapeutic relationship. Exercise 7, "Working With the Client's Internal Conflict," provides introductory skills for working with internal conflict in the context of psychedelic-assisted therapy. Exercise 8, "Addressing Transference," teaches how to develop awareness of transference and to improve one's ability to tolerate and gently investigate the emotions as they arise. Exercise 9, "Navigating Strong Emotions," teaches how to explore intense feelings that may arise in PAT compassionately. Exercise 10, "Making Sense of the Experience: Integration I," teaches skills to make insights gained during altered states of consciousness become embodied in a way that leads to meaningful change in one's worldview and behaviors. Exercise 11, "Working With Disappointment: Integration II," teaches how to manage feelings of disappointment in PAT compassionately and productively. Exercise 12, "Embodying Insights: Integration III," teaches how to encourage integration after psychedelic medicine sessions.

A Note About Vocal Tone, Facial Expression, and Body Posture

Humanistic-experiential therapies in general, and PAT in particular, strongly attend to the nonverbal and paralinguistic cues expressed by both client and therapist. The empathic process of PAT involves careful moment-by-moment reading by the therapist of the client's message as communicated through both verbal expression and nonverbal styles. The therapist in turn is coached and trained to be aware of their tone of voice, facial expression, and body posture to convey the attitudes of warmth, empathy, genuine curiosity, and openness through their moment-by-moment responding.

Each one of the PAT skill and response types covered in the book is delivered with a particular therapeutic tone that cannot be completely conveyed through the written medium. We highly recommend that therapists pay attention to how they might be coming across to the client. For instance, paying attention to verbal cues such as tone of voice, facial expressions, and how one's nervous system may be informing the delivery of the message. Often, the words may seem right, but the energy that they are wrapped in can feel unsafe or incongruent. Ideally, the therapist will attune to the client, and in a similar way, when the client is dysregulated, they will attune to the therapist. In this way, when members of the therapeutic alliance feel safe enough to be authentic and to mirror unconditional positive regard in the process, the relationship promotes congruence (trustworthiness) and is mutually beneficial.

It is useful for PAT learners to watch recorded examples of themselves doing the practice exercises and to self-evaluate from this more objective vantage point. Furthermore, we also recommend students seek peer evaluation, providing another objective sounding board in their skill development process.

The Role of Deliberate Practice in PAT Training

The use of psychoactive substances for healing and wellness is deeply rooted in Indigenous cultures, where extensive training and supervision, often spanning many years, are required to facilitate medicine-assisted ceremonies. As PAT gains recognition in the Western context, it is crucial for Western-trained practitioners to approach it with humility and recognize themselves as novices in this field for a significant period of time. Developing personal and professional awareness, regulation skills, intuitive capacities, empathic development, somatic approaches, and the confidence to navigate challenging situations takes years of dedicated practice.

To ensure safety, foster humility, and build trustworthiness, ongoing mentorship and receiving feedback are imperative. The practice examples provided in this book can be tailored to various training programs, offering tangible scenarios that enable students to apply theory to practice.

Many PAT training programs recommend, and some require, that therapists personally experience nonordinary states of consciousness, obtain personal experience as a client in PAT, or both. These experiences can be achieved by engaging in PAT or other methods such as specific forms of breathwork (e.g., Grof, 2019). Engaging in experiential training fosters an intuitive understanding of nonordinary spaces that cannot be fully achieved through observation alone. It cultivates a form of intuition in nonordinary spaces that is difficult to attain through observation alone. The core aspects of experiential training, as outlined by Greenberg and Goldman (1988) in the context of psychotherapy training, are also applicable to PAT. These aspects include didactic learning, skills training, experiential engagement, and personal growth. Experiential training provides an opportunity to explore one's reactions to the strong emotional content often present in PAT (Shulgin, 2019), which can help practitioners develop the "person of the therapist" and inner skills of psychotherapy (e.g., Aponte & Kissil, 2016; Rousmaniere, 2019).

It is important to note that the skills presented in this book are foundational and not intended to be exhaustive. Deliberate practice, although valuable, should not be the sole method for acquiring proficiency in PAT. A comprehensive training process involves acquiring theoretical knowledge, discussing how to apply theory to practice amid complex scenarios, observing and studying PAT sessions with real clients, deliberate practice applying theory to practice through role-play, engaging in personal and experiential growth work as a therapist, and receiving supervision of one's work with real clients.

Overview of the Book's Structure

This book is organized into three parts. Part I contains this chapter and Chapter 2, which provides basic instructions on how to perform these exercises. We found through testing that providing too many instructions upfront overwhelmed trainers and trainees, and as a result, they skipped past them. Therefore, we kept these instructions as brief and simple as possible to focus only the most essential information that trainers and trainees will need to get started with the exercises. Further guidelines for getting the most about deliberate practice are provided in Chapter 3, and additional instructions for monitoring and adjusting the difficulty of the exercises are provided in Appendix A. **Do not skip the instructions in Chapter 2 and be sure to read the additional guidelines**

and instructions in Chapter 3 and Appendix A once you are comfortable with the basic instructions.

Part II contains the 12 skill-focused exercises, which are ordered based on their stage of therapy and difficulty: beginner, intermediate, and advanced (see Table 1.1). The first two exercises focus on somatic skills that apply to all the other skills in this book. The following 10 exercises are presented in the order that PAT is performed: the preparation session, the psychedelic medicine session, and the integration session. Although the skills are presented in this order, all the skills in this book can be essential in all stages of PAT.

Each exercise contains a brief overview, example client–therapist interactions to help guide trainees, step-by-step instructions for conducting that exercise, and a list of criteria for mastering the relevant skill. The client statements and sample therapist responses are then presented, also organized by difficulty (beginner, intermediate, and advanced). The statements and responses are presented separately so that the trainee playing the therapist has more freedom to improvise responses without being influenced by the sample responses, which should only be turned to if the trainee has difficulty improvising their own responses. PAT trainees are invited to run through the sample transcript with one playing the therapist and the other playing the client to get a feel for how a session might unfold.

The last two exercises in Part II provide opportunities to practice the 12 skills within simulated psychotherapy sessions. Exercise 13 provides a sample psychotherapy session transcript in which the PAT skills are used and clearly labeled, thereby demonstrating how they might flow together in an actual therapy session. PAT trainees are invited to run through the sample transcript with one playing the therapist and the other playing the client in order to get a feel for how a session might unfold. Exercise 14 provides suggestions for undertaking mock sessions, as well as client profiles ordered by difficulty (beginner, intermediate, and advanced) that trainees can use for improvised role-plays.

Part III contains Chapter 3, which provides additional guidance for trainers and trainees. While Chapter 2 is more procedural, Chapter 3 covers big-picture issues. It highlights six key points for getting the most out of deliberate practice and describes the importance of appropriate responsiveness, attending to trainee well-being and respecting their privacy, and trainer self-evaluation, among other topics.

Three appendixes conclude this book. Appendix A provides instructions for monitoring and adjusting the difficulty of each exercise as needed. It provides a Deliberate Practice Reaction Form for the trainee playing the therapist to complete to indicate whether the exercise is too easy or too difficult. Appendix B includes a Deliberate Practice Diary Form that can be used during a training session's final evaluation to process the trainees' experiences. However, its primary purpose is to give trainees a format to explore and record their experiences while engaging in additional, between-session deliberate practice activities without the supervisor. Appendix C presents a sample syllabus demonstrating how the 12 deliberate practice exercises and other support material can be integrated into a wider PAT training course. Instructors may choose to modify the syllabus or pick elements of it to integrate into their own courses.

Downloadable versions of this book's appendixes, including a color version of the Deliberate Practice Reaction Form, can be found in the "Clinician and Practitioner Resources" tab online (https://www.apa.org/pubs/books/deliberate-practice-psychedelic-assisted-therapy).

Instructions for the Therapeutic Approach for Psychedelic-Assisted Therapy Deliberate Practice Exercises

This chapter provides basic instructions that are common to all the exercises in this book. More specific instructions are provided in each exercise. Chapter 3 also provides important guidance for trainees and trainers that will help them get the most out of deliberate practice. Appendix A offers additional instructions for monitoring and adjusting the difficulty of the exercises as needed after getting through all the client statements in a single difficulty level, including a Deliberate Practice Reaction Form the trainee playing the therapist can complete to indicate whether they found the statements too easy or too difficult. **Difficulty assessment is an important part of the deliberate practice process and should not be skipped.**

Overview

The deliberate practice exercises in this book involve role-plays of hypothetical situations in therapy. It is expected that psychedelic-assisted therapy (PAT) providers will work in pairs to deliver PAT, which provides a unique opportunity to co-create an ongoing peer assessment practice. Aligning with this unique opportunity, the role-play involves three people: One trainee role-plays the therapist, another trainee role-plays the client, and the trainer (professor/supervisor) provides a self- and peer-evaluation framework and observes and provides feedback on their process. Alternately, a third peer can observe and provide feedback. Having students record their sessions also provides a more objective vantage point for students to self-assess their practice.

This book provides a script for each role-play, each with a client statement and also an example therapist response. The client statements are graded in difficulty from beginning to advanced, although these difficulty grades are only estimates. The actual perceived difficulty of client statements is subjective and varies widely by trainee. For example, some trainees may experience a stimulus of a client being angry to be easy

https://doi.org/10.1037/0000399-002

Deliberate Practice in Psychedelic-Assisted Therapy, by S. Dames, A. Penn, M. Williams, J. A. Zamaria, T. Rousmaniere, and A. Vaz

to respond to, whereas another trainee may experience it as very difficult. Thus, it is important for trainees to provide difficulty assessments and adjustments to ensure that they are practicing at the right difficulty level: neither too easy nor too hard.

Time Frame

We recommend a 90-minute time block for every exercise, structured roughly as follows:

- First 20 minutes: Orientation. The trainer explains the PAT skill and demonstrates the exercise procedure with a volunteer trainee.

- Middle 50 minutes: Trainees perform the exercise in pairs. The trainer or a peer provides feedback throughout this process and monitors/adjusts the exercise's difficulty as needed after each set of statements (see Appendix A for more information about difficulty assessment).

- Final 20 minutes: Review, feedback, and discussion.

Preparation

1. Every trainee will need their own copy of this book.

2. Each exercise requires the trainer to fill out a Deliberate Practice Reaction Form after completing all the statements from a single difficulty level. This form is available in the "Clinician and Practitioner Resources" tab online (https://www.apa.org/pubs/books/deliberate-practice-psychedelic-assisted-therapy) and in Appendix A.

3. Trainees are grouped into pairs. One volunteers to role-play the therapist and one to role-play the client (they will switch roles after 15 minutes of practice).

4. The role of the trainer can be to provide direct feedback to the trainee pair, to create a supportive and structured feedback process that empowers trainees to provide constructive feedback to one another (promoting an ongoing peer evaluation practice), or a hybrid of the two approaches. Furthermore, it can be helpful to record the sessions and to have trainees review the recording to provide a more fulsome self and peer feedback process.

The Role of the Trainer

The primary responsibilities of the trainer are to ensure trainees are receiving objective feedback on their process. This can be done by the following:

1. Providing a self and peer assessment framework to encourage compassionate feedback practice. Setting trainees' expectations to engage in peer evaluation as a lifelong career practice is important to improve safety, accountability, and ongoing professional development.

2. Providing corrective feedback, which includes both information about how well the trainees' response met expected criteria and any necessary guidance about how to improve the response.

3. Reminding trainees to do difficulty assessments and adjustments after each level of client statements is completed (beginning, intermediate, and advanced).

How to Practice

Each exercise includes its own step-by-step instructions. Trainees should follow these instructions carefully, as every step is important.

Skill Criteria

Each of the first 12 exercises focuses on one essential PAT skill with two to three skill criteria that describe the important components or principles for that skill.

The goal of the role-play is for trainees to practice improvising responses to the client statement in a manner that (a) is attuned to the client, (b) meets skill criteria as much as possible, and (c) feels authentic for the trainee. Trainees are provided scripts with example therapist responses to give them a sense of how to incorporate the skill criteria into a response. **It is important, however, that trainees do not read the example responses verbatim in the role-plays!** Therapy is highly personal and improvisational; the goal of deliberate practice is to develop trainees' ability to improvise within a consistent framework. Memorizing scripted responses would be counterproductive for helping trainees learn to perform therapy that is responsive, authentic, and attuned to each individual client.

Our team of authors collaboratively wrote the scripted example responses. However, trainees' personal style of therapy may differ slightly or greatly from that in the example scripts. It is essential that, over time, trainees develop their own style and voice, while simultaneously being able to intervene according to the model's principles and strategies. To facilitate this, the exercises in this book were designed to maximize opportunities for improvisational responses informed by the skill criteria and ongoing feedback. Trainees will note that some of the scripted responses do not meet all the skill criteria: These responses are provided as examples of flexible application of PAT skills in a manner that prioritizes attunement with the client.

If the trainee doesn't feel comfortable with the scenarios, we recommend you continue practicing until you develop more ease in your process. With more ease, your ability to attune, intuitively respond, and remain authentic will be far greater.

Review, Feedback, and Discussion

The review and feedback sequence after each role-play has these two elements:

- First, the trainee who played the client **briefly** shares how it felt to be on the receiving end of the therapist response. This can help assess how well trainees are attuning with the client.

- Second, the trainer or peer assessor provides **brief** feedback (less than 1 minute) based on the skill criteria for each exercise. Keep feedback specific, behavioral, and brief to preserve time for skill rehearsal. If one trainer is teaching multiple pairs of trainees, the trainer walks around the room, observing the pairs and offering brief feedback. When the trainer is not available, the trainee playing the client gives peer feedback to the therapist, based on the skill criteria and how it felt to be on the receiving end of the intervention. Alternatively, a third trainee can observe and provide feedback.

Trainers (or peers) should remember to keep all feedback specific and brief and not to veer into discussions of theory. There are many other settings for extended discussion of PAT theory and research. In deliberate practice, it is of utmost importance to maximize time for continuous behavioral rehearsal via role-plays.

Final Evaluation

After both trainees have role-played the client and the therapist, the trainer provides an evaluation. Participants should engage in a short group discussion based on this evaluation. This discussion can provide ideas for where to focus homework and future deliberate practice sessions. To this end, Appendix B presents a Deliberate Practice Diary Form, which can also be downloaded from the "Clinician and Practitioner Resources" tab online (https://www.apa.org/pubs/books/deliberate-practice-psychedelic-assisted-therapy). This form can be used as part of the final evaluation to help trainees process their experiences from that session with the supervisor. However, it is designed primarily to be used by trainees as a template for exploring and recording their thoughts and experiences between sessions, particularly when pursuing additional deliberate practice activities without the supervisor, such as rehearsing responses alone or if two or more trainees want to practice the exercises together—perhaps with another trainee filling the supervisor's role. Then, if they want, the trainees can discuss these experiences with the supervisor at the beginning of the next training session.

Deliberate Practice Exercises for Psychedelic-Assisted Therapy Skills

This section of the book provides 12 deliberate practice exercises for essential psychedelic-assisted therapy (PAT) skills. These exercises are organized in a developmental sequence, from those that are more appropriate for someone just beginning PAT training to those who have progressed to a more advanced level. Although we anticipate that most trainers would use these exercises in the order we have suggested, some trainers may find it more appropriate to their training circumstances to use a different order. We also provide two comprehensive exercises that bring together the PAT skills using an annotated PAT session transcript and mock PAT sessions.

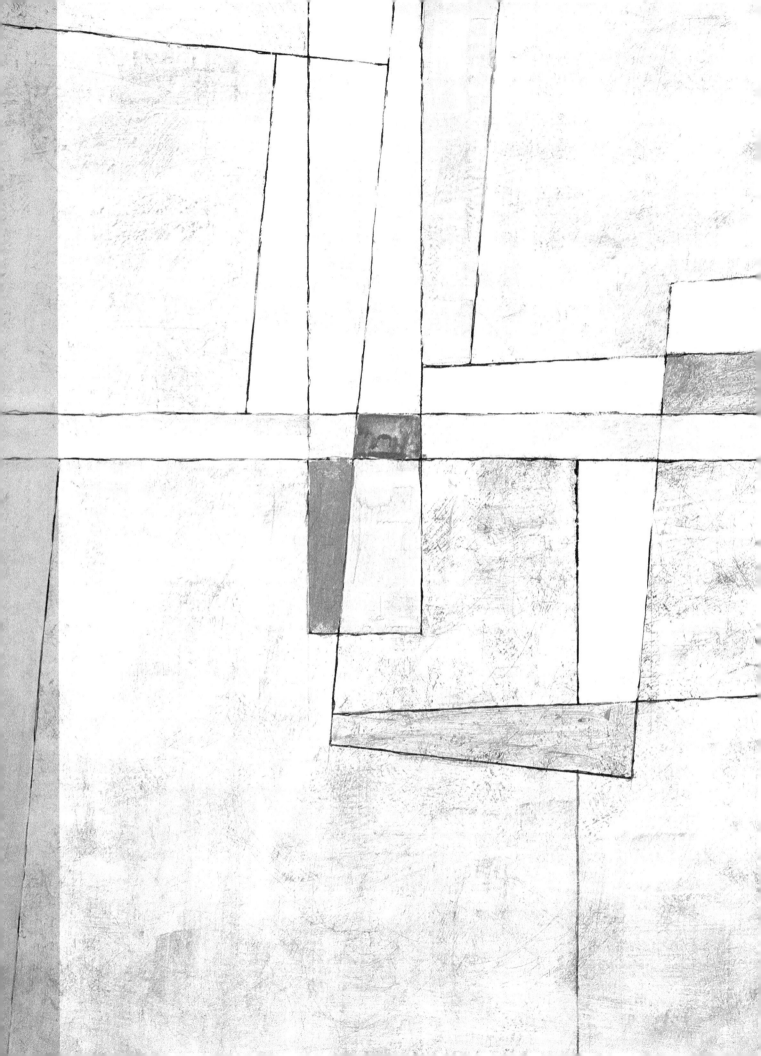

Redirecting to the Body

Preparations for Exercise 1

1. Read the instructions in Chapter 2.

2. Download the Deliberate Practice Reaction Form and the Deliberate Practice Diary Form at https://www.apa.org/pubs/books/deliberate-practice-psychedelic-assisted-therapy (see the "Clinician and Practitioner Resources" tab; also available in Appendixes A and B, respectively).

Skill Description

Skill Difficulty Level: Beginner

This exercise is designed to help guide clients tune into their body in the therapeutic encounter. This is one of the most fundamental skills in psychedelic-assisted therapy (PAT) and is used throughout every stage of therapy. Tending to bodily sensations and emotions can help clients shift away from fixating on solutions of the mind (Maté, 2011; van der Kolk, 2015). This shift of lens can help clients experience therapy from a different perspective—from figuring it out at the level of the mind to listening in at the level of the body. Tuning into their somatic experiences can help clients break away from over-identifying with past belief systems (e.g., shame and guilt cycles) and rigid life roles, such as feeling victim to circumstances (Ogden & Fisher, 2015). Becoming aware of somatic sensations in the moment can interrupt the automatic cognitive loops, creating a space between the event and the client's interpretation, which enables the client to shift from unconscious reaction to conscious choice. This can open the door to a greater ability to refriend/reparent the less developed or avoided parts of the client's self (J. Fisher, 2017).

https://doi.org/10.1037/0000399-003

Deliberate Practice in Psychedelic-Assisted Therapy, by S. Dames, A. Penn, M. Williams, J. A. Zamaria, T. Rousmaniere, and A. Vaz

The therapist should improvise a response to each client statement following these skill criteria:

1. **Acknowledge/validate the client's stated concern or experience.** In this first skill criterion, the counselor highlights the emotional response and core need/value they hear embedded in what the client is sharing. Use your active listening skills to consider the underlying meaning, which is not always explicitly stated by clients. This first step is essential because it ensures that you have adequately understood the emotion and motivating desire that is driving the client's reaction and because the client may not have considered this material that lies beneath the presenting concern.

2. **Direct inwardly: Invite the client to feel and articulate the bodily sensations they are currently experiencing.** The next step is to invite the client to consider how they might honor their emotions further in the situation that is presenting. Sometimes clients' emotions align easily with the story presenting on the surface of the therapeutic encounter, and other times they are best served by gently directing them inwardly, despite the temptation to stay in the surface story. To elicit the emotions that relate to the client's presenting concern, the therapist can invite them to revisit the event through imagery (e.g., "When you think back to when this happened . . ."; "When you imagine yourself in that scenario again . . ."). Because trauma resides in the body, this practice of revisiting the felt senses of the body is an important part of tending to old wounds that remain attached to the surface narratives.

SKILL CRITERIA FOR EXERCISE 1

1. Acknowledge and validate the client's stated concern or experience.
2. Direct inwardly: Invite the client to feel and articulate the bodily sensations they are currently experiencing.

Examples of Redirecting to the Body

Example 1

CLIENT: [*anxious*] To be honest, I feel really nervous being here.

THERAPIST: I can understand how this experience might make you feel vulnerable. (Criterion 1) How do you experience this nervousness in your body right now? (Criterion 2)

Example 2

CLIENT: [*irritated*] It was so rude that she interrupted the debrief like that during my group therapy session. It's like she doesn't care about anyone else in the room. It's all about her.

THERAPIST: I can imagine it triggering some irritation in your body to have the group agreements broken like that. (Criterion 1) When you imagine her interrupting you in the debrief, how does your body respond? What emotions are you noticing? (Criterion 2)

Example 3

CLIENT: [*afraid*] I don't know who I am anymore. I am totally freaking out right now.

THERAPIST: It sounds like you are experiencing some intense fear right now. (Criterion 1) What does "freaking out" feel like in your body? (Criterion 2)

INSTRUCTIONS FOR EXERCISE 1

Step 1: Role-Play and Feedback

- The client says the first beginner client statement. The therapist **improvises** a response based on the skill criteria.
- The trainer (or, if not available, the client) provides **brief** feedback based on the skill criteria.
- The client then repeats the same statement, and the therapist again improvises a response. The trainer (or client) again provides brief feedback.

Step 2: Repeat

- Repeat Step 1 for all the statements **in the current difficulty level** (beginner, intermediate, or advanced).

Step 3: Assess and Adjust Difficulty

- The therapist completes the Deliberate Practice Reaction Form (see Appendix A) and decides whether to make the exercise easier or harder or to repeat the same difficulty level.

Step 4: Repeat for Approximately 15 Minutes

- Repeat Steps 1 to 3 for at least 15 minutes.
- The trainees then switch therapist and client roles and start over.

Now it's your turn! Follow Steps 1 and 2 from the exercise instructions.

Remember: The goal of the role-play is for trainees to practice improvising responses to the client statements in a manner that (a) uses the skill criteria and (b) feels authentic for the trainee. **Example therapist responses for each client statement are provided at the end of this exercise. Trainees should attempt to improvise their own responses before reading the examples.**

BEGINNER-LEVEL CLIENT STATEMENTS FOR EXERCISE 1
Beginner Client Statement 1
[Sad] I'm still feeling really down about the breakup with my boyfriend.
Beginner Client Statement 2
[Anxious] To be honest, I feel really nervous being here.
Beginner Client Statement 3
[Annoyed] I can't believe they called me out like that during my group therapy session. I felt so singled out.
Beginner Client Statement 4
[Embarrassed] I can't believe I said that in front of everyone in the group. I'll never be able to show my face there again.
Beginner Client Statement 5
[Surprise, smiling] Since our last session, I keep catching myself smiling. This is so unusual for me!

 Assess and adjust the difficulty before moving to the next difficulty level (see Step 3 in the exercise instructions).

INTERMEDIATE-LEVEL CLIENT STATEMENTS FOR EXERCISE 1
Intermediate Client Statement 1
[Sadness] Every time I think about ending the relationship with my partner, I feel overwhelmed by sadness.
Intermediate Client Statement 2
[Shame] I feel like such a terrible person. I've made such awful decisions in my life and hurt people, and now I'm paying for them.
Intermediate Client Statement 3
[Scared] My past experience with psychedelics felt traumatizing. I'm just frightened that this experience will make things worse.
Intermediate Client Statement 4
[Angry] I'm feeling really energized. Like I need to get up, throw something . . . hit something!
Intermediate Client Statement 5
[Grief] I've been feeling waves of grief about losing my daughter. It's been hard to get out of bed this past week.

 Assess and adjust the difficulty before moving to the next difficulty level (see Step 3 in the exercise instructions).

ADVANCED-LEVEL CLIENT STATEMENTS FOR EXERCISE 1
Advanced Client Statement 1
[Confusion/disembodiment] I don't know what's happening to me right now. I can't feel anything anymore.
Advanced Client Statement 2
[Irritated] It was so rude that she interrupted the debrief like that during my group therapy session. It's like she doesn't care about anyone else in the room. It's all about her.
Advanced Client Statement 3
[Lonely] I'm afraid to let others in, but I'm so tired of feeling alone in the world.
Advanced Client Statement 4
[Regretful] I don't know how I could hurt my own child like that. I wish I could take it all back.
Advanced Client Statement 5
[Skeptical] Nothing has ever worked for me. Why would this therapy be any different?

 Assess and adjust the difficulty here (see Step 3 in the exercise instructions). If appropriate, follow the instructions to make the exercise even more challenging (see Appendix A).

Example Therapist Responses: Redirecting to the Body

Remember: Trainees should attempt to improvise their own responses before reading the example responses. **Do not read the following responses verbatim unless you are having trouble coming up with your own responses!**

EXAMPLE RESPONSES TO BEGINNER-LEVEL CLIENT STATEMENTS FOR EXERCISE 1
Example Response to Beginner Client Statement 1
It makes so much sense that you're still feeling this. (Criterion 1) When you turn your attention to how this is feeling in your body as you describe this loss, what sensations and emotions are you noticing right now? (Criterion 2)
Example Response to Beginner Client Statement 2
I can understand how this experience might make you feel vulnerable. (Criterion 1) How do you experience this nervousness in your body right now? (Criterion 2)
Example Response to Beginner Client Statement 3
I can hear some irritation, and maybe even some hurt by how the facilitator handled the situation. (Criterion 1) When you remember that moment, notice what is happening in your body. What physical sensations and emotions are you noticing? (Criterion 2)
Example Response to Beginner Client Statement 4
It sounds like you are feeling embarrassed about what happened. I can imagine you feel really vulnerable right now. (Criterion 1) How does it feel in your body when you imagine speaking to the group about your experience? (Criterion 2)
Example Response to Beginner Client Statement 5
As you describe your experience, I find myself smiling too. What a pleasant surprise! (Criterion 1) I see you are smiling now too. At this moment, how does this smile show up in your body below the neck? Can you describe the sensation and emotion that comes with the smile? (Criterion 2)

EXAMPLE RESPONSES TO INTERMEDIATE-LEVEL CLIENT STATEMENTS FOR EXERCISE 1

Example Response to Intermediate Client Statement 1

Oh, when you describe your experience, I feel a heaviness in my chest. It sounds really difficult. (Criterion 1) When you imagine ending the relationship with your partner, what shows up in your body? Describe the sensation of sadness—its texture, color, location, movement. (Criterion 2)

Example Response to Intermediate Client Statement 2

It sounds like a lot of strong feelings are coming to the surface. Sometimes in this state, we find ourselves reviewing our lives, and it brings up strong feelings, sometimes even shame. (Criterion 1) What happens in your body as you experience those feelings of shame? (Criterion 2)

Example Response to Intermediate Client Statement 3

It makes a lot of sense that you feel so apprehensive, maybe even scared to try this form of therapy based on your past experience. (Criterion 1) When you think about what happened in the past, and the potential for something similar to happen again, can you describe the quality of the physical sensations that show up in your body? Can you describe an emotion that is paired with the sensations? (Criterion 2)

Example Response to Intermediate Client Statement 4

It's possible that all this energy is some anger coming up for you right now. (Criterion 1) Let's try to explore this feeling a little more. Can you tell me where you're feeling this anger and energy in your body? (Criterion 2)

Example Response to Intermediate Client Statement 5

To not want to get out of bed, you must feel so overwhelmed by it all. (Criterion 1) This grief that you speak of, can you revisit it now? How is it showing up in your body? What other emotions are you noticing amid the waves of grief? (Criterion 2)

EXAMPLE RESPONSES TO ADVANCED-LEVEL CLIENT STATEMENTS FOR EXERCISE 1
Example Response to Advanced Client Statement 1
It sounds like you're feeling confused and unsure right now. (Criterion 1) Stay with this experience. I wonder if that confusion, or if any of the feelings you're having, have a physical location? (Criterion 2)
Example Response to Advanced Client Statement 2
I can imagine it triggering some irritation in your body to have the group agreements broken like that. (Criterion 1) When you imagine her interrupting you in the debrief, how does your body respond? What emotions are you noticing? (Criterion 2)
Example Response to Advanced Client Statement 3
When you describe feeling alone in the world, I feel a heaviness in my heart. It sounds like you are longing for more. (Criterion 1) When you allow yourself to drop into feeling "alone in the world," in terms of physical sensations, how does it show up in your body? What emotions accompany the physical sensations? (Criterion 2)
Example Response to Advanced Client Statement 4
As a parent, I can imagine the experience of regret and perhaps even self-doubt is really heavy for you. (Criterion 1) When you think about how your body reacted in that past moment, what arises in your body in the present moment? Describe the physical sensations that accompany the story. What emotions are you noticing? (Criterion 2)
Example Response to Advanced Client Statement 5
It sounds like you may be feeling skeptical about getting the help you need? (Criterion 1) Can you name one or two emotions that come up now, as you sit with the uncertainty of what lies ahead? (Criterion 2)

Compassionately Witnessing Strong Emotions

Preparations for Exercise 2

1. Read the instructions in Chapter 2.

2. Download the Deliberate Practice Reaction Form and the Deliberate Practice Diary Form at https://www.apa.org/pubs/books/deliberate-practice-psychedelic-assisted-therapy (see the "Clinician and Practitioner Resources" tab; also available in Appendixes A and B, respectively).

Skill Description

Skill Difficulty Level: Beginner

The act of compassionate witnessing refers to the therapist's mirroring of unconditional positive regard. This skill promotes a greater ability for the client to notice, work with, and share the emotional content and experience that is coming up in their body (Neff, 2011). This sharing of the client's felt experience, and the therapist offering what is arising in their own body in response, underscores that the client is not alone (Fosha et al., 2019). This skill is particularly relevant in psychedelic-assisted therapy (PAT), where intense emotions and experiences often arise in the client. This is a fundamental skill in PAT and is used throughout every stage of therapy.

Compassionate witnessing requires the therapist's genuine curiosity. It involves the therapist watching from a calm place, listening with their body, and holding awareness of not only the words spoken but also body language, tone of voice, emotions expressed, and energy present (Desmond, 2015). To absorb this information from all of the senses requires the practitioner to drop below the narrative of the surface story so they can attend to and respond from the wisdom of their body and avoid being distracted by the felt pressure to craft a "smart" response.

https://doi.org/10.1037/0000399-004

Deliberate Practice in Psychedelic-Assisted Therapy, by S. Dames, A. Penn, M. Williams, J. A. Zamaria, T. Rousmaniere, and A. Vaz

When the client feels unconditional positive regard, their concerns of being judged and of the felt need to say the right words dissipate. Through new eyes, where there are no expectations of what is to come or value statements of what is deemed worthy, the therapist cultivates the relational trust required for the client to show up authentically. When met with genuine unconditional positive regard, clients develop the relational security that can be described as secure attachment, and the corrective healing process deepens.

Compassionate witnessing requires the therapist to be fully present in the moment, listening deeply through the sensations of the body, rather than listening to respond with culturally conditioned responses such as advice giving, interpreting, educating, and consoling, which often flow from a mind more focused on "fixing" than being fully present and connected to what is arising moment by moment.

This exercise will help therapists use their own experience in a clinically productive manner during PAT. In moments when the therapist experiences countertransference, perhaps becoming emotionally charged themselves, they may find that they can no longer observe as a calm witness. When this happens, especially when facilitating groups, it can be helpful to make the implicit explicit by acknowledging the emotions that are coming up for the therapist. Transparency often neutralizes the charge in that moment, promoting nonjudgmental compassion for self and others. Countertransference most commonly takes the form of emotional attachment to relieving the client's suffering (i.e., feeling responsible for their healing and wellbeing). In this work that is built on empathy, we need to maintain acute clarity that we do not take on the emotions and suffering of others or responsibility for their cure or resolution. True compassionate witnessing retains individuation to be a still witness for others, for their inner healing intelligence to lead the way. We do not collude with their alienating narratives, nor do we fuse with their distress, scrambling to fix it, reduce it, or paper over it with affirmations and encouragement.

The therapist should improvise a response to each client statement using the following skill criteria:

1. **Share sensations/emotions arising in you in response to the client's statements (i.e., somatic resonance).** In this first skill criterion, you, as therapist, highlight your own sensations and emotions that arose in response to what was shared. Use your deep listening skills and take note of specific words that you felt in your body and piqued your curiosity, as well as the felt sense that presented as you were listening. This communication is essential because it provides a sympathetic mirror for the other—for instance, "When you spoke about losing your daughter, I felt a sinking in my chest." This kind of response communicates that they are seen and heard, that their experience carries meaning in the world beyond themselves.

2. **Reflect or inquire about some aspect of what the client may be longing for or is deeply important to them.** Although it may be tempting to engage in the client's narrative with conversational or objective exploration, this is not the practice here. Remain connected to the experience in the body and sense the message of their heart that can be detected in their narrative. For instance, if a client speaks of an argument with a partner who was not taking their feelings into account and was insisting on their own way, you might inquire, "It sounds like you really wanted to be heard and to have some sense of mutuality in the way decisions were being made." Even though this is offered in declarative sentence structure, the background intention and tone of voice must embody the statement as an inquiry. We are never telling clients what they are experiencing but may make a statement for the purpose of inquiring and inviting correction or confirmation.

SKILL CRITERIA FOR EXERCISE 2
1. Share sensations/emotions arising in you in response to the client's statements (i.e., somatic resonance).
2. Reflect or inquire about some aspect of what the client may be longing for or is deeply important to them.

Examples of Compassionately Witnessing Strong Emotions

Example 1

CLIENT: [*fearful*] I'm terrified that my spouse will leave me. I don't want to be alone.

THERAPIST: When I heard you say that you were terrified, I felt a tightening in my upper chest. (Criterion 1) Having support and companionship must feel essential to you. Is what I'm saying close to what you feel? (Criterion 2)

Example 2

CLIENT: [*joyful*] I haven't felt this good for years. I can't stop smiling!

THERAPIST: It sure sounds like you have been waiting for this kind of relief for a long time. (Criterion 2) Watching you smile is bringing a smile to my face, and I'm feeling lighter myself. (Criterion 1) Say more about the changes, if you would. (Criterion 2)

Example 3

CLIENT: [*anxious*] I feel a sense of impending doom all the time these days. I'm always waiting for the next shoe to drop.

THERAPIST: Hearing your anticipation of impending doom, I have this vision of a dark cloud washing over me, and a tightness in my throat. (Criterion 1) And tell me if I'm on target . . . I get the sense that you'd love some peace in your body rather than the bracing and contraction you are living with day to day. (Criterion 2)

INSTRUCTIONS FOR EXERCISE 2
Step 1: Role-Play and Feedback
<ul><li>The client says the first beginner client statement. The therapist **improvises** a response based on the skill criteria.</li><li>The trainer (or, if not available, the client) provides **brief** feedback based on the skill criteria.</li><li>The client then repeats the same statement, and the therapist again improvises a response. The trainer (or client) again provides brief feedback.</li></ul>
Step 2: Repeat
<ul><li>Repeat Step 1 for all the statements **in the current difficulty level** (beginner, intermediate, or advanced).</li></ul>
Step 3: Assess and Adjust Difficulty
<ul><li>The therapist completes the Deliberate Practice Reaction Form (see Appendix A) and decides whether to make the exercise easier or harder or to repeat the same difficulty level.</li></ul>
Step 4: Repeat for Approximately 15 Minutes
<ul><li>Repeat Steps 1 to 3 for at least 15 minutes.</li><li>The trainees then switch therapist and client roles and start over.</li></ul>

Now it's your turn! Follow Steps 1 and 2 from the exercise instructions.

Remember: The goal of the role-play is for trainees to practice improvising responses to the client statements in a manner that (a) uses the skill criteria and (b) feels authentic for the trainee. **Example therapist responses for each client statement are provided at the end of this exercise. Trainees should attempt to improvise their own responses before reading the example responses.**

BEGINNER-LEVEL CLIENT STATEMENTS FOR EXERCISE 2
Beginner Client Statement 1
[Joyful] I haven't felt this good for years. I can't stop smiling!
Beginner Client Statement 2
[Fearful] I'm terrified that my spouse will leave me. I don't want to be alone.
Beginner Client Statement 3
[Sad] I feel sad right now. Actually, I feel sad all the time these days.
Beginner Client Statement 4
[Peaceful] I've never felt this calm inside.
Beginner Client Statement 5
[Anxious] I feel a sense of impending doom all the time these days. I'm always waiting for the next shoe to drop.

✋ **Assess and adjust the difficulty before moving to the next difficulty level (see Step 3 in the exercise instructions).**

INTERMEDIATE-LEVEL CLIENT STATEMENTS FOR EXERCISE 2
Intermediate Client Statement 1
[Giddy] I don't know what I'm laughing at, but I can't stop giggling.
Intermediate Client Statement 2
[Apprehensive] I'm not so sure about this. I don't know if this was a good idea.
Intermediate Client Statement 3
[Guilty] I've been such a terrible parent.
Intermediate Client Statement 4
[Irritated] I'm feeling so impatient. This therapy feels like a highly structured process with a lot of waiting, and I don't like waiting!
Intermediate Client Statement 5
[Panicked] I'm starting to feel kind of freaked out, like I want to get out of here.

Assess and adjust the difficulty before moving to the next difficulty level (see Step 3 in the exercise instructions).

ADVANCED-LEVEL CLIENT STATEMENTS FOR EXERCISE 2
Advanced Client Statement 1
[Hyperarousal] This is too much. I don't think I can handle all these thoughts and feelings right now.
Advanced Client Statement 2
[Hyperarousal] It's all just too much to hold. Now, I'm numb, and can't seem to reconnect.
Advanced Client Statement 3
[Grief] I just can't get on top of this grief that I'm feeling.
Advanced Client Statement 4
[Disgusted] I can't believe they did that. The whole situation sickens me.
Advanced Client Statement 5
[Embarrassed] I'm such a mess right now. I can't believe I'm letting people see me like this in group therapy.

 Assess and adjust the difficulty here (see Step 3 in the exercise instructions). If appropriate, follow the instructions to make the exercise even more challenging (see Appendix A).

Example Therapist Responses: Compassionately Witnessing Strong Emotions

Remember: Trainees should attempt to improvise their own responses before reading the example responses. **Do not read the following responses verbatim unless you are having trouble coming up with your own!** (Later, as an exercise, you can try reading them verbatim and feeling how these words resonate, or not, for you. Notice what you like about them and how you'd need to change the language to feel more natural and authentic to who you are.)

EXAMPLE RESPONSES TO BEGINNER-LEVEL CLIENT STATEMENTS FOR EXERCISE 2
Example Response to Beginner Client Statement 1
I can feel the smile on my face seeing your smile, and I'm feeling lighter myself. (Criterion 1) Am I right to sense that it is pretty sweet for you to have some real joy after all this time? (Criterion 2)
Example Response to Beginner Client Statement 2
When I hear that you feel terrified, I've got a burning feeling in my upper chest. (Criterion 1) As you imagine being alone, are you longing for some sense of stability and security? (Criterion 2)
Example Response to Beginner Client Statement 3
And I get the sense that this sadness is wearing you down. (Criterion 2) I'm sure feeling a tenderness in my heart as I sit in this felt sense of sadness with you. (Criterion 1)
Example Response to Beginner Client Statement 4
I can feel a sense of stillness wash over me as you say that. (Criterion 1) I get the sense that this stillness you are experiencing is a welcome break from what you might normally experience in everyday life. Does this resonate with your experience? (Criterion 2)
Example Response to Beginner Client Statement 5
I'd imagine that is an exhausting way to live, so much anxiety and painful anticipation. (Criterion 2) I can feel a tightness in my throat as you name it. (Criterion 1)

EXAMPLE RESPONSES TO INTERMEDIATE-LEVEL CLIENT STATEMENTS FOR EXERCISE 2
Example Response to Intermediate Client Statement 1
I sure can't suppress the smile I feel as you laugh. (Criterion 1) The joy is just bubbling up right now, it seems. Does it feel like joy to you, or something different? (Criterion 2)
Example Response to Intermediate Client Statement 2
You're noticing feelings of apprehension, which is really normal to experience when stepping away from what is familiar and ordinary. (Criterion 2) As you express these feelings, I notice tingles running up the back of my neck. Where does it show up for you? (Criterion 1)
Example Response to Intermediate Client Statement 3
It sounds like you're feeling guilty and regret related to how you've dealt with your kids, and at the same time I hear a lot of care for their well-being. (Criterion 2) There's certainly a tenderness in me as you say that. (Criterion 1)
Example Response to Intermediate Client Statement 4
I can feel your sense of urgency (Criterion 1) and can totally understand how it would be irritating to feel like you lack control in some aspects of this therapy process. (Criterion 2)
Example Response to Intermediate Client Statement 5
Yeah, it's really common to feel afraid, just wanting some solid ground when our perceptions and feelings go through this big shift on the substance. (Criterion 2) And, what I want you to hear is that I have a real sense of calm as I have complete trust that you are doing really well and this phase will pass. (Criterion 1)

EXAMPLE RESPONSES TO ADVANCED-LEVEL CLIENT STATEMENTS FOR EXERCISE 2
Example Response to Advanced Client Statement 1
Yes, this is really scary right now. (Criterion 2) Notice and just breathe with me now, deeply and slowly. My heart is slowing just a bit as we breathe this way. (Criterion 1)
Example Response to Advanced Client Statement 2
I see that. And I notice feeling very still in this moment. (Criterion 1) As you feel the numbness, is it providing you some relief or is it creating something different? (Criterion 2)
Example Response to Advanced Client Statement 3
[Pause] I really feel a heaviness as I sit with you in that grief. (Criterion 1) Am I hearing a sense of hopelessness or desire for movement forward with all this sadness? (Criterion 2)
Example Response to Advanced Client Statement 4
Sounds like you're pretty disgusted with what happened. (Criterion 2) Just hearing you say it causes a twist in my gut. (Criterion 1)
Example Response to Advanced Client Statement 5
Sounds like you are having a hard time being kind to yourself right now, and at the same time, I think I hear a part of you that is shocked and maybe even a bit pleased that you are taking the risk to be real in the group. (Criterion 2) I'm sure delighted seeing you show up so fully! (Criterion 1)

Exploring Intentions and Expectations

Preparations for Exercise 3

1. Read the instructions in Chapter 2.

2. Download the Deliberate Practice Reaction Form and the Deliberate Practice Diary Form at https://www.apa.org/pubs/books/deliberate-practice-psychedelic-assisted-therapy (see the "Clinician and Practitioner Resources" tab; also available in Appendixes A and B, respectively).

Skill Description

Skill Difficulty Level: Beginner

Expectations focus on outcomes. Intentions focus on process. We cannot control the outcomes, but with an intentional process, we can influence them.

In psychedelic-assisted therapy, therapists explore client's intentions and expectations in preparation sessions and at the beginning of each psychedelic medicine session. Setting explicit intentions is an important part of laying the therapeutic groundwork in the process of psychedelic therapy. The psychedelic experience is informed by one's expectations and intentions, which is called the "set" (i.e., mindset) in the commonly used description of the "set and setting" of the therapeutic process (Grof, 2000). By setting intentions and managing one's expectations, the client consciously cultivates their frame of mind according to what they hope to achieve, or perhaps release, in the psychedelic-assisted therapy (PAT) experience. This provides a north star of sorts, facilitating a greater likelihood that they will move closer to their desired goals. To set an intention, clients lean into what is immediately present for them in the body, noticing what feels especially true and pressing in that moment, with a focus on the felt sense in the body.

https://doi.org/10.1037/0000399-005

Deliberate Practice in Psychedelic-Assisted Therapy, by S. Dames, A. Penn, M. Williams, J. A. Zamaria, T. Rousmaniere, and A. Vaz

Expectations refer to the beliefs that something will or should happen, regarding relational boundaries and anticipated outcomes. As such, much like an intention, expectations can serve as a self-fulfilling prophecy, informing the reality of where we are heading—whether we consciously want to move there or not (Kirsch, 1997; Shapiro & Shapiro, 1997). They can also serve as an unchecked assumption that sets clients up for frustration and disappointment. It is important that clients' expectations of the experience are made explicit. This helps therapists and clients consciously manage expectations, which cultivates greater empowerment and choice in the clients' experiences (Constantino et al., 2018).

Finally, no matter how carefully one considers their intentions and expectations, the intelligence of the body is often a wiser guide than the logic of the mind (Ogden & Fisher, 2015; van der Kolk, 2015). With this in mind, it is wise to hold intentions lightly and to be open to surprise, accepting that what arises is exactly what is called for in that moment, without needing to control the process or the outcome.

The counselor should improvise a response to each client statement following these skill criteria:

1. **Reflect the client's underlying intentions or expectations (making the implicit explicit).** In this first skill criterion, the counselor makes the subtle more explicit to promote clarity and a greater capacity for the client to reframe consciously, where helpful. This first step is essential because it ensures that you have adequately understood the intentions or expectations that are driving the client's reaction. This can help clients who may not have considered that their perception of a successful therapy experience hinges on specific hopes and expectations that may not be realistic or beneficial in their healing experience.

2. **Clarify if the client's expectations are realistic.** A lot of media reports of PAT have described clients having life-changing experiences that can almost make PAT sound like a miracle cure. Although the effects of PAT may be profound, if the client's goals are not realistic, then they are likely setting themselves up for disappointment or feeling like a personal failure. Thus, it is important for the therapist to clarify whether the client's goals are realistic.

3. **Invite the client to elaborate on what lies beneath the surface story.** In many cultures, especially in the West, image, achievements, and external praise are often prioritized over one's innate values and desires. Clients may be prone to think of lofty intentions that may not be congruent with their actual values and desires. Furthermore, clients may often put more trust on external solutions, or advice from others, than their own intuition. To promote inner healing intelligence requires an ongoing practice of looking beneath the surface story of what initially presents. Exploring what lies beneath the intentions and expectations to the most authentic truth is important to promote clients' congruence and agency to develop a strong foundation in the therapeutic process.

SKILL CRITERIA FOR EXERCISE 3

1. Reflect the client's underlying intentions or expectations (making the implicit explicit).
2. Clarify if the client's expectations are realistic.
3. Invite the client to elaborate on what lies beneath the surface story.

Examples of Exploring Intentions and Expectations

Example 1

CLIENT: [*sad*] I just want to get my partner back.

THERAPIST: I hear that you wish for this process to help you get back what you've lost. (Criterion 1) We can't be sure of what they will do in the future. (Criterion 2) What qualities of self would need to change for you to "get your partner back"? What is holding you back from manifesting these qualities now? (Criterion 3)

Example 2

CLIENT: [*calm*] I want to explore the realm of the spiritual, talk to angels and ancestors, that sort of thing. Does that count as an intention?

THERAPIST: I hear that connecting with your spiritual side is important for your journey. (Criterion 1) Indeed, it's not uncommon for people using psychedelics to describe their experience as somehow spiritual. (Criterion 2) Can you say a little more about what you mean by a spiritual experience? If a connection with your spiritual nature does come up in the session, what do you hope comes of it? Ideally, how might such an experience affect you, your life, your relationships? (Criterion 3)

Example 3

CLIENT: [*anxious*] After years of struggle with PTSD [posttraumatic stress disorder] symptoms, my intention in this upcoming therapy session is to finally be free of it.

THERAPIST: I'm hearing that a successful session may hinge on the expectation that you will be cured of PTSD symptoms. (Criterion 1) Research has shown psychedelic therapy to help many people with PTSD. However, it can often take more than one session. (Criterion 2) What would it feel like for you if your recovery takes longer than one session? (Criterion 3)

INSTRUCTIONS FOR EXERCISE 3
Step 1: Role-Play and Feedback
• The client says the first beginner client statement. The therapist **improvises** a response based on the skill criteria. • The trainer (or, if not available, the client) provides **brief** feedback based on the skill criteria. • The client then repeats the same statement, and the therapist again improvises a response. The trainer (or client) again provides brief feedback.
Step 2: Repeat
• Repeat Step 1 for all the statements **in the current difficulty level** (beginner, intermediate, or advanced).
Step 3: Assess and Adjust Difficulty
• The therapist completes the Deliberate Practice Reaction Form (see Appendix A) and decides whether to make the exercise easier or harder or to repeat the same difficulty level.
Step 4: Repeat for Approximately 15 Minutes
• Repeat Steps 1 to 3 for at least 15 minutes. • The trainees then switch therapist and client roles and start over.

Now it's your turn! Follow Steps 1 and 2 from the exercise instructions.

Remember: The goal of the role-play is for trainees to practice improvising responses to the client statements in a manner that (a) uses the skill criteria and (b) feels authentic for the trainee. **Example therapist responses for each client statement are provided at the end of this exercise. Trainees should attempt to improvise their own responses before reading the example responses.**

BEGINNER-LEVEL CLIENT STATEMENTS FOR EXERCISE 3
Beginner Client Statement 1
[Sad] I just want to get my partner back.
Beginner Client Statement 2
[Anxious] No matter what I do, there is an inner critic that picks it apart. I want to feel good enough!
Beginner Client Statement 3
[Determined] On the other side of this, I want to experience more joy in life.
Beginner Client Statement 4
[Determined] I'm tired of always looking for what's wrong. I want to cultivate more gratitude in my life.
Beginner Client Statement 5
[Anxious] I'm hoping after all this, I won't feel so anxious all the time.

 Assess and adjust the difficulty before moving to the next difficulty level (see Step 3 in the exercise instructions).

INTERMEDIATE-LEVEL CLIENT STATEMENTS FOR EXERCISE 3
Intermediate Client Statement 1
[Desperate] I've been reading all these stories in the news of veterans and other people receiving this treatment and that it is working like a miracle cure. This is supposed to be some kind of magic bullet, right? As you know, I feel like I've tried everything for my depression with no success. This is my last-ditch effort—it just has to work to get rid of my depression.
Intermediate Client Statement 2
[Sad] I want to know what is beneath this eating disorder that has been haunting me for so many years.
Intermediate Client Statement 3
[Conflicted] I really am hoping that psychedelic therapy can help me with my anxiety. But my wife thinks this is a waste of time and might even make things worse.
Intermediate Client Statement 4
[Anxious] I am feeling so awful, this therapy better work right away!
Intermediate Client Statement 5
[Depressed] I have tried everything; this is my last hope.

 Assess and adjust the difficulty before moving to the next difficulty level (see Step 3 in the exercise instructions).

ADVANCED-LEVEL CLIENT STATEMENTS FOR EXERCISE 3
Advanced Client Statement 1
[Anxious] After years of struggle with PTSD symptoms, my intention in this upcoming therapy session is to finally be free of it.
Advanced Client Statement 2
[Calm] I want to explore the realm of the spiritual, talk to angels and ancestors, that sort of thing. Does that count as an intention?
Advanced Client Statement 3
[Depressed] I've been in therapy since I was 10, and nothing has worked. I don't think this will work either.
Advanced Client Statement 4
[Hopeful] I want to get super high and feel great!
Advanced Client Statement 5
[Anxious] My friend recommended this kind of therapy, but honestly I'm worried that it could make me crazy.

 Assess and adjust the difficulty here (see Step 3 in the exercise instructions). If appropriate, follow the instructions to make the exercise even more challenging (see Appendix A).

Example Therapist Responses: Exploring Intentions and Expectations

Remember: Trainees should attempt to improvise their own responses before reading the example responses. **Do not read the following responses verbatim unless you are having trouble coming up with your own responses!**

EXAMPLE RESPONSES TO BEGINNER-LEVEL CLIENT STATEMENTS FOR EXERCISE 3
Example Response to Beginner Client Statement 1
I hear that you wish for this process to help you get back what you've lost. (Criterion 1) We can't be sure of what they will do in the future. (Criterion 2) What qualities of self would need to change for you to "get your partner back"? What is holding you back from manifesting these qualities now? (Criterion 3)
Example Response to Beginner Client Statement 2
I'm hearing you acknowledge that life is messy and that you'd like to find a place of peace within the messiness. That perhaps perfection is perfectly imperfect. (Criterion 1) Some people achieve this kind of change through psychedelic therapy. (Criterion 2) I'm wondering how living "good enough" in your day-to-day life might look and feel differently than it does now? (Criterion 3)
Example Response to Beginner Client Statement 3
It sounds like your intention is to cultivate more joy in your life. (Criterion 1) That is a potentially realistic expectation. (Criterion 2) What obstacles might be preventing you from feeling more joy now? (Criterion 3)
Example Response to Beginner Client Statement 4
It sounds like you would like to switch out the lens from which you view life through, from what is wrong to what is right. (Criterion 1) That is a potentially realistic expectation. (Criterion 2) When you remember back to a time when you experienced genuine gratitude for something in your life, what did that feel like in your body? How might your day-to-day life feel or look different if you felt more gratitude in your life? (Criterion 3)
Example Response to Beginner Client Statement 5
I can imagine it is tiring to be managing so much anxiety in your day-to-day life, and that you'd like this process to bring about some relief. (Criterion 1) Many people experience a reduction in anxiety symptoms from psychedelic therapy. (Criterion 2) Sometimes it can be helpful to better understand the belief system or context that is at the root of the anxiety. Do you have a sense of that now, or is this something you'd like to explore in the session? (Criterion 3)

EXAMPLE RESPONSES TO INTERMEDIATE-LEVEL CLIENT STATEMENTS FOR EXERCISE 3

Example Response to Intermediate Client Statement 1

That would truly be fantastic if you could take a psychedelic and it would instantly cure your depression. (Criterion 1) Although we do occasionally see truly miraculous results, I worry that you may have unrealistic expectations. Depression is often reduced after psychedelic therapy, but it takes time and hard work. (Criterion 2) I'm curious how you feel hearing this? (Criterion 3)

Example Response to Intermediate Client Statement 2

It sounds like you're really interested in understanding this part of yourself better. (Criterion 1) This is a realistic expectation for psychedelic therapy. (Criterion 2) How do you think your relationship with the eating disorder would be different if you understood what was beneath it? Do you have a sense of what has stopped you from being able to understand its underpinnings up until now? (Criterion 3)

Example Response to Intermediate Client Statement 3

So it seems like you're hoping that psychedelic therapy can help you with your anxiety, but your wife has concerns about whether this is safe. (Criterion 1) Research has shown that psychedelic therapy can help many people with anxiety. With proper screening and careful treatment, psychedelic therapy can be very safe. (Criterion 2) What would your life look like with less anxiety? (Criterion 3)

Example Response to Intermediate Client Statement 4

It sounds like you want this therapy to help you immediately. (Criterion 1) Although that can occasionally happen, it often takes time and work for the greatest benefits to be realized. (Criterion 2) What would a successful treatment look like to you? (Criterion 3)

Example Response to Intermediate Client Statement 5

It sounds like there is a lot riding on this treatment. (Criterion 1) While psychedelic therapy can be effective for many people, there are also some people who feel fewer benefits. (Criterion 2) If this treatment were to work, how might you feel differently, or what would it allow you to do that you are not able to do right now? (Criterion 3)

EXAMPLE RESPONSES TO ADVANCED-LEVEL CLIENT STATEMENTS FOR EXERCISE 3

Example Response to Advanced Client Statement 1

I'm hearing that a successful session may hinge on the expectation that you will be cured of PTSD symptoms. (Criterion 1) Research has shown psychedelic therapy to help many people with PTSD. However, it can often take more than one session. (Criterion 2). What would it feel like for you if your recovery takes longer than one session? (Criterion 3)

Example Response to Advanced Client Statement 2

I hear that connecting with your spiritual side is important for your journey. (Criterion 1) Indeed, it's not uncommon for people using psychedelics to describe their experience as somehow spiritual. (Criterion 2) Can you say a little more about what you mean by a spiritual experience? If a connection with your spiritual nature does come up in the session, what do you hope comes of it? Ideally, how might such an experience affect you, your life, your relationships? (Criterion 3)

Example Response to Advanced Client Statement 3

When things have been difficult like this for a long time, it can be hard to imagine that things can be different. It's totally fine for you to be wary or skeptical of this process. I appreciate your honesty. (Criterion 1) While psychedelic therapy is often effective at helping people with depression, there is always a chance that it may not help. (Criterion 2) Depression can be complex, and it can take time for us to embody new ways of "seeing" and "being" in the world in our everyday behaviors. I wonder how your life might look and feel different for you to feel some initial progress in this area. Do you have a sense of what a small step forward might look and feel like? (Criterion 3)

Example Response to Advanced Client Statement 4

I hear that you want to get high and feel great. (Criterion 1) Most people feel very different when they take a psychedelic substance, and it is impossible to predict what your experience will be. We call it a "nonordinary state of consciousness." You might have lots of different feelings come up for you. Some of them you might describe as happy, light, or "high." Other feelings may be sad or challenging at times. (Criterion 2) How do you feel hearing that we cannot predict your experience? (Criterion 3)

Example Response to Advanced Client Statement 5

I hear that you have some fear that this experience could make you crazy, which is understandable given how many scary messages we receive about drugs. (Criterion 1) Psychedelic therapy can be very safe when proper screen and safety precautions are taken. (Criterion 2) When you imagine "not coming back," what are you afraid will change, or will be lost in this process? And perhaps equally important, what are you hoping will change or be lost in the process? (Criterion 3)

Cultural Considerations: Racially and Ethnically Diverse Communities

Preparations for Exercise 4

1. Read the instructions in Chapter 2.

2. Download the Deliberate Practice Reaction Form and the Deliberate Practice Diary Form at https://www.apa.org/pubs/books/deliberate-practice-psychedelic-assisted-therapy (see the "Clinician and Practitioner Resources" tab; also available in Appendixes A and B, respectively).

Skill Description

Skill Difficulty Level: Beginner

Psychedelic therapy puts clients at an increased level of vulnerability. One of the therapeutic mechanisms of psychedelic therapy involves the quieting of the nervous system and/or ego, so that the client can move beneath the surface of life, into a deep embodied healing process. It hampers the normal psychological protections that many racialized people have had to develop to navigate in the world, and as a result, they may feel defenseless. Therefore, the development of relational trust is imperative. If therapists do not understand the unique needs of clients who have experienced racism, it can put them at additional risk of harm (M. T. Williams et al., 2020). Furthermore, cultural themes often arise during psychedelic experiences, and missing the opportunity to address them can impede the integration process. Thus, it is important that all clinicians seek cultural understanding as a basic mechanism of effective therapy (Davis et al., 2018).

North America is becoming more diverse over time. In the next 20 years, in the United States, non-Hispanic White people are projected to become a minority group (U.S. Census Bureau, 2014). In the next 10 years in Canada, visible minorities will make up a third of the population (Statistics Canada, 2017).

https://doi.org/10.1037/0000399-006

Deliberate Practice in Psychedelic-Assisted Therapy, by S. Dames, A. Penn, M. Williams, J. A. Zamaria, T. Rousmaniere, and A. Vaz

Our culture informs our values and worldview. Our race refers to our observable human traits (appearance based). Our ethnicity, on the other hand, is the expression of our unique cultural identity. It is important to consider the difference between race and ethnicity because ethnicity serves as a positive construct that can promote a sense of identity and belonging, whereas race deliberately places people into boxes, based on appearance and presumed heritage (M. T. Williams, 2020).

Although few therapists would consider themselves racist, many will perpetuate racism without realizing it. The most important component of cultural safety is humility, which cultivates an open curiosity to take direction from the client, rather than from assumptions that may or may not be accurate (Davis et al., 2018). For instance, well-intentioned therapists may say something that they believe is culturally relevant but is a hurtful misperception or generalization (Constantine, 2007). As such, developing awareness of our assumptions and biases is imperative before administering these therapies to people from culture(s) different from our own (J. Harris et al., 2024).

Additionally, different cultures can experience and express mental health symptoms differently, and stigma related to psychedelic therapy varies (Sue & Sue, 2017). Therapists who are working with persons of color are encouraged to ask directly about their experiences of racism before the psychedelic medicine session. Asking about cultural stigma is also important because feelings of shame can inhibit one's ability to trust the medicine and the therapeutic process. Feeling guarded during a psychedelic experience can inhibit the ability to surrender or let go. Speaking about these experiences makes the implicit explicit, so that the client's fears are addressed. This is an important component of building the trust necessary for the therapeutic container to feel safe.

We strongly believe every therapist needs cultural safety training as a basic foundation to begin building their capacity to work safely with clients. A critical component of developing a safe relational container to support psychedelic therapies requires an honest assessment of one's biases, an open-hearted curiosity, and ongoing open dialogues with clients about how race, ethnicity, culture, and religion inform how they make meaning of their life and therapy experience (Hook et al., 2013).

This exercise is not meant to have therapists memorize responses because this would not be congruent or authentic, and congruence is a requirement in the development of trust in the therapeutic alliance. Rather, this exercise is meant to help learners identify blind spots, discomforts, and triggers that can lead to subconscious projections and help learners find ways to respond that feel authentic and demonstrate humility in the process.

Note: If any of the statements do not feel safe for you as the therapist, please choose alternative statements that do feel safe. The therapist should improvise a response to each client statement following these skill criteria:

1. **Promote cultural safety and show cultural humility by conveying a desire not to assume the client's experience as well as to learn from them.** Therapists should never assume that they know what is best for clients in any situation. No matter the amount of training or life experience the therapist may have, this is a good time to check one's assumptions. Assumptions based on stereotypes can lead to harmful and unnecessary prejudices, and as such, cultural humility is essential. Although the client will generally know more about their own culture than you do, it's also important to remember that ethnic identity development can be a challenging process for anyone, no matter their race or ethnicity. People often start at a stage where they don't think much about their race and ethnicity, and over time, they decide what this aspect of their identity means to them. A stronger, positive ethnic identity protects people of color from

some of the harms of racism (M. T. Williams et al., 2012, 2018). Therapists should not assume clients have this all figured out, and in fact, feelings of shame and internalized racism are common during this process. It's important that therapists work with clients of color to understand where the client is on their journey and then, if necessary, help strengthen their ethnic identity.

2. **Emphasize that the client and their cultural worldview will be respected by conveying a desire to adapt therapy to better respect the client's needs and cultural worldview.** This can be achieved by showing respect to the client at all times. You should invite the client to share any concerns they have about the process so that they can be explicitly addressed before the session. Additionally, if there are cultural practices or objects of care that can be included, this is a good way to promote familiarity and safety in the therapeutic process. Inviting the client to include rituals that are familiar to them shows you respect their beliefs, can promote a sense of safety and grounding, and can help them integrate insights into their daily routine.

SKILL CRITERIA FOR EXERCISE 4

1. Promote cultural safety and show cultural humility by conveying a desire not to assume the client's experience and to learn from them.
2. Emphasize that the client and their cultural worldview will be respected by conveying a desire to adapt therapy to better respect the client's needs and cultural worldview.

Examples of Cultural Considerations: Racially and Ethnically Diverse Communities

Example 1

CLIENT: [*anxious*] I grew up learning that, in my culture, we were discouraged from making big expressions of our emotions. But in the videos I've seen of this kind of therapy, it seems like people are crying and yelling, and I'm afraid if I don't do that, I won't be doing it right.

THERAPIST: I'd like to support you to express yourself in a way that feels congruent with your cultural preferences. That feels like an important—perhaps even imperative—part of your experience. (Criterion 1) Please don't feel any pressure to express your emotions in any particular way. (Criterion 2)

Example 2

CLIENT: [*worried*] I can't get past this idea that these sacred medicines were taken from my people in the process of colonization, and now the same system that controls their use appears to have reduced them to the consumption of chemicals. I'm worried these feelings will impact the session.

THERAPIST: Thank you for sharing that with me. It feels important to acknowledge that the brutal history of colonization is interwoven with the suffering of your people. I don't want to assume that I know what is best for you in this situation. (Criterion 1) However,

I do wonder if these feelings may be an important part of your therapy process, not necessarily a hindrance to it. Let's talk about some ways that we can work together to navigate these feelings if they come up in session. (Criterion 2)

Example 3

CLIENT: [*anxious*] I don't feel safe with White people.

THERAPIST: That makes sense. A lot of White people harm people of color, knowingly and unknowingly. I don't want to assume. . . . But would it be fair to say that you or people you care about have been hurt by White people? (Criterion 1) How might we tailor this situation to help you feel safe? (Criterion 2)

INSTRUCTIONS FOR EXERCISE 4

Step 1: Role-Play and Feedback

- The client says the first beginner client statement. The therapist **improvises** a response based on the skill criteria.
- The trainer (or, if not available, the client) provides **brief** feedback based on the skill criteria.
- The client then repeats the same statement, and the therapist again improvises a response. The trainer (or client) again provides brief feedback.

Step 2: Repeat

- Repeat Step 1 for all the statements **in the current difficulty level** (beginner, intermediate, or advanced).

Step 3: Assess and Adjust Difficulty

- The therapist completes the Deliberate Practice Reaction Form (see Appendix A) and decides whether to make the exercise easier or harder or to repeat the same difficulty level.

Step 4: Repeat for Approximately 15 Minutes

- Repeat Steps 1 to 3 for at least 15 minutes.
- The trainees then switch therapist and client roles and start over.

Now it's your turn! Follow Steps 1 and 2 from the exercise instructions.

Remember: The goal of the role-play is for trainees to practice improvising responses to the client statements in a manner that (a) uses the skill criteria and (b) feels authentic for the trainee. **Example therapist responses for each client statement are provided at the end of this exercise. Trainees should attempt to improvise their own responses before reading the example responses.**

BEGINNER-LEVEL CLIENT STATEMENTS FOR EXERCISE 4
Beginner Client Statement 1
[Curious] Have you ever worked with Indigenous clients?
Beginner Client Statement 2
[Concerned] In my culture, emotional expression can be loud at times. I'm worried that it may bother other people if I'm too loud.
Beginner Client Statement 3
[Worried] I grew up learning that, in my culture, we were discouraged from making big expressions of our emotions. But in the videos I've seen of this kind of therapy, it seems like people are crying and yelling, and I'm afraid if I don't do that, I won't be doing it right.
Beginner Client Statement 4
[Anxious] I am afraid that I might get arrested for this if someone finds out. Our community is always a target when it comes to drugs.
Beginner Client Statement 5
[Calm] In my culture, we are taught to wash our face to help us transition from ceremony. I'd like to honor the teachings of my Elders.

🤚 **Assess and adjust the difficulty before moving to the next difficulty level (see Step 3 in the exercise instructions).**

INTERMEDIATE-LEVEL CLIENT STATEMENTS FOR EXERCISE 4

Intermediate Client Statement 1

[Anxious] I don't feel safe with White people.

Intermediate Client Statement 2

[Apprehensive] Is there any way I can have a Black therapist?

Intermediate Client Statement 3

[Anxious] In my culture, we sometimes say that sadness is because we've dishonored our ancestors. I'm afraid that my ancestors might show up during my journey.

Intermediate Client Statement 4

[Concerned] The music that you were just playing is considered really sacred in my culture, and it just seemed like it was background here. Could you not play that during my session?

Intermediate Client Statement 5

[Sad] My dream is to walk into a room and for a therapist to see the real me and not to avoid the issue of race.

 Assess and adjust the difficulty before moving to the next difficulty level (see Step 3 in the exercise instructions).

ADVANCED-LEVEL CLIENT STATEMENTS FOR EXERCISE 4
Advanced Client Statement 1
[Anxious] I am a Muslim, and we are not supposed to ingest intoxicating substances. Will this make me intoxicated?
Advanced Client Statement 2
[Worried] I can't get past this idea that these sacred medicines were taken from my people in the process of colonization, and now the same system that now controls their use appears to have reduced them to the consumption of chemicals. I'm worried these feelings will impact the session.
Advanced Client Statement 3
[Distrustful] It's hard to take advice from someone who looks a lot like the same people who treat me like I'm a lesser human because of my skin color.
Advanced Client Statement 4
[Irritated] You said that we are all one and color doesn't matter. It does matter, and it's racist for you to say that.
Advanced Client Statement 5
[Anxious] My husband is really against this kind of thing. These substances are just not part of our culture.

🛑 **Assess and adjust the difficulty here (see Step 3 in the exercise instructions). If appropriate, follow the instructions to make the exercise even more challenging (see Appendix A).**

Example Therapist Responses: Cultural Considerations: Racially and Ethnically Diverse Communities

Remember: Trainees should attempt to improvise their own responses before reading the example responses. **Do not read the following responses verbatim unless you are having trouble coming up with your own responses!**

EXAMPLE RESPONSES TO BEGINNER-LEVEL CLIENT STATEMENTS FOR EXERCISE 4
Example Response to Beginner Client Statement 1
I have [or have not] worked with Indigenous clients, but Indigenous People come from so many different cultures and traditions, I certainly don't want to make any assumptions. (Criterion 1) What do you want me to know about you and your culture that will help me support you on this journey? (Criterion 2)
Example Response to Beginner Client Statement 2
I'd like to support you to express yourself in a way that feels congruent with your cultural preferences. That feels like an important, perhaps even imperative, part of your experience. (Criterion 1) Please don't feel any pressure to express your emotions in any particular way. (Criterion 2)
Example Response to Beginner Client Statement 3
I want to be clear, there's no "right" way to do this therapy. Of course we want you to feel safe, and we'll ensure that. (Criterion 1) But whatever comes up for you, and in whatever way, is fine with us, be it big or small. (Criterion 2)
Example Response to Beginner Client Statement 4
I understand that you're worried about the idea of taking a drug that is, in most cases, illegal. I hear that it's a huge problem how your community is profiled and targeted by law enforcement for drug offenses. (Criterion 1) I'm really glad you brought this up, and if you continue to have concerns about this or other aspects of your safety, I encourage you to bring them up to me as soon as you feel comfortable doing so, so that we can think through them together. (Criterion 2)
Example Response to Beginner Client Statement 5
I'm grateful that you brought this up. I'd like our time together to reflect an environment and process that respects your culture and elders. (Criterion 1) We can integrate the face-washing tradition into our work. Are there any other practices or objects we can include that would help you feel like you are honoring your cultural teachings? (Criterion 2)

EXAMPLE RESPONSES TO INTERMEDIATE-LEVEL
CLIENT STATEMENTS FOR EXERCISE 4

Example Response to Intermediate Client Statement 1

That makes sense. A lot of White people harm people of color, knowingly and unknowingly. I don't want to assume. . . . But would it be fair to say that you or people you care about have been hurt by White people? (Criterion 1) How might we tailor this situation to help you feel safe? (Criterion 2)

Example Response to Intermediate Client Statement 2

I wish we had a Black therapist to offer you. I acknowledge that I may have limitations in my ability to understand your experience. (Criterion 1) Are you worried that there is something important I won't understand because I am not Black? I'd like to understand every part of your experience as a Black person so I can authentically join you in this journey. (Criterion 2)

Example Response to Intermediate Client Statement 3

It's really important to me that people understand their experience in a way that makes sense to them. I'd like to learn more about this part of your culture because this sounds like a very important way that you understand your feelings. (Criterion 1) As we continue our conversation, I'd like to encourage you to share more about your culture and how I can be supportive of your journey. (Criterion 2)

Example Response to Intermediate Client Statement 4

I can certainly see how that would bother you, and if you like, we can take that out. (Criterion 1) Would it be helpful to look at the rest of the playlist to see if you have any strong feelings about the other music that we'll be using? (Criterion 2)

Example Response to Intermediate Client Statement 5

I think what I'm hearing is that when a therapist doesn't bring up your race, it erases that part of your experience, or at least doesn't make room for it in therapy. I don't want to assume though—is this part of what you're saying? (Criterion 1) Now that you've made this clear, I'd like to be more supportive. If it's clear for you, how might I be more explicit about the impacts and influence of your race in our time together? If not clear, I welcome your feedback as I feel my way through how to best support you in this area. (Criterion 2)

EXAMPLE RESPONSES TO ADVANCED-LEVEL CLIENT STATEMENTS FOR EXERCISE 4

Example Response to Advanced Client Statement 1

Thank you for sharing this really important religious standard with me. I can understand why you don't want this treatment to violate your faithfulness, and I want to help support you in that. (Criterion 1) I can't make a determination if psychedelics are intoxicating, but I can tell you that they have a range of effects that can alter your experience of thinking, emotions, and physical sensations. I would like you to be as informed as possible going into this, so I'll go through all the common effects of psychedelics with you. Then I hope you can make a determination if participation in this treatment would be in violation of your religion. (Criterion 2)

Example Response to Advanced Client Statement 2

Thank you for sharing that with me. It feels important to acknowledge that the brutal history of colonization is interwoven with the suffering of your people. I don't want to assume that I know what is best for you in this situation. (Criterion 1) However, I do wonder if these feelings may be an important part of your therapy process, not necessarily a hindrance to it. Let's talk about some ways that we can work together to navigate these feelings if they come up in session. (Criterion 2)

Example Response to Advanced Client Statement 3

I'd like to thank you for being so honest with me. It takes a lot of courage, and integrity to be transparent about where you are at right now, and your feelings are so understandable! Recognizing we are arriving here with different cultural backgrounds, I may inadvertently say or do something that doesn't land well for you in our time together. (Criterion 1) Please let me know if that happens. Speaking to these tensions is an opportunity to heal harms from relational wounds of the past. (Criterion 2)

Example Response to Advanced Client Statement 4

Oh my goodness, you are absolutely right! I am so sorry I said that. I can see how that could be dismissive of your experience as a person of color, and I regret my words. I was trying to convey that a person's worth should not be tied to their race, which I thought would help put you at ease, but I see I really failed in my attempt to communicate this, and perhaps you are now less comfortable with me. (Criterion 1) I truly appreciate you bringing this to my attention, and this means I will need to work that much harder to earn your trust. (Criterion 2)

Example Response to Advanced Client Statement 5

I can imagine that could feel really uncomfortable. I'd like to understand your concern better. (Criterion 1) Are you concerned that your husband is not in support of you doing this work, or because the substances aren't part of your culture? Are there any ways that we can help you feel more comfortable or confident about our work together? (Criterion 2)

Boundaries and Informed Consent

Preparations for Exercise 5

1. Read the instructions in Chapter 2.

2. Download the Deliberate Practice Reaction Form and the Deliberate Practice Diary Form at https://www.apa.org/pubs/books/deliberate-practice-psychedelic-assisted-therapy (see the "Clinician and Practitioner Resources" tab; also available in Appendixes A and B, respectively).

Skill Description

Skill Difficulty Level: Intermediate

Psychedelics can evoke strong emotions, including feelings of idealization, love, and sexual attraction, which may be directed toward the therapist (Grof, 2019). Because this is so common, it is wise for the therapist to anticipate that these feelings may arise and to be prepared to respond appropriately. As such, it is important for the therapist to clarify boundaries before the session and to reiterate them throughout.

Informed consent describes the process for which clients are provided with all the information they need, including the potential risks and benefits, to be able to consent fully to participate in psychedelic therapy. This includes describing the details of the therapeutic process, the therapy environment, a typical and atypical client experience, the expectation of the client, and the roles of the therapy team. There must be adequate time to review the consent form and to have all their questions answered before signing the treatment consent form. When done successfully, informed consent helps clients feel more empowered (promoting agency, dignity, and autonomy), establishes a therapeutic alliance between the therapists and the client, reduces the risk of

https://doi.org/10.1037/0000399-007

Deliberate Practice in Psychedelic-Assisted Therapy, by S. Dames, A. Penn, M. Williams, J. A. Zamaria, T. Rousmaniere, and A. Vaz

inadvertent harms that result from misunderstandings, and promotes transparency, and thereby integrity, in the therapy process. It is the responsibility of the therapist to ensure that consent is informed, ongoing and can be withdrawn or changed at any time.

The client must be competent to provide consent (i.e., reading level, age, sound mind). Finally, the client's cultural lens must be considered to ensure that the content and delivery method of consent aligns with the client's ability to understand the content, and that the manner of seeking consent is aligned with their ways of knowing.

Certain activities are always prohibited in psychedelic-assisted therapy, such as sexual activity, communicating with outside parties during a session, leaving the session before completion, aggression, nudity, driving after the session, and taking other medicines without prior approval or vetting by therapist or clinician. Therapists should explain the rationale for why these rules apply to all participants, so clients do not feel that it is personal and to promote buy-in for the agreements within the therapeutic alliance.

It can be helpful to remember that those who have experience in nonordinary states of consciousness will be more able to engage in "informed" consent because they have a lived experience of their sense of agency in the psychedelic space. Those with past experiences have had an opportunity to establish some trust in the process, and as such, may have more tolerance for ambiguity. For those who do not have life experience, it is important to remember that the uncertainty hampers trust in the process. To establish more certainty, the therapy process should be structured enough to promote a sense of predictability and control going into the session. Any variances from the structure that was agreed on should be at the client's discretion—again, always reminding the client that they are in the driver's seat of their experience.

The goal of this exercise is to help trainees become more comfortable and fluent in addressing challenging questions and boundary issues that may arise throughout psychedelic-assisted therapy. For this exercise, it might be particularly useful to do a routine review of the example therapist responses provided at the end. We've found that these example responses often help trainees get a clearer sense for the types of roles and boundaries usually communicated during psychedelic-assisted treatments.

Finally, it is important to remember that even though the nature of consent is well defined in one moment, it is wise never to assume it applies to all moments. As such, the ongoing weaving of consent throughout the therapeutic process is imperative.

The therapist should improvise a response to each client statement following these skill criteria:

1. **Acknowledge the client's concern.** The therapist conveys clear understanding or normalizing of the client's concern, without avoiding challenging topics being present. This helps create a trusting working alliance, where the therapist starts by honoring what is arising for the client.

2. **Clarify agreements, roles, and boundaries related to the client's concern.** The therapist conveys what is to be expected in therapy, as well as the expected role of the therapist and the client throughout the process. By transitioning from vague to specific, consent becomes informed. Importantly, if a client requests a prohibited activity, clarify what is prohibited and explain why. As described earlier, certain activities are always prohibited in psychedelic-assisted therapy, such as sexual activity, communicating with outside parties during a session, leaving the session before completion, aggression, nudity, driving after the session, and taking other medicines without prior approval/vetting by the clinician. Therapists should explain the rationale for why these rules apply to all participants, so clients do not feel that it is personal.

SKILL CRITERIA FOR EXERCISE 5

1. Acknowledge the client's concern.
2. Clarify agreements, roles, and boundaries related to the client's concern. (Note: If a prohibited activity is requested, clarify what is prohibited and explain why.)

Examples of Boundaries and Informed Consent

Example 1

CLIENT: [*nervous*] Every time I use a psychedelic, I get turned on. What happens if I'm feeling sexual here?

THERAPIST: Thank you for asking. This isn't at all uncommon, so it's important that we talk about it. (Criterion 1) While sexual feelings may arise as a natural component of your experience, therapy never includes sex. If sexual feelings arise, it is my role to help you understand where these feelings are coming from, without ever engaging in sexual activity with you. (Criterion 2)

Example 2

CLIENT: [*warm*] I like hugs. I'll take as many as I can get in the session.

THERAPIST: Thank you for letting me know. (Criterion 1) Hugs can make people feel really safe sometimes during these sessions. At the same time, sometimes you may find your feelings may change due to where you are on your journey. So, to make sure you remain in the driver's seat, we will always ask for consent before giving you a hug. (Criterion 2)

Example 3

CLIENT: [*anxious*] Can my partner be here with me during the psychedelic medicine session?

THERAPIST: That's a great question. A lot of people ask if and how their partners can be integrated into this process. (Criterion 1) Typically, psychedelic medicine sessions are confidential, only including the therapy team and the client. However, with your consent, this is something we can arrange. During the session, if at any point you'd like for your loved one to step out, it's important that you know that you can change your mind at any time, and we will support your decision. (Criterion 2)

INSTRUCTIONS FOR EXERCISE 5
Step 1: Role-Play and Feedback
• The client says the first beginner client statement. The therapist **improvises** a response based on the skill criteria.   • The trainer (or, if not available, the client) provides **brief** feedback based on the skill criteria.   • The client then repeats the same statement, and the therapist again improvises a response. The trainer (or client) again provides brief feedback.
Step 2: Repeat
• Repeat Step 1 for all the statements **in the current difficulty level** (beginner, intermediate, or advanced).
Step 3: Assess and Adjust Difficulty
• The therapist completes the Deliberate Practice Reaction Form (see Appendix A) and decides whether to make the exercise easier or harder or to repeat the same difficulty level.
Step 4: Repeat for Approximately 15 Minutes
• Repeat Steps 1 to 3 for at least 15 minutes.   • The trainees then switch therapist and client roles and start over.

Now it's your turn! Follow Steps 1 and 2 from the exercise instructions.

Remember: The goal of the role-play is for trainees to practice improvising responses to the client statements in a manner that (a) uses the skill criteria and (b) feels authentic for the trainee. **Example therapist responses for each client statement are provided at the end of this exercise. Trainees should attempt to improvise their own responses before reading the example responses.**

BEGINNER-LEVEL CLIENT STATEMENTS FOR EXERCISE 5
Beginner Client Statement 1
[Worried] I worry I'll feel attracted to you during our psychedelic session. If that happens, would it be okay for us to cuddle?
Beginner Client Statement 2
[Frightened] If I feel afraid, would it be okay to hold your hand? I might even need a hug at some point.
Beginner Client Statement 3
[Curious] I'm sure you guys take these all the time, right? How have psychedelics worked for you?
Beginner Client Statement 4
[Nervous] So, once I sign this informed consent, I guess that's it, right? No turning back now!
Beginner Client Statement 5
[Warm] I like hugs. I'll take as many as I can get in the session.

🤚 **Assess and adjust the difficulty before moving to the next difficulty level (see Step 3 in the exercise instructions).**

INTERMEDIATE-LEVEL CLIENT STATEMENTS FOR EXERCISE 5
Intermediate Client Statement 1
[Hopeful] I know I feel really grateful during psychedelic sessions. There's a real chance I'll want to call my boss during the session and thank her for how supportive she has been through this difficult time.
Intermediate Client Statement 2
[Curious] I noticed on Facebook that you and I have a lot of mutual friends. Do you ever tell them about your work with clients?
Intermediate Client Statement 3
[Nervous] I'm uncomfortable having a male in the room during my session.
Intermediate Client Statement 4
[Excited] If you haven't noticed by now, I'm feeling really turned on!
Intermediate Client Statement 5
[Worried] One of the things that made me choose you as a therapist was the articles that I read where you talked about providing psychedelic therapy, but I'm a little worried that you're going to talk about me in articles like that in the future.

 Assess and adjust the difficulty before moving to the next difficulty level (see Step 3 in the exercise instructions).

ADVANCED-LEVEL CLIENT STATEMENTS FOR EXERCISE 5
Advanced Client Statement 1
[Nervous] I don't want anyone touching me during the session.
Advanced Client Statement 2
[Worried] I had a friend who had a therapist turn him in to child protective services because of something he said in a session. Could that happen here?
Advanced Client Statement 3
[Worried] I'm worried I'll get uncomfortable during the psychedelic session and want to leave in the middle of it.
Advanced Client Statement 4
[Worried] I've heard in the news that people can get sexually abused when they take these medicines.
Advanced Client Statement 5
[Curious] Every time I use a psychedelic, I get turned on. What happens if I'm feeling sexual here?

🛑 **Assess and adjust the difficulty here (see Step 3 in the exercise instructions). If appropriate, follow the instructions to make the exercise even more challenging (see Appendix A).**

Example Therapist Responses: Boundaries and Informed Consent

Remember: Trainees should attempt to improvise their own responses before reading the example responses. **Do not read the following responses verbatim unless you are having trouble coming up with your own responses!**

EXAMPLE RESPONSES TO BEGINNER-LEVEL CLIENT STATEMENTS FOR EXERCISE 5
Example Response to Beginner Client Statement 1
It's normal to experience a range of feelings during psychedelic medicine sessions, including attraction to those in the room with us. (Criterion 1) My role is to help you explore these feelings in a way that honors the intentions and agreements we discussed before the session. Any activity that may be perceived as crossing into sexualized territory would be a violation of trust in our therapeutic alliance, which will impact safety. In psychedelic medicine sessions, to protect participants, we agree to not engage in any form of activity that could feel sexualized. (Criterion 2)
Example Response to Beginner Client Statement 2
I hear that you feel like you might need some physical reassurance during the session, and you can absolutely ask for this kind of support at any point in the session. (Criterion 1) We will never touch you without your permission, and the touch would never be sexual. In the session, you can ask for this touch, or you can hold out your hand. You can always say stop or ask that we stop holding your hand. If you can't speak clearly during the session, you can simply pull your hand back and we'll get the message. (Criterion 2)
Example Response to Beginner Client Statement 3
I'm not surprised that you might think that. (Criterion 1) But the way we use psychedelics here is not for fun, but as medicine. The idea is to take them only at certain times to address a specific issue—for example, for improving mental health, gaining insight, or improving well-being. I have tried psychedelics before, as part of my training and in a legal context, and I learned a lot from it. (Criterion 2)
Example Response to Beginner Client Statement 4
By signing this consent form, you are not legally obligated to do anything. This is a form that I provide to everyone to make sure they understand the process and what to expect. (Criterion 1) You don't lose any of your rights by signing because it's not a contract or a waiver. It is really offered here to make sure that I am doing my job by letting you know all the possible risks and challenges you might encounter so you can make an informed choice about moving forward. You can still change your mind about participating in psychedelic-assisted therapy at any time. (Criterion 2)
Example Response to Beginner Client Statement 5
I hear you, thank you for letting me know. (Criterion 1) Sometimes hugs can make people feel really safe during these sessions. At the same time, sometimes you may find your feelings may change due to where you are on your journey. So, to make sure you remain in the driver's seat, we will always ask for consent before giving you a hug. (Criterion 2)

EXAMPLE RESPONSES TO INTERMEDIATE-LEVEL CLIENT STATEMENTS FOR EXERCISE 5

Example Response to Intermediate Client Statement 1

It is common to have insights and experience strong feelings during the session. How wonderful to be experiencing gratitude for the support you've had. (Criterion 1) It's important that you wait until after the session is over before you contact anyone, so that you are making the decision in your ordinary state of mind. Making these decisions while you are in an altered and more vulnerable state of consciousness can cause unnecessary stress after the session. To protect participants, all sexualized activity is prohibited in psychedelic medicine sessions. You can absolutely take these insights and feelings with you. Expressing yourself after the session is an excellent way to integrate what happened in the session in your daily life. (Criterion 2)

Example Response to Intermediate Client Statement 2

It's true that it's kind of a small world, and I'm not surprised we may know some of the same people. (Criterion 1) But you can be assured that I don't talk casually about my clients and never talk about them in public settings. If I do seek consultation from professional colleagues, I would change your name and anything that could be used to identify you. Your identity and private information are confidential within our clinic. (Criterion 2)

Example Response to Intermediate Client Statement 3

Thank you for raising this important concern. We can absolutely honor your request. (Criterion 1) As we co-develop a safe space for your session, I'd like to celebrate how you are voicing your boundaries in a way that exercises self-compassion and promotes trust and predictability. (Criterion 2)

Example Response to Intermediate Client Statement 4

It's not uncommon for people to feel some sexual arousal or emotional closeness when they've taken this medicine. (Criterion 1) It's my job as a therapist to help you understand where these feelings are coming from, without actually engaging in sexual activity with you. If you'd be open to talking about the feelings, we can explore what's coming up for you. (Criterion 2)

Example Response to Intermediate Client Statement 5

Thank you for sharing that concern. It's valid. Please know that the cases I described in those articles were a mash-up of different people, and nothing in them could be used to identify the people involved. (Criterion 1) I'll never share your name or things that could be used to identify you without your permission. Everything we talk about here is confidential. (Criterion 2)

EXAMPLE RESPONSES TO ADVANCED-LEVEL CLIENT STATEMENTS FOR EXERCISE 5

Example Response to Advanced Client Statement 1

I applaud how you are using your voice in this request. It's really important that you feel empowered to set boundaries that help you feel ready and safe as you prepare for your session. (Criterion 1) To ensure we are honoring your request, while also supporting your needs in the session, I'd like to ask you a clarifying question. When strong emotions come up for processing, touch can be a tangible way to remind the body that it is not alone in the experience. From this perspective, in the session, if you experience a want or need for your body to be comforted in the session, how would you like us to respond in that moment? (Criterion 2)

Example Response to Advanced Client Statement 2

That's a great question. (Criterion 1) In general, what we talk about in therapy is totally confidential. There are a few key exceptions where I'd have to break confidentiality. One would be if you said you wanted to harm someone else. I'm bound to warn that person. Another would be if you told me that you were going to hurt yourself and we weren't able to come up with a plan to keep you safe. In that case, I'd want to admit you to a hospital to keep you safe. The final situation, which may have been what happened to your friend, is if I learn that a child or an adult that can't take care of themselves is being harmed. In that situation, I'm what's called a mandated reporter, and I have to let child protective or adult protective services know so that they can keep that person safe. I realize that's a lot. Do you have any questions about these exceptions to confidentiality? (Criterion 2)

Example Response to Advanced Client Statement 3

I am so sorry that you are not feeling comfortable. It sometimes happens that psychedelics contribute to feelings of unease or anxiety. (Criterion 1) Since you have recently taken the medication, I am afraid that you cannot leave right now. Remember when we talked about how you are required to stay here until the medicine wears off? Leaving before the session has completed is prohibited. That is because psychedelics can impair your judgment, so we need to keep an eye on you to make sure you stay safe until it is out of your system. That being said, maybe there are a few things we can do to make you more comfortable until it is over [suggest breathing exercises or lying down; offer water, fan, blanket, benzodiazepine, etc., based on the client's specific issue]. (Criterion 2)

Example Response to Advanced Client Statement 4

This is a really unfortunate occurrence. Thanks for bringing it up. Let's just take a moment to address this. (Criterion 1) Therapy never includes any kind of sexual contact. This is why it is so critical to have a therapist who is skilled and trustworthy. I want to reassure you that we are not going to violate your boundaries during this process. We know how very harmful sexual contact with clients is, which is why we clarify up front that this is an important boundary that we will always uphold. We are here to help you heal, not cause you more suffering. (Criterion 2)

Example Response to Advanced Client Statement 5

Thank you for asking. This isn't at all uncommon, so it's important that we talk about it. (Criterion 1) While sexual feelings may arise as a natural component of your experience, therapy never includes sex. If sexual feelings arise, it is my role to help you understand where these feelings are coming from, without actually engaging in sexual activity with you. (Criterion 2)

Responding to Relational Ruptures

Preparations for Exercise 6

1. Read the instructions in Chapter 2.

2. Download the Deliberate Practice Reaction Form and the Deliberate Practice Diary Form at https://www.apa.org/pubs/books/deliberate-practice-psychedelic-assisted-therapy (see the "Clinician and Practitioner Resources" tab; also available in Appendixes A and B, respectively).

Skill Description

Skill Difficulty Level: Intermediate

The success of all models of psychotherapy depends on a strong therapeutic relationship that is characterized by trust, positive regard, and agreement on the goals and tasks of therapy (Eubanks-Carter et al., 2015). In psychedelic-assisted therapy (PAT), the intensity and vulnerability of the psychedelic experience makes it especially important that the client feels safe with their therapist (Shulgin & Shulgin, 1990, 2002). Like all forms of therapy, in PAT clients can experience ruptures in the therapeutic relationship (Stolaroff, 2020). Ruptures can be caused by miscommunication, misattunement, or many other reasons.

The goal of responding to a rupture is to help re-create safety within the therapeutic relationship. This is done by acknowledging the impact of the interaction with empathy and demonstrating curiosity about the client's experience, which may vary significantly from person to person. When indicated, it can be important to express accountability for the therapist's action or inaction as well. The consequences of a therapeutic rupture are often difficult to predict and require humility to allow the client's experience to take priority over a therapist's defensiveness, hurt, or disagreement. Regardless of the

https://doi.org/10.1037/0000399-008

Deliberate Practice in Psychedelic-Assisted Therapy, by S. Dames, A. Penn, M. Williams, J. A. Zamaria, T. Rousmaniere, and A. Vaz

source of the rupture, repair always begins with a desire to understand more about what took place from the client's perspective (Eubanks-Carter et al., 2015; Safran & Muran, 2000).

In terms of a process to navigate ruptures, and to facilitate relational repair, nonviolent communication (Rosenberg, 2015) is a well-vetted framework that helps reestablish connection through empathy and creating connection around four aspects of awareness. These include articulating observations, identifying feelings, identifying universal human needs, and making requests. In this exercise, we employ empathic engagement through compassionate witnessing and focus on responding to observations with acknowledgment of the client's perceptions and further inviting expression of feelings by inviting the client to share their subjective experience of the event.

The therapist should improvise a response to each client statement following these skill criteria:

1. **Acknowledge the client's experience and empathically reflect their concerns.** Our aim is to make the implicit explicit so that there is a shared understanding of what is on the relational table. It's important to separate our evaluations, biases, and judgments from the description of what we are objectively observing. For instance, instead of saying "Clearly, you're upset," one might say, "I'm seeing your tears and hear the quivering in your voice." You may also act as a compassionate witness by offering empathic reflection and your own somatic resonance—for instance, "Are you feeling cautious and wanting to protect yourself right now? I feel a sudden shift in my gut and am very curious about it."

2. **Invite the client to share their subjective experience related to the rupture.** Respond with a question or statement that invites the client to offer more of their subjective experience related to the rupture.

SKILL CRITERIA FOR EXERCISE 6

1. Acknowledge the client's experience and empathically reflect their concerns.
2. Invite the client to share their subjective experience related to the rupture.

Examples of Therapists Navigating Relational Ruptures

Example 1

CLIENT: [*hurt*] Last session, you got my girlfriend's name wrong, and that really bothered me. It felt like you weren't paying attention.

THERAPIST: Oh, I remember something didn't feel right as I spoke of her, and I regret not paying better attention to that. (Criterion 1) How did that feel for you? Do you worry that I might be missing some important parts of your story? (Criterion 2)

Example 2

CLIENT: [*sad*] This is kind of hard to say, but you've been late to all our sessions this month. Sometimes I wonder if you even care.

THERAPIST: [*sighs*] Thank you for bringing that up. I do want to acknowledge my pattern of lateness and apologize for that. (Criterion 1) I feel sad to hear you question my caring about you. And yet, I can appreciate how my lateness lands for you that way. Would you tell me more about what is coming up for you? (Criterion 2)

Example 3

CLIENT: [*doubtful*] There is no way that you as a cisgender man can understand my experience as a trans person.

THERAPIST: It makes total sense you don't trust that I can appreciate your experience. I hear you. Only someone with your background is truly going to have a lived experience of what you have been through. (Criterion 1) That being said, I am here with you right now and I want nothing more than to help you to feel safe and understood. If you're willing to give it a go, I hope I can earn your trust as we spend some time together. Is there something you'd be willing to share with me about what you've experienced that you think would be helpful for me to know, as we go into this work together? (Criterion 2)

INSTRUCTIONS FOR EXERCISE 6
Step 1: Role-Play and Feedback
• The client says the first beginner client statement. The therapist **improvises** a response based on the skill criteria. • The trainer (or, if not available, the client) provides **brief** feedback based on the skill criteria. • The client then repeats the same statement, and the therapist again improvises a response. The trainer (or client) again provides brief feedback.
Step 2: Repeat
• Repeat Step 1 for all the statements **in the current difficulty level** (beginner, intermediate, or advanced).
Step 3: Assess and Adjust Difficulty
• The therapist completes the Deliberate Practice Reaction Form (see Appendix A) and decides whether to make the exercise easier or harder or to repeat the same difficulty level.
Step 4: Repeat for Approximately 15 Minutes
• Repeat Steps 1 to 3 for at least 15 minutes. • The trainees then switch therapist and client roles and start over.

Now it's your turn! Follow Steps 1 and 2 from the instructions.

Remember: The goal of the role-play is for trainees to practice improvising responses to the client statements in a manner that (a) uses the skill criteria and (b) feels authentic for the trainee. **Example therapist responses for each client statement are provided at the end of this exercise. Trainees should attempt to improvise their own responses before reading the example responses.**

BEGINNER-LEVEL CLIENT STATEMENTS FOR EXERCISE 6
Beginner Client Statement 1
[Hurt] Last session, you got my girlfriend's name wrong, and that really bothered me. It felt like you weren't paying attention.
Beginner Client Statement 2
[Uncertain] Sorry, I'm a little taken aback by what you just said. It feels like you're judging me really harshly.
Beginner Client Statement 3
[Angry] This is the third time my dosing session has been pushed back. This is so unprofessional, and clearly you don't care a thing about the people you say you want to help.
Beginner Client Statement 4
[Offended] Why does this psychedelic therapy have to be so expensive? Am I just a paycheck to you guys?
Beginner Client Statement 5
[Hurt] I heard you talking to your receptionist about me when I was leaving last week, and you used the wrong pronouns. I shouldn't have to correct my therapist of all people!

 Assess and adjust the difficulty before moving to the next difficulty level (see Step 3 in the exercise instructions).

INTERMEDIATE-LEVEL CLIENT STATEMENTS FOR EXERCISE 6
Intermediate Client Statement 1
[Sad] This is kind of hard to say, but you've been late to all our sessions this month. Sometimes I wonder if you even care.
Intermediate Client Statement 2
[Shame] Every time you mention my abuse history, I feel really ashamed. It makes me just close up inside.
Intermediate Client Statement 3
[Angry] This is bullshit, I'm sick of you asking me how I feel all the time. Is that the only thing you know how to say?
Intermediate Client Statement 4
[Irritated] I feel like I'm just going in circles each time we talk, and every time I express frustration, you dismiss my feelings.
Intermediate Client Statement 5
[Disgust] I can't believe how that therapist talked to me while I was experiencing strong emotions in the medicine session. It felt directive and dismissive of what was coming up for me.

 Assess and adjust the difficulty before moving to the next difficulty level (see Step 3 in the exercise instructions).

ADVANCED-LEVEL CLIENT STATEMENTS FOR EXERCISE 6
Advanced Client Statement 1
[Anxious] I know you like feedback, so you should know that our work felt off today . . . but I'm not sure I want to talk about it.
Advanced Client Statement 2
[Angry] That was a really abrupt ending last session. I know we only have an hour, but I was kind of in the middle of something. That's been on my mind, and I'm a little pissed off about it.
Advanced Client Statement 3
[Frustrated] I just don't think you know how to help me. This whole "being mindful of my inner experience" thing seems bogus.
Advanced Client Statement 4
[Doubtful] There is no way that you as a cisgender man can understand my experience as a trans person.
Advanced Client Statement 5
[Angry] I explicitly asked to not be touched, and someone touched my foot during the session. How am I supposed to trust you all?

Assess and adjust the difficulty here (see Step 3 in the exercise instructions). If appropriate, follow the instructions to make the exercise even more challenging (see Appendix A).

Example Therapist Responses: Responding to Relational Ruptures

Remember: Trainees should attempt to improvise their own responses before reading the example responses. **Do not read the following responses verbatim unless you are having trouble coming up with your own responses!**

EXAMPLE RESPONSES TO BEGINNER-LEVEL CLIENT STATEMENTS FOR EXERCISE 6
Example Response to Beginner Client Statement 1
Oh, I remember something didn't feel right as I spoke of her, and I regret not paying better attention to that. (Criterion 1) How did that feel for you? Do you worry that I might be missing some important parts of your story? (Criterion 2)
Example Response to Beginner Client Statement 2
I can see that something important just happened. I'm so glad you've stopped me so we can talk more about what's happening for you right now. (Criterion 1) Can you tell me more about what part landed as judgmental? (Criterion 2)
Example Response to Beginner Client Statement 3
I can completely appreciate why you'd be upset about this. Frankly, I'm pretty frustrated about it myself. (Criterion 1) I know it can be hard to wait when you have been suffering for so long. Would you be willing to tell me more about how this is impacting you? (Criterion 2)
Example Response to Beginner Client Statement 4
Therapy can be really expensive. It sounds like this financial outlay leaves you questioning the value of the therapy and our motivations. (Criterion 1) If I am right on either count, can you say more about your doubts and concerns? (Criterion 2)
Example Response to Beginner Client Statement 5
Thank you for telling me—I want to do better, and I'm really sorry about that. I do hear that you want our relationship to be truly safe and respectful for you. (Criterion 1) How are you feeling as you hear my response at this point? (Criterion 2)

EXAMPLE RESPONSES TO INTERMEDIATE-LEVEL CLIENT STATEMENTS FOR EXERCISE 6

Example Response to Intermediate Client Statement 1

Thank you for bringing that up. I do want to acknowledge my pattern of lateness and apologize for that. (Criterion 1) I feel sad to hear you question my caring about you. And yet, I can appreciate how my lateness lands for you that way. Would you tell me more about what is coming up for you about it? (Criterion 2)

Example Response to Intermediate Client Statement 2

I can understand how my acknowledgment of such a painful time in your life would bring up feelings of vulnerability. I appreciate the courage it takes for you to share this with me. (Criterion 1) Tell me more about the closing up—what is that like? (Criterion 2)

Example Response to Intermediate Client Statement 3

Okay, I see that I am asking about your feelings over and over and that is really uncomfortable for you. Thank you for letting me know. (Criterion 1) It is a bit of a dilemma for me because I see emotion at the core of what you're working on. Can you help me see this more from your perspective? (Criterion 2)

Example Response to Intermediate Client Statement 4

I am so glad that you are sharing this with me. I want to understand my impact with you. Dismissing your experience is certainly not what I want to have happen. (Criterion 1) Can you give me an example of our interaction that left you feeling this way so we can look at it together? (Criterion 2)

Example Response to Intermediate Client Statement 5

I'm so glad you are voicing these concerns. Working with these relational tensions is an important part of the healing process. (Criterion 1) I'd like to know more about how this interaction impacted you. As you recall that experience again, what emotions are coming up for you? (Criterion 2)

EXAMPLE RESPONSES TO ADVANCED-LEVEL **CLIENT STATEMENTS FOR EXERCISE 6**
Example Response to Advanced Client Statement 1
I appreciate your honesty, and I know it's tough sometimes when sessions feel off. (Criterion 1) Certainly we don't need to talk about it right now if you don't want to. If you feel safe talking about this in the future, that could be very helpful. Often the things we don't want to share are the very things we need to talk about to move ahead. (Criterion 2)
Example Response to Advanced Client Statement 2
I too regret how I ended the session last week, and I appreciate you bringing this up. (Criterion 1) I want to fully understand, what was that like for you when we ended so abruptly? (Criterion 2)
Example Response to Advanced Client Statement 3
I'm sorry you're not experiencing change the way you'd like so far, and thanks for letting me know what's on your mind. (Criterion 1) Sometimes getting to the right place is a winding road, and mindfulness may not be the right path right now. Let's step back a moment and talk about what might be more helpful. (Criterion 2)
Example Response to Advanced Client Statement 4
I'm sorry the triggers for your sadness are even showing up right here in my office. (Criterion 1) Would you be willing to say more about what happens inside when you think I am showing off? (Criterion 2)
Example Response to Advanced Client Statement 5
I'm really glad you said something. Being able to trust is absolutely core to this work. I can see why you'd be upset, and I will circle back to the team to learn from this. (Criterion 1) Can we talk more about the thoughts and feelings coming up for you about that touch happening? (Criterion 2)

Working With the Client's Internal Conflict

Preparations for Exercise 7

1. Read the instructions in Chapter 2.

2. Download the Deliberate Practice Reaction Form and the Deliberate Practice Diary Form at https://www.apa.org/pubs/books/deliberate-practice-psychedelic-assisted-therapy (see the "Clinician and Practitioner Resources" tab; also available in Appendixes A and B, respectively).

Skill Description

Skill Difficulty Level: Intermediate

Multiplicity of mind is a natural and commonplace feature of the human condition. It refers to the idea that our minds are made up of distinct feeling states, sometimes referred to as "parts" or "self-states" (Elliott & Greenberg, 1997). We can be of two or more minds about something. We can desire connection with, and space from, the same person. We can experience love and hate toward the same thing. Although all these parts of our mind are attempting to help us remain safe, they can be at odds with each other about how this is accomplished. For example, when we are hurt, one part of us may have the urge to reach out for help from friends or family. However, we also may have the urge to shut down or withdraw to prevent us from being vulnerable, especially if we have a trauma history.

One of the benefits of psychedelics is the potential to sharpen our awareness of our multiplicity. If done in the right set and setting, psychedelics allow us to examine our disparate parts with a curious and compassionate intention (Grof, 2019; Shulgin, 2019).

https://doi.org/10.1037/0000399-009

Deliberate Practice in Psychedelic-Assisted Therapy, by S. Dames, A. Penn, M. Williams, J. A. Zamaria, T. Rousmaniere, and A. Vaz

Working with multiplicity in psychotherapy is sometimes called "parts work" (Kellogg & Garcia Torres, 2021). In this exercise, we are working with the following three components of parts work:

- identifying the emerging parts in conflict,
- validating all parts, and
- understanding the parts and their resulting conflict.

For those that want to do a deeper dive into parts work, there are a variety of models, such as emotion-focused therapy (Goldman & Greenberg, 2015), schema therapy (Arntz & Jacob, 2017), or internal family systems (Schwartz & Sweezy, 2019). Whatever the model you are working with, when working with split off parts, it's important that clients understand that any resistance that shows up comes from past trauma, and that defenses were originally formed to protect, not to harm.

In this exercise, therapists will focus on recognizing that a part is showing up, validating that it is a normal part of the healing process, and inquiring about the function or experience of the parts. The therapist should improvise a response to each client statement following these skill criteria:

1. **Identify the emerging parts of self.** In this first step, the therapist tentatively reflects the main self-parts that may be emerging or represented in the client's statement. For example, if the client describes being hopeful and worried about treatment, the therapist can translate this into "parts language" by stating: "So, it's like a part of you is hopeful about this process, while another part of you is scared and worried." Through identifying the different parts of self, we are promoting the mindful detachment required to step back from the emotions in the moment, to gain a better understanding of how to care for the wound beneath it.

2. **Validate the conflicting parts.** This step involves normalizing and validating the internal conflict as an organic part of the human experience. When the emerging part has been validated and the process is normalized, it feels less threatening, enabling a greater ability to lean into the conflict with curiosity. Validating the part of self that is showing up promotes self-compassion through a reparenting or a refriending process. Examples of this step include saying the following to the part:

   "I see you."

   "I understand why you had to do what you did."

   "I appreciate how you have been trying to protect yourself."

3. **Inquire about the function or experience of the parts.** Once the parts of self have been identified and validated, the next step is to investigate the impetus of the conflicted part that is showing up. For example, the therapist can ask what might be the underlying function or need of the part coming up or ask what it feels like to be in contact with a part. By exploring the part with curiosity, it promotes nonattachment (mitigating the risk of overidentifying with it), and the self-compassion and awareness required to nurture the wound or belief system that is keeping the part of self separate (and thereby in conflict) from the whole.

SKILL CRITERIA FOR EXERCISE 7

1. Identify the emerging parts of self.
2. Validate the conflicting parts.
3. Inquire about the function or experience of the parts.

Examples of Working With the Client's Internal Conflict

Example 1

CLIENT: [*hopeful and afraid*] Part of me really wants to do this psychedelic medicine session to get well, but part of me is really afraid right now.

THERAPIST: I'm hearing there are a few parts of your self emerging right now, one that is afraid and one that is hopeful. (Criterion 1) It's completely normal for the more fearful parts of ourselves to emerge when we are confronted with something that we don't know and that we can't control. A lot of people feel the exact same way you do in the minutes, hours, days, and weeks leading up to their psychedelic medicine session. (Criterion 2) When you consider what lies beneath the fear you are feeling, what are you sensing? (Criterion 3)

Example 2

CLIENT: [*hopeful and distrusting*] I am feeling so terrified right now. I feel the psychedelic medicine totally kicking in now. I know rationally that you are here to help and protect me, but I have this horrible fear that you are really trying to kill me.

THERAPIST: I'm so glad you are sharing this with me, this fear you are experiencing sounds overwhelming. (Criterion 2) I'm hearing that there is a part of you that wants to believe in the process, and another that doesn't trust it. (Criterion 1) Let's tend to this fearful part. When you ask the fearful part what it wants you to know, what is reflected back to you? (Criterion 3)

Example 3

CLIENT: [*longing and repulsion*] I long to be more intimate with my partner, but when it happens, it's like I become allergic to him. Everything in me feels repulsed by his touch. I can see how much it hurts him.

THERAPIST: It sounds like you have two parts of self emerging, one that is longing for connection, and one that is afraid of connection. (Criterion 1) That must be confusing! (Criterion 2) When you ask the part of yourself what it is afraid of, what impression are you getting? (Criterion 3)

INSTRUCTIONS FOR EXERCISE 7
Step 1: Role-Play and Feedback
• The client says the first beginner client statement. The therapist **improvises** a response based on the skill criteria. • The trainer (or, if not available, the client) provides **brief** feedback based on the skill criteria. • The client then repeats the same statement, and the therapist again improvises a response. The trainer (or client) again provides brief feedback.
Step 2: Repeat
• Repeat Step 1 for all the statements **in the current difficulty level** (beginner, intermediate, or advanced).
Step 3: Assess and Adjust Difficulty
• The therapist completes the Deliberate Practice Reaction Form (see Appendix A) and decides whether to make the exercise easier or harder or to repeat the same difficulty level.
Step 4: Repeat for Approximately 15 Minutes
• Repeat Steps 1 to 3 for at least 15 minutes. • The trainees then switch therapist and client roles and start over.

Now it's your turn! Follow Steps 1 and 2 from the exercise instructions.

Remember: The goal of the role-play is for trainees to practice improvising responses to the client statements in a manner that (a) uses the skill criteria and (b) feels authentic for the trainee. **Example therapist responses for each client statement are provided at the end of this exercise. Trainees should attempt to improvise their own responses before reading the example responses.**

BEGINNER-LEVEL CLIENT STATEMENTS FOR EXERCISE 7
Beginner Client Statement 1
[Afraid and hopeful] Part of me really wants to do this psychedelic medicine session to get well, but part of me is really afraid right now.
Beginner Client Statement 2
[Trusting and distrusting] Part of me knows that these things take time, but another part feels like I was tricked to believe it would work this time, and mad at myself for falling for it again.
Beginner Client Statement 3
[Angry and ashamed] There is a part of me that is really angry a lot of the time and sees how other people always screw up and hurt me. There's also another part that realizes how I screw up and hurt people too. I kind of hate that part of myself.
Beginner Client Statement 4
[Afraid and hopeful] You know, this sounds weird, but I'm almost afraid of this treatment working. A part of me is afraid of getting better because then I wouldn't have something to blame my messed up life on.
Beginner Client Statement 5
[Want and fear] I know I need to change, and I want to change! But there is this part of me that just doesn't trust that I'll be okay if I do.

 Assess and adjust the difficulty before moving to the next difficulty level (see Step 3 in the exercise instructions).

INTERMEDIATE-LEVEL CLIENT STATEMENTS FOR EXERCISE 7

Intermediate Client Statement 1

[Accepting and guilty] My dad never allowed me to engage in the performing arts, which I have always been drawn to. He told me that's what gay people do, and that if I was gay, I would not be welcome in our home. I got into sports to keep the peace, but it never fed me. Now, when I try to embrace this part of myself, I feel guilty—like it's wrong, and it keeps me from letting loose.

Intermediate Client Statement 2

[Afraid and hopeful] I am feeling so terrified right now. I feel the psychedelic medicine totally kicking in now. I know rationally that you are here to help and protect me, but I have this horrible fear that you are really trying to kill me.

Intermediate Client Statement 3

[Insecure and secure] I keep thinking that there's a "right" way to do this psychedelic medicine therapy. And there are certain things you're going to want me to talk about, and if I don't, I'm going to disappoint you. And another part of me says, "Screw it, it's my therapy."

Intermediate Client Statement 4

[Vulnerable and protective] My whole life I've been at the brunt of other people's anger, and now I've become the angry person that is causing harm to others. I'm so ashamed of myself.

Intermediate Client Statement 5

[Curious and skeptical] I know you believe in this stuff, and I want to too, but there is a part of me that is like, "Really?! This can't be for real." While I'm feeling curious, the doubts are causing me to wonder if I am setting myself up for disappointment.

 Assess and adjust the difficulty before moving to the next difficulty level (see Step 3 in the exercise instructions).

ADVANCED-LEVEL CLIENT STATEMENTS FOR EXERCISE 7
Advanced Client Statement 1
[Longing and repulsion] I long to be more intimate with my partner, but when it happens, it's like I become allergic to him. Everything in me feels repulsed by his touch. I can see how much it hurts him.
Advanced Client Statement 2
[Longing and skeptical] I've always had this pull toward spirituality, but in my home of origin, any mention of such things was a recipe for ridicule. I'm ready to explore that part of myself, but it still feels like a childhood fantasy.
Advanced Client Statement 3
[Excited and afraid] I feel some excitement for the potential of what could happen in the session, but I've been disappointed so many times, I'm afraid to hope.
Advanced Client Statement 4
[Decisive and afraid] I know what is holding me back now. It was so clear to me in the session. But when I think about doing what I think I need to do to get unstuck, I feel sick— like something terrible might happen if I do it.

🛑 **Assess and adjust the difficulty here (see Step 3 in the exercise instructions). If appropriate, follow the instructions to make the exercise even more challenging (see Appendix A).**

Example Therapist Responses: Working With the Client's Internal Conflict

Remember: Trainees should attempt to improvise their own responses before reading the example responses. **Do not read the following responses verbatim unless you are having trouble coming up with your own responses!**

EXAMPLE RESPONSES TO BEGINNER-LEVEL CLIENT STATEMENTS FOR EXERCISE 7
Example Response to Beginner Client Statement 1
I'm hearing there are a few parts of your self emerging right now, one that is afraid, and one that is hopeful. (Criterion 1) It's completely normal for the more fearful parts of ourselves to emerge when we are confronted with something that we don't know and that we can't control. A lot of people feel the exact same way you do in the minutes, hours, days, and weeks leading up to their psychedelic medicine session. (Criterion 2) When you consider what this fearful part is protecting you from right now, what is your impression? (Criterion 3)
Example Response to Beginner Client Statement 2
It sounds like a part of you wants to trust the process, but you're also experiencing some distrust, based on past disappointments. (Criterion 1) It makes sense that this protective part of yourself is coming forward. (Criterion 2) With your permission, I'd like to explore the feelings that are coming forward right now. Would that be okay? Imagine this part that feels tricked and mad at yourself. When you ask this part what it wants you to know, what is reflected back to you? (Criterion 3)
Example Response to Beginner Client Statement 3
So I think I'm hearing that there are parts of you that feel hurt and parts of you that feel angry, and as a result, hurt others. Is that accurate? (Criterion 1) It is really common for us to unconsciously perpetuate the hurt within us, but with awareness, you are developing an ability to interrupt the pattern. (Criterion 2) What's it like to both feel and inflict pain? (Criterion 3)
Example Response to Beginner Client Statement 4
So there are parts that want to get better and other parts that are afraid of changing and getting better? (Criterion 1) It is common for parts of ourselves to be in conflict like this, and it can feel like a battle inside at times. (Criterion 2) What's that conversation like between those two parts of you? (Criterion 3)
Example Response to Beginner Client Statement 5
What a powerful insight that is. (Criterion 2) It sounds like a part of you knows what you want, but another part of you is afraid to reach for it. It must feel like an internal tug of war. (Criterion 1) Imagine talking to the part of yourself that is holding back. You might even close your eyes, to focus inwardly. When you ask what it is trying to protect you from, what is reflected back to you? (Criterion 3)

EXAMPLE RESPONSES TO INTERMEDIATE-LEVEL CLIENT STATEMENTS FOR EXERCISE 7

Example Response to Intermediate Client Statement 1

Hearing about your upbringing, it makes a lot of sense that there is a part of yourself that longs to be accepted, and another part of yourself that feels like such acceptance is forbidden. (Criterion 1) This is a common act of survival for children, and all humans for that matter! (Criterion 2) When you imagine yourself as a little boy, longing to get lost in performative arts, but afraid of rejection if he does, what do you think he needs to hear right now? (Criterion 3)

Example Response to Intermediate Client Statement 2

I'm so glad you are sharing this with me, this fear you are experiencing sounds overwhelming. (Criterion 2) I'm hearing that there is a part of you that wants to believe in the process, and another that doesn't trust it. (Criterion 1) Let's tend to this fearful part. When you ask this part what it wants you to know, what is reflected back to you? (Criterion 3)

Example Response to Intermediate Client Statement 3

I'm hearing there are parts of you that want to please other people and other parts that want you to please yourself. (Criterion 1) You know, that actually makes a lot of sense. (Criterion 2) Can you tell me what it's like to be feeling both of those parts right now? (Criterion 3)

Example Response to Intermediate Client Statement 4

I really admire your courage to face this inner conflict. (Criterion 2) It sounds like you're feeling caught between a protective part of self and a vulnerable part of self. I wonder if they are both rooted in the same unhealed wound. (Criterion 1) When you imagine talking to this part of you that feels angry and asking what it is trying to protect you from, what is your impression? (Criterion 3)

Example Response to Intermediate Client Statement 5

It sounds like there is part of you that is hopeful, and yet there is still a part of you that is afraid of opening yourself up to disappointment. (Criterion 1) This is totally understandable. When facing something that feels new and uncertain, it is completely normal to feel both vulnerable and protective at the same time. (Criterion 2) What would it look like for you to hold space for the part that is uncertain, while also holding space for the part that is curious and hopeful? (Criterion 3)

EXAMPLE RESPONSES TO ADVANCED-LEVEL CLIENT STATEMENTS FOR EXERCISE 7

Example Response to Advanced Client Statement 1

It sounds like you have two parts of self emerging, one that is longing for connection, and one that is afraid of connection. (Criterion 1) That must be confusing! (Criterion 2) When you ask the part of yourself what it is afraid of, what impression are you getting? (Criterion 3)

Example Response to Advanced Client Statement 2

I can totally understand how one part of you is longing to feel spiritually connected, and another part of you feels skeptical, or even unsafe at the thought of trusting it. (Criterion 1) It makes sense this is coming up. These protective mechanisms often become woven into our belief systems. (Criterion 2) I wonder what it would be like to imagine that you are a guesthouse for all these parts of self that represent you. When you imagine welcoming this part of yourself home, how does it feel? (Criterion 3)

Example Response to Advanced Client Statement 3

It sounds like you are feeling conflicted by wanting to hope, but not trusting it at the same time. (Criterion 1) I imagine this is confusing for you. (Criterion 2) To prepare for the session, we will discuss intentions and expectations, which can help reduce the risk of disappointment. Before we go there, I'd like to explore this internal conflict you're experiencing. What would it look like to enjoy the excitement, while also making space for the part of yourself that feels let down from past expectations? (Criterion 3)

Example Response to Advanced Client Statement 4

It sounds like a part of you is inspired and clear on the path forward, and another part of you is afraid of stepping into unfamiliar territory. (Criterion 1) That makes a lot of sense. It's common for these various parts of self to feel conflicted at times, which can create a lot of tension within you. (Criterion 2) Sometimes it can help to explore these parts of self, such as the age you were when they came to be, and what they want you to know about them. When you imagine asking this part of yourself how old it is, listening to your intuition, what is reflected back to you? (Criterion 3)

Addressing Transference

Preparations for Exercise 8

1. Read the instructions in Chapter 2.

2. Download the Deliberate Practice Reaction Form and the Deliberate Practice Diary Form at https://www.apa.org/pubs/books/deliberate-practice-psychedelic-assisted-therapy (see the "Clinician and Practitioner Resources" tab; also available in Appendixes A and B, respectively).

Skill Description

Skill Difficulty Level: Intermediate

Transference refers to the unconscious redirection of one's feelings onto another person. Transference is common in all types of psychotherapy. As "non-specific amplifiers of the psyche" (Grof, 2019, p. 78), psychedelics can facilitate or amplify transference. In psychedelic medicine sessions, the client's feelings about someone in their past or present are frequently projected onto the therapist. Bringing the client's projections into their conscious awareness can facilitate self-reflection, growth, and healing (McWilliams, 2004).

If unaddressed, transference can impede the development of trust and safety in the therapeutic relationship. Furthermore, it can lead to a compromise in professional boundaries and role ambiguity and can impact the client's ability to see and address the relational patterns that are hampering their progress (Safran, 2012). Although difficult at times, it is imperative to address transference potentially related to past discrimination, identity, and privilege, which can be an ongoing source of distrust in the therapeutic relationship, such as assumptions around race, age, gender, religion, ethnicity, disability, income, and so on.

---

https://doi.org/10.1037/0000399-010

Deliberate Practice in Psychedelic-Assisted Therapy, by S. Dames, A. Penn, M. Williams, J. A. Zamaria, T. Rousmaniere, and A. Vaz

When made explicit, the awareness of transference provides opportunities to practice feeling and expressing old emotions within a new, safe context (Levenson et al., 2023). The client has an opportunity to redo or rewrite a relational story of the past by reallocating and reframing what is happening in the moment to tend to the source of dissonance beneath the presenting feelings. Some basic strategies to manage transference as it arises include gently bringing awareness to the pattern, exploring the feelings beneath the anxiety and resulting defenses that present on the surface, and to improve one's ability to tolerate and gently investigate the emotions as they arise.

This exercise focuses on addressing three main types of transference phenomena: idealized transference, negative transference, and erotic transference.

Idealized transference happens when the practitioner is viewed as enlightened or as the only one who can effectively engage in the healing process with the participant. Because psychedelics can lead to reduced feelings of fear and increased feelings of love and connection, the participant may believe that their progress is because of the practitioner, rather than their healing process or inner healing intelligence. If this projection is not addressed, it can prevent the participant from realizing their own capacity for healing.

Negative transference happens when impressions and assumptions from threatening past relationships are placed on to the therapist. These can be related to dynamics such as neglect or abuse from a parent or caregiver, feeling less important than a sibling, or judgment from a past therapist, for example. The reminder of past adverse relationships can activate negative feelings in the present-day relationship with the therapist. This type of transference may also show up as fear of rejection, where the client wonders if they are safe, will be accepted, and allowed to express themselves authentically. If the transference is not identified, the confusion can lead to a relational rupture in the therapeutic alliance. However, when worked with consciously, the client can recognize that such projections are not personal. This creates an opportunity to acknowledge the old wound that is coming up for healing and to tend to it compassionately.

Erotic transference happens when reenactments of early life impulses and fantasies emerge in the therapy session and a desire for closeness to the therapist is felt by the client as sexual interest or arousal toward the therapist. In this situation, it is critical that the therapist maintains impeccable boundaries while avoiding remarks that may feel shaming to the patient. It should be made clear that therapeutic relationships never involve sexual contact, even if erotic transference is present.

The therapist should improvise a response to each client statement following these skill criteria:

1. **Make a process comment highlighting the client's transference feelings or thoughts toward the therapist.** In this first skill criterion, the therapist makes a process comment highlighting how the client may be perceiving the therapist, or feelings coming up toward the therapist. The purpose here is to gently promote awareness of the transference phenomena that may be taking place. By doing so, you redirect emotions and make the implicit an explicit part of the therapeutic process. In this exercise, the therapist addresses the three types of transference phenomena described previously: idealized transference, negative transference, and erotic transference.

2. **Invite further exploration.** The therapist can work with and even leverage transference to help the client move through chronic relational patterns that may be holding them back in their daily life. By exploring the roots of the relational distortion, clients develop the awareness required to reframe, rewrite, or upgrade the belief systems that inform their perspective and resulting behaviors.

SKILL CRITERIA FOR EXERCISE 8

1. Make a process comment highlighting the client's transference feelings or thoughts toward the therapist.
2. Invite further exploration.

Examples of Addressing Transference

Example 1

CLIENT: [*fearful; negative transference*] I feel like I really have to get better from this treatment and if I don't, you're going to be really disappointed with me.

THERAPIST: I know that you came to this treatment really wanting to get better, and I can imagine having these negative thoughts of me being disappointed might be scary for you. (Criterion 1) Can we talk about what feelings are emerging right now for you, especially around disappointment? (Criterion 2)

Example 2

CLIENT: [*playful; erotic transference*] In the last session, I felt really turned on . . .

THERAPIST: It is not uncommon for the body to experience sexual arousal during the session, and I appreciate you sharing that you felt that so that we can discuss it. (Criterion 1) Psychotherapy never involves sexual contact, but it can be valuable to learn from your experience. Looking back to the experience, what emotions are coming up for you about it now? (Criterion 2)

Example 3

CLIENT: [*joy; idealized transference*] I am so grateful you were here for me though this session. I love you so much. I can't even put into words how much love I feel for you right now.

THERAPIST: You're feeling really safe with me right now. We often feel love toward people who make us feel safe. (Criterion 1) Could you tell me what is happening right now that is making you feel this safe? (Criterion 2)

INSTRUCTIONS FOR EXERCISE 8
Step 1: Role-Play and Feedback
<ul><li>The client says the first beginner client statement. The therapist **improvises** a response based on the skill criteria.</li><li>The trainer (or, if not available, the client) provides **brief** feedback based on the skill criteria.</li><li>The client then repeats the same statement, and the therapist again improvises a response. The trainer (or client) will again provide brief feedback.</li></ul>
Step 2: Repeat
<ul><li>Repeat Step 1 for all the statements **in the current difficulty level** (beginner, intermediate, or advanced).</li></ul>
Step 3: Assess and Adjust Difficulty
<ul><li>The therapist completes the Deliberate Practice Reaction Form (see Appendix A) and decides whether to make the exercise easier or harder or to repeat the same difficulty level.</li></ul>
Step 4: Repeat for Approximately 15 Minutes
<ul><li>Repeat Steps 1 to 3 for at least 15 minutes.</li><li>The trainees then switch therapist and client roles and start over.</li></ul>

Now it's your turn! Follow Steps 1 and 2 from the exercise instructions.

Remember: The goal of the role-play is for trainees to practice improvising responses to the client statements in a manner that (a) uses the skill criteria and (b) feels authentic for the trainee. **Example therapist responses for each client statement are provided at the end of this exercise. Trainees should attempt to improvise their own responses before reading the examples.**

BEGINNER-LEVEL CLIENT STATEMENTS FOR EXERCISE 8
Beginner Client Statement 1
[Insecure; negative transference] I feel like I really have to get better from this treatment and if I don't, you're going to be really disappointed with me.
Beginner Client Statement 2
[Anxious during psychedelic medicine session; negative transference] I think you are here to take advantage of me, just like everyone else has. I know you want something.
Beginner Client Statement 3
[Anxious to please; idealized transference] I want to give you this piece of artwork that I made after our last session. It really captures how I felt in that last moment. I was hoping maybe you'd hang it up in your office.
Beginner Client Statement 4
[Longing; idealized transference] When you were sitting next to me during the session, you seemed so calm and at peace, I figured you must meditate, like, all the time. I just hope that someday I can be as calm and centered as you are.
Beginner Client Statement 5
[Longing; idealized transference] I was thinking about the way you looked at me during the session, and how kind your face was, and how accepting your eyes were. And I was just thinking about how lucky your kids are to have a parent like you. I wish I was your child.

 Assess and adjust the difficulty before moving to the next difficulty level (see Step 3 in the exercise instructions).

INTERMEDIATE-LEVEL CLIENT STATEMENTS FOR EXERCISE 8
Intermediate Client Statement 1
[Playful; erotic transference] In the last session, I felt really turned on . . .
Intermediate Client Statement 2
[Longing; idealized transference] I just wish my partner was more like you.
Intermediate Client Statement 3
[Anxious; negative transference] I realized after our last session that I'm really an angry person and that I'm not very easy to be around. Heck, you probably don't even like to be around me.
Intermediate Client Statement 4
[Unworthy; idealized and negative transference] So after our prep session, I went home and googled you. I really didn't realize what a big deal you are in this field. I feel like I'm kind of wasting your time doing therapy with me.
Intermediate Client Statement 5
[Hostile; negative transference] You know, you were just sitting there all calm and closed eyes like some kind of Buddha while I was really suffering. You're just totally self-absorbed with this idea that you're always calm and composed.

🕐 **Assess and adjust the difficulty before moving to the next difficulty level (see Step 3 in the exercise instructions).**

ADVANCED-LEVEL CLIENT STATEMENTS FOR EXERCISE 8

Advanced Client Statement 1

[Anxious admiration; idealization transference] I am so grateful you were here for me through this session. I love you so much. I can't even put into words how much love I feel for you right now.

Advanced Client Statement 2

[Intimate/lustful during the psychedelic medicine session; erotic transference] I felt very sexual, in a way I have never felt before. I want to be closer to you. Will you hold me in your arms right now?

Advanced Client Statement 3

[Skeptical; negative transference] Look, I really don't want to do all this chit-chat with you. If I'm honest, I kind of think you therapists are kind of nosy. Can't we just let the medicine do its thing, and dispense with all the psychobabble?

Advanced Client Statement 4

[Bashful; erotic and negative transference] When I went to the bathroom during the session, I realized I was kind of turned on. I wanted to tell you when we came back in the room, but I figured you'd get weirded out, so I tried to distract myself until it went away.

Advanced Client Statement 5

[Offended; negative transference] You know, I'm tired of you White people just taking other people's spiritual practices and acting like you made them up. Like that dreamcatcher on the wall over there. Are you native? I'm a quarter Cherokee, and I think that's offensive.

 Assess and adjust the difficulty here (see Step 3 in the exercise instructions). If appropriate, follow the instructions to make the exercise even more challenging (see Appendix A).

Example Therapist Responses: Addressing Transference

Remember: Trainees should attempt to improvise their own responses before reading the example responses. **Do not read the following responses verbatim unless you are having trouble coming up with your own responses!**

EXAMPLE RESPONSES TO BEGINNER-LEVEL CLIENT STATEMENTS FOR EXERCISE 8
Example Response to Beginner Client Statement 1
I know that you came to this treatment really wanting to get better, and I can imagine having these negative thoughts of me being disappointed might be scary for you. (Criterion 1) Can we talk about what feelings are emerging right now for you, especially around disappointment? (Criterion 2)
Example Response to Beginner Client Statement 2
I'm hearing a concern that I'm just here to take something from you. I can imagine that must not feel very safe. (Criterion 1) Sometimes that feeling can come up because something like that has happened at another time in your life. Would you be open to exploring this together? (Criterion 2)
Example Response to Beginner Client Statement 3
Aw, that's really lovely. It sounds like your last session was really important to you and some feelings came up toward me and our work. (Criterion 1) I'm wondering if you could share with me why it's important to you for me to put it up in the office? (Criterion 2)
Example Response to Beginner Client Statement 4
It sounds like my calm presence was helpful to you and that's something you'd like to be able to do for yourself. (Criterion 1) I wonder if you'd be willing to talk about the challenges of finding that kind of calm within yourself? (Criterion 2)
Example Response to Beginner Client Statement 5
It sounds like you had some really powerful feelings about being cared for in our session. (Criterion 1) Could we spend some time talking about what that felt like and what's coming up for you now? (Criterion 2)

| **EXAMPLE RESPONSES TO INTERMEDIATE-LEVEL** |
| **CLIENT STATEMENTS FOR EXERCISE 8** |

Example Response to Intermediate Client Statement 1

It is not uncommon for the body to experience sexual arousal during the session, and I appreciate you sharing that you felt this so we can discuss it. (Criterion 1) Looking back to the experience, what emotions are coming up for you about it now? (Criterion 2)

Example Response to Intermediate Client Statement 2

I notice you're feeling really positive about me. It's common in this process to develop feelings of safety that you may be longing for in your day-to-day life. (Criterion 1) Let's think about what is helping you feel safe in this context to provide insight into what you might be longing for more of in your day-to-day relationships. (Criterion 2)

Example Response to Intermediate Client Statement 3

That's a really big realization. It sounds like you're afraid that your anger may hurt me too? (Criterion 1) As you're letting me know of this realization, can you say more about what feelings may be coming up toward me? (Criterion 2)

Example Response to Intermediate Client Statement 4

It sounds like the work I've done in this field brought up some feelings for you around your own worth. (Criterion 1) We can explore this a little more. Would you be open to that? (Criterion 2)

Example Response to Intermediate Client Statement 5

I'm sorry. Thank you for sharing that with me. It sounds like when I was sitting next to you, you felt like I was disconnected from what was going on with you at that moment. I can imagine that must have hurt, and I appreciate you being willing to share that vulnerability with me. (Criterion 1) Would you be willing to explore that feeling a little more with me? (Criterion 2)

EXAMPLE RESPONSES TO ADVANCED-LEVEL CLIENT STATEMENTS FOR EXERCISE 8
Example Response to Advanced Client Statement 1
I'm really glad that you're feeling safe with me right now. We often feel love toward people that make us feel safe. (Criterion 1) Could you tell me what is happening right now that is making you feel this safe? (Criterion 2)
Example Response to Advanced Client Statement 2
I hear you are feeling safe and wanting to be close to me right now. (Criterion 1) In a therapeutic relationship, we can feel very close, and even have sexual feelings, without acting on them. While psychotherapy never includes sexual contact, it can be valuable to learn from sexual feelings. Would you be open to discussing the sexual feelings you are having? (Criterion 2)
Example Response to Advanced Client Statement 3
I hear you that we get into a lot of personal material, and that can feel pretty vulnerable. (Criterion 1) I'm wondering how it feels to share these personal aspects of your life with me? (Criterion 2)
Example Response to Advanced Client Statement 4
It sounds like you experienced sexual feelings and then anxiety around our relationship. You know, that's not uncommon, and while I'm sorry you didn't feel comfortable bringing it up in the session, I'm glad that you're talking about it now. (Criterion 1) While psychotherapy never includes sexual contact, it can be valuable to learn from sexual feelings. Would you be open to exploring some of the feelings that came up around the fact that you were a little turned on during the session? (Criterion 2)
Example Response to Advanced Client Statement 5
I really appreciate you being willing to be candid with me, and I hear that you're angry. (Criterion 1) Would you be willing to talk about what's coming up for you right now around this? (Criterion 2)

Navigating Strong Emotions

Preparations for Exercise 9

1. Read the instructions in Chapter 2.

2. Download the Deliberate Practice Reaction Form and the Deliberate Practice Diary Form at https://www.apa.org/pubs/books/deliberate-practice-psychedelic-assisted-therapy (see the "Clinician and Practitioner Resources" tab; also available in Appendixes A and B, respectively).

Skill Description

Skill Difficulty Level: Advanced

When intense emotions arise in the present, they often include feelings, beliefs, or stuck energy that was too painful to process in the past. From this vantage point, it can be a good sign when strong emotions come up during psychedelic therapy. The rise of intense affect may signal that our bodies now feel secure enough to metabolize an emotion that was previously overwhelming.

When emotions cannot be felt and expressed, we can become incongruent, often resulting in internalized, maladaptive shame (Greenberg & Paivio, 2003). This shame can then create an internal noise that serves as a chronic form of stress or anxiety. One antidote to maladaptive shame is the development of self-compassion toward oneself and one's emotions (Gilbert, 2010). This exercise will help therapists promote this healing process by inviting the client's emotions into the psychedelic therapy process and promoting self-compassion.

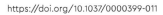

https://doi.org/10.1037/0000399-011

Deliberate Practice in Psychedelic-Assisted Therapy, by S. Dames, A. Penn, M. Williams, J. A. Zamaria, T. Rousmaniere, and A. Vaz

A focus on emotions in psychedelic-assisted therapy (PAT) generally has the following goals in mind:

- Increase awareness and learn to describe the felt experience of emotions in the body.

- Recognize that the felt experience of emotions is often a necessary step in therapy.

- Expand one's window of tolerance for strong emotions through regulation and self-compassion practices.

- Evaluate how to work with emotions more consciously, shifting from reacting to them to acting on them.

- Reduce the risk of ongoing maladaptive coping reactions by improving one's felt sense of support and security.

- Develop alternative coping mechanisms such as self-regulation and seeing help that reduce the risk of unconscious patterned reactions.

Practicing responding to strong emotions also provides an opportunity for therapists to explore their reactions to the strong emotional content often present in PAT (Shulgin, 2019). This can help therapists develop the "person of the therapist" and inner skills of psychotherapy (e.g., Aponte & Kissil, 2016; Rousmaniere, 2019).

The therapist should improvise a response to each client statement following these skill criteria:

1. **Acknowledge or normalize the client's emotion.** In this first skill criterion, the therapist turns the focus away from the content of the client statement and instead acknowledges or normalizes their emotional experience. This first step is essential because oftentimes the focus on the story is more accessible and comfortable and, as a result, is a frequent distraction from the felt sense of the experience.

2. **Promote self-compassion.** For the purposes of this exercise, the therapist has three options to choose from to promote the client's self-compassion.

   - **Option 1:** Helping the client regulate the body, such as engaging in paced breathing.

   - **Option 2:** Encouraging curiosity toward the strong emotion, like a mysterious guest, rather than overidentifying with it or resisting it.

   - **Option 3:** Helping the client dialogue with the emotion in a loving way, like they would a "dear other."

SKILL CRITERIA FOR EXERCISE 9

1. Acknowledge or normalize the client's emotion.
2. Promote self-compassion by using one of the following tasks:
   - Option 1: Help the client regulate the body.
   - Option 2: Encourage curiosity toward the strong emotion.
   - Option 3: Help the client dialogue with the emotion.

Examples of Navigating Strong Emotions

Note: Underlined text is to be read aloud by the person playing the client to provide context.

Example 1

Just before the psychedelic medicine session

CLIENT: [*breathing fast*] I just don't know if I can do this. I thought I was ready, but I'm having a full-on panic attack right now.

THERAPIST: I can hear the fear you are experiencing in this time of uncertainty, and I'm noticing that you are breathing really fast right now. (Criterion 1) Before we go any further, let's support your body. Can we take some nice, slow breaths together? As we are slowly breathing together, where are you noticing this sense of "panic" in your body right now? (Criterion 2, Option 1: Regulate the body)

Example 2

After the psychedelic medicine session

CLIENT: [*angry*] There was a time in the session when I just imagined all the people in my life looking at me like I was a baby. And then I found myself angry for some reason, like I just wanted to tell all of them to go to hell. Come to think of it, I push people that love me away all the time.

THERAPIST: That was a big experience, and it sounds like it's still resonating for you. (Criterion 1) I'm wondering what this anger that is showing up in those moments is all about? Where do you think it comes from? (Criterion 2, Option 2: Encourage curiosity)

Example 3

In the middle of the psychedelic medicine session

CLIENT: [*angry*] I am feeling so angry about what happened to me! I just want to smash something, and then I feel guilty for having such violent fantasies.

THERAPIST: It sounds like you're experiencing intense emotions around this, and it's totally natural to have a desire to express it. (Criterion 1) Can you imagine actually talking directly to your anger? When you imagine asking the anger what it's trying to protect you from, what does it say in response? (Criterion 2, Option 3: Dialogue with the emotion)

INSTRUCTIONS FOR EXERCISE 9

Step 1: Role-Play and Feedback

- The client says the first beginner client statement. The therapist **improvises** a response based on the skill criteria.
- The trainer (or, if not available, the client) provides **brief** feedback based on the skill criteria.
- The client then repeats the same statement, and the therapist again improvises a response. The trainer (or client) again provides brief feedback.

Step 2: Repeat

- Repeat Step 1 for all the statements **in the current difficulty level** (beginner, intermediate, or advanced).

Step 3: Assess and Adjust Difficulty

- The therapist completes the Deliberate Practice Reaction Form (see Appendix A) and decides whether to make the exercise easier or harder or to repeat the same difficulty level.

Step 4: Repeat for Approximately 15 Minutes

- Repeat Steps 1 to 3 for at least 15 minutes.
- The trainees then switch therapist and client roles and start over.

Now it's your turn! Follow Steps 1 and 2 from the exercise instructions.

Remember: The goal of the role-play is for trainees to practice improvising responses to the client statements in a manner that (a) uses the skill criteria and (b) feels authentic for the trainee. **Example therapist responses for each client statement are provided at the end of this exercise. Trainees should attempt to improvise their own responses before reading the example responses.**

   Note: Underlined text is to be read aloud by the person playing the client to provide context.

BEGINNER-LEVEL CLIENT STATEMENTS FOR EXERCISE 9
Beginner Client Statement 1
Just before the psychedelic medicine session
[Breathing fast] I just don't know if I can do this. I thought I was ready, but I'm having a full-on panic attack right now.
Beginner Client Statement 2
Just before the dosing session
[Frustrated] The last session was so hard. I felt sick and angry most of the time. If that's what it's going to be like again today, I'm out!
Beginner Client Statement 3
Early in the psychedelic medicine session
[Gripping chest and holding breath] No! No! I can't let go. I won't. It feels like a giant knot in my chest, weighing, no, holding me down. It's trying to loosen, but . . . I can't, I'm afraid to let go.
Beginner Client Statement 4
Early in the psychedelic medicine session
[Nauseous] My stomach is in knots. I feel so sick right now.
Beginner Client Statement 5
Early in the psychedelic medicine session
[Afraid] Oh God, something is very wrong. I've made a massive mistake. How do I make this stop?!

 Assess and adjust the difficulty before moving to the next difficulty level (see Step 3 in the exercise instructions).

INTERMEDIATE-LEVEL CLIENT STATEMENTS FOR EXERCISE 9
Intermediate Client Statement 1
Early in the psychedelic medicine session
[Laughing uncontrollably] This is all so silly! What am I doing here? On a psychedelic, listening to music on a Tuesday? Nothing to see here! What a joke. Life is just a big joke!
Intermediate Client Statement 2
Early in the psychedelic medicine session
[Afraid] I feel like I am wearing a tight suit that is growing smaller by the minute. It's taking my breath away.
Intermediate Client Statement 3
In the middle of the psychedelic medicine session
[Shouting and smiling] I love you! I love you all! It's all so beautiful! I'm so beautiful. You're so beautiful!
Intermediate Client Statement 4
In the middle of the psychedelic medicine session
[Anxious] I don't want to go there! I can't—I don't want to!
Intermediate Client Statement 5
In the middle of the psychedelic medicine session
[Angry] I am feeling so angry about what happened to me! I just want to smash something, and then I feel guilty for having such violent fantasies.

 Assess and adjust the difficulty before moving to the next difficulty level (see Step 3 in the exercise instructions).

ADVANCED-LEVEL CLIENT STATEMENTS FOR EXERCISE 9
Advanced Client Statement 1
After the psychedelic medicine session
[Ashamed] When I was remembering the abuse during the session, I just felt so upset with myself and thought, "Why did I let her do that to me?! Why didn't you get away?!"
Advanced Client Statement 2
After the psychedelic medicine session
[Sad] There was a moment during the session where I just felt nothing but love. It was amazing—bright, warm, expansive. And then, this dark presence seemed to come in around the edges, and I heard a voice. It was my own voice, saying, "What the fuck do you think you're doing? You're not allowed to feel this!" and that's when I started to cry because I thought I'll never feel love like that again.
Advanced Client Statement 3
After the psychedelic medicine session
[Angry] There was a time in the session when I just imagined all the people in my life looking at me like I was a baby. And then I found myself angry for some reason, like I just wanted to tell all of them to go to hell. Come to think of it, I push people away all the time that love me.
Advanced Client Statement 4
After the psychedelic medicine session
[Angry] After the session yesterday, I had this really strong feeling toward my boss. You know how I told you how my ex-husband always used to take me for granted? Well, I realized that's exactly the same thing I felt about my boss. I just want to go in tomorrow and tell him to stuff it!
Advanced Client Statement 5
After the psychedelic medicine session
[Happy] You know how I told you in the prep sessions that my mind is always trying to figure out what to do next, and how that kind of fuels my anxiety? Well, during the session yesterday, there was this period of time where that just stopped for a while, and it was so delightful!

 Assess and adjust the difficulty here (see Step 3 in the exercise instructions). If appropriate, follow the instructions to make the exercise even more challenging (see Appendix A).

Example Therapist Responses: Navigating Strong Emotions

Remember: Trainees should attempt to improvise their own responses before reading the example responses. **Do not read the following responses verbatim unless you are having trouble coming up with your own responses!**

EXAMPLE RESPONSES TO BEGINNER-LEVEL CLIENT STATEMENTS FOR EXERCISE 9
Example Response to Beginner Client Statement 1
I can hear the fear you are experiencing in this time of uncertainty, and I'm noticing that you are breathing really fast right now. (Criterion 1) Before we go any further, let's support your body. Can we take some nice, slow breaths together? As we are breathing together, where are you noticing this sense of "panic" in your body right now? (Criterion 2, Option 1: Regulate the body)
Example Response to Beginner Client Statement 2
I can understand why you'd be afraid to go through that again. It sounds like your body had a lot of fear and anger to move through. (Criterion 1) As you feel this sensation, imagine it is a part of yourself that is longing to come out of the shadows, but it's afraid. When you ask this part of you what it is afraid of, what's coming up for you? (Criterion 2, Option 3: Dialogue with the emotion)
Example Response to Beginner Client Statement 3
I can see how difficult this is for you. When I hear you share your experience, in my body, I feel a heaviness, even a gripping in my chest. (Criterion 1) When you imagine this knot, and the fear you have of it loosening, I wonder what you fear will happen if it unravels to the point that it is gone. How do you feel about slowly breathing into the fear that may be holding the knot in place? (Criterion 2, Option 1: Regulate the body)
Example Response to Beginner Client Statement 4
Oh, that sounds really uncomfortable. It is possible this is related to the digestion of the medicine, but I wonder if what you're experiencing might be tied to an emotion that is showing itself physically. (Criterion 1) How do you feel about engaging with the discomfort like you would a dear friend, seeking clarity about what it wants you to know? (Criterion 2, Option 3: Dialogue with the emotion)
Example Response to Beginner Client Statement 5
It's totally normal for your body to feel afraid of the uncertainty in this first medicine session. I'm right here with you. (Criterion 1) How do you feel about wrapping your arms around your chest, holding yourself in a big hug? (Criterion 2, Option 1: Regulate the body) As you start to settle, what are you noticing in your body right now? (Criterion 2, Option 2: Encourage curiosity)

EXAMPLE RESPONSES TO INTERMEDIATE-LEVEL CLIENT STATEMENTS FOR EXERCISE 9

Example Response to Intermediate Client Statement 1

Something seems humorous, maybe even absurd, right now! Enjoy these laughs! (Criterion 1) What tickled you so much? Why do you think this is coming up? (Criterion 2, Option 2: Encourage curiosity)

Example Response to Intermediate Client Statement 2

It sounds like this emotion is really difficult, even scary to feel. I'd like to explore these sensations more, without shutting them down. But first, let's take care of your body. (Criterion 1) If you're okay with it, I'd like to breathe with you for a moment, to help your body feel regulated and safe while these feelings are present. How do you feel about that? (Criterion 2, Option 1: Regulate the body)

Example Response to Intermediate Client Statement 3

I can't help but feel swept up in the joy that is emanating from you right now. It sounds like you're having some powerful insights and strong emotions. (Criterion 1) When you are ready to share, I'd like to hear about what's showing up for you and what this joy feels like in your body. (Criterion 2, Option 2: Encourage curiosity)

Example Response to Intermediate Client Statement 4

I see that there's something powerful coming up for you right now. (Criterion 1) Stay with the feeling, if you can. I suspect it's coming up for a reason. Try taking some deep, full breaths with me, breathing in the feeling, holding it, and breathing it out. (Criterion 2, Option 1: Regulate the body) After that, let me know how it might feel to put some words to the experience you're having right now. (Criterion 2, Option 2: Encourage curiosity)

Example Response to Intermediate Client Statement 5

It sounds like you're experiencing intense emotions around this, and it's totally natural to have a desire to express it. (Criterion 1) Can you imagine actually talking directly to your anger? When you imagine asking the anger what it's trying to protect you from, what does it say in response? (Criterion 2, Option 3: Dialogue with the emotion)

EXAMPLE RESPONSES TO ADVANCED-LEVEL
CLIENT STATEMENTS FOR EXERCISE 9

Example Response to Advanced Client Statement 1

So it sounds like there was this part of you that wanted to protect that younger part of yourself, that younger you that was abused? (Criterion 1) Sometimes, when we feel this later in life, it can almost feel like we betrayed our younger selves. I wonder how that lands in your body when I frame your experience this way? (Criterion 2, Option 2: Encourage curiosity)

Example Response to Advanced Client Statement 2

Oh, that's so intense. I really appreciate you sharing that with me. How are you doing with this today? I notice you're holding your chest. I'm wondering if that's where you're feeling this right now? (Criterion 1) Okay, it's great you noticed that. I'm wondering if we could just take a moment and breathe into that feeling together and see what you notice. (Criterion 2, Option 1: Regulate the body)

Example Response to Advanced Client Statement 3

That was a big experience, and it sounds like it's still resonating for you. (Criterion 1) I'm wondering what this anger that is showing up in those moments is all about? Where do you think it comes from? (Criterion 2, Option 2: Encourage curiosity)

Example Response to Advanced Client Statement 4

It sounds like some really important feelings—some real anger—came up for you! You made a really important connection yesterday between what was going on in your marriage and what's going on at your job now. (Criterion 1) I'm wondering if we could spend some time today engaging with the anger that you felt. If you imagine this anger knocking at your body's door with an important message, what do you think it's trying to tell you? (Criterion 2, Option 3: Dialogue with the emotion)

Example Response to Advanced Client Statement 5

Ah, that's wonderful. It sounds like you felt some long-overdue relief and delight! (Criterion 1) Did you notice if you felt anything different in your body when that happened? Maybe close your eyes, focus on your body again, and see if you can remember what that felt like? (Criterion 2, Option 2: Encourage curiosity)

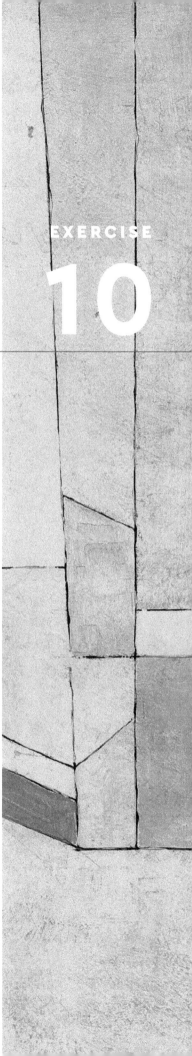

Making Sense of the Experience: Integration I

Preparations for Exercise 10

1. Read the instructions in Chapter 2.

2. Download the Deliberate Practice Reaction Form and the Deliberate Practice Diary Form at https://www.apa.org/pubs/books/deliberate-practice-psychedelic-assisted-therapy (see the "Clinician and Practitioner Resources" tab; also available in Appendixes A and B, respectively).

Skill Description

Skill Difficulty Level: Advanced

Psychedelic integration is the part of the therapeutic process when insights gained during altered states of consciousness become embodied in a way that leads to meaningful change in one's worldview and behaviors (Grof, 2000). Conversely, if one does not integrate, insights remain at a cognitive level but do not impact one's belief systems or change one's perspective enough to inform future behaviors and ways of being.

The integration phase of the psychedelic process is about meaning making (Stolaroff, 1994). It's the journey after the journey. This leg of the journey is just as important as the psychedelic medicine session. When successful, the integration process increases the chances of a psychedelic session leading to lasting change (Shulgin & Shulgin, 2002). Key features of effective integration include the following:

- Exploring visual, physical, or psychological experiences to gain deeper insights from the psychedelic medicine session.
- Using lessons that emerge in the psychedelic medicine session to implement positive change in one's daily life and relationships.
- Allowing strong emotions that arise from past trauma to be felt and released.

https://doi.org/10.1037/0000399-012

Deliberate Practice in Psychedelic-Assisted Therapy, by S. Dames, A. Penn, M. Williams, J. A. Zamaria, T. Rousmaniere, and A. Vaz

- Embracing one's new understanding of self and others.
- Tracking progress toward goals.
- Developing a plan to maintain momentum and accountability for lasting change.
- Managing desire for further psychedelic use.
- Setting intentions for future experiences.

In an integration session, it's important to engage in active listening, demonstrating and cultivating a nonjudgmental, trusting, and accepting container in which your client can share their experience. Exploration of the experience can promote deeper meaning making. It's important to reiterate that the psychedelic and integration process is a time-released experience that unfolds at the pace of readiness and trust. It is normal for people to experience ups and downs on the path to integration. Finally, sometimes in the afterglow of an intense psychedelic experience, clients may want to make major life changes. Generally, it is recommended that they first take at least a month to settle into new ways of being and feeling before making any major decisions about their life (Grof, 2000).

The therapist should improvise a response to each client statement following these skill criteria:

1. **Appreciate and validate the client's perspective.** Express appreciation for the client's disclosure and validate their concerns.

2. **Respond with a question or statement that invites the client to make meaning of their psychedelic medicine experience.** Common therapist questions that invite for client meaning making include the following:

   - Ask the client to describe their experience, from the come up, to the peak, to the come down.

   - Ask the client what they learned from their experience.

   - Ask if there were challenging or frightening parts of the experience.

   - Explore how "set and setting" played a role in how the psychedelic experience unfolded.

SKILL CRITERIA FOR EXERCISE 10
1. Appreciate and validate the client's perspective.
2. Respond with a question or statement that invites the client to make meaning of their psychedelic medicine experience.

Examples of Making Sense of the Experience: Integration I

Example 1

CLIENT: [*confused*] That was a really profound experience yesterday. I wrote a lot down last night, but I'm still trying to make sense of everything. I don't really know where to start.

THERAPIST: I hear from you how meaningful yesterday felt. I think it makes great sense to take your time to unpack some of what you explored and what was revealed to you during your experience. (Criterion 1) I also understand that it feels complex and also difficult to know where to start. Perhaps just begin with wherever you may find yourself today. If there are any parts of the experience that you feel drawn to putting words to, or where there is a curiosity or an urgency, you might start in any of those places. (Criterion 2)

Example 2

CLIENT: [*surprised*] I had no idea that stuff was going to come up yesterday about my family.

THERAPIST: Yeah, thank you for bringing that up. It seemed like such a powerful dialogue you were having with yourself. (Criterion 1) Can you put a little more language to what that part of the experience was like for you, and what impact that experience might have on your life moving forward? (Criterion 2)

Example 3

CLIENT: [*sad and guilty*] You asked me about when I was struggling and crying during the session. That was when I was trying to protect my son from this demon, and then I realized the demon was me and the depression that I seem to have given him.

THERAPIST: Wow, that's a really powerful experience. I appreciate you sharing that with me. (Criterion 1) How was it for you to both be able to appreciate your son's depression but also feel responsible for it? (Criterion 2)

INSTRUCTIONS FOR EXERCISE 10
Step 1: Role-Play and Feedback
• The client says the first beginner client statement. The therapist **improvises** a response based on the skill criteria.   • The trainer (or, if not available, the client) provides **brief** feedback based on the skill criteria.   • The client then repeats the same statement, and the therapist again improvises a response. The trainer (or client) again provides brief feedback.
Step 2: Repeat
• Repeat Step 1 for all the statements **in the current difficulty level** (beginner, intermediate, or advanced).
Step 3: Assess and Adjust Difficulty
• The therapist completes the Deliberate Practice Reaction Form (see Appendix A) and decides whether to make the exercise easier or harder or to repeat the same difficulty level.
Step 4: Repeat for Approximately 15 Minutes
• Repeat Steps 1 to 3 for at least 15 minutes.   • The trainees then switch therapist and client roles and start over.

Now it's your turn! Follow Steps 1 and 2 from the exercise instructions.

Remember: The goal of the role-play is for trainees to practice improvising responses to the client statements in a manner that (a) uses the skill criteria and (b) feels authentic for the trainee. **Example therapist responses for each client statement are provided at the end of this exercise. Trainees should attempt to improvise their own responses before reading the example responses.**

BEGINNER-LEVEL CLIENT STATEMENTS FOR EXERCISE 10
Beginner Client Statement 1
[Confused] That was a really profound experience yesterday. I wrote a lot down last night, but I'm still trying to make sense of everything. I don't really know where to start.
Beginner Client Statement 2
[Guilty] I kept seeing my late wife in the session and feeling so guilty. I was so cold to her when we were married. I was so caught up in what I thought was important back then.
Beginner Client Statement 3
[Sad] I had this flash of a memory from my childhood. I was a baby actually, lying in my crib crying. And no one came for me.
Beginner Client Statement 4
[Afraid] I had this moment where I realized that I feel the same sense of threat and strong desire to avoid strong women in my life as I did when I was a little girl, avoiding my mom's anger and eventual rejection. No wonder I break a sweat whenever my boss walks in!
Beginner Client Statement 5
[Relieved] Oh man, I remember when the medicine started to kick in and I thought, "Oh no, this is going to be terrible. I can't control this," and then I just let go, and it was the most amazing feeling, like I was floating peacefully.

🛑 **Assess and adjust the difficulty before moving to the next difficulty level (see Step 3 in the exercise instructions).**

INTERMEDIATE-LEVEL CLIENT STATEMENTS FOR EXERCISE 10
Intermediate Client Statement 1
[Surprised] I had no idea that stuff was going to come up yesterday about my family.
Intermediate Client Statement 2
[Afraid] I can't shake this feeling I had in the session last week. It was me as a kid, trapped in a box by myself. It was dark and I was scared. The intensity of it passed eventually, but in a subtle way, that feeling hasn't left me.
Intermediate Client Statement 3
[Self-compassionate] The part of the session that stood out to me most was that dialogue with my younger part. It was so profound. It's like I've had this little kid inside me, this little version of me, ever since I was little, and I finally heard their voice yesterday.
Intermediate Client Statement 4
[Ashamed] For the first time I can remember, I saw my own beauty. I saw how hard I've been on my body, and then the shame rushed in.
Intermediate Client Statement 5
[Self-compassionate] I know this is going to sound weird, but I saw myself as an old person during the session, and I was telling myself now, "What the hell are you waiting for? Live your life, silly!"

 Assess and adjust the difficulty before moving to the next difficulty level (see Step 3 in the exercise instructions).

ADVANCED-LEVEL CLIENT STATEMENTS FOR EXERCISE 10
Advanced Client Statement 1
[Sad and guilty] You asked me about when I was struggling and crying during the session. That was when I was trying to protect my son from this demon, and then I realized the demon was me and the depression that I seem to have given him.
Advanced Client Statement 2
[Longing] I saw my grandmother and she was speaking to me, telling me things about her life that were also true about my life. She seemed so real, but was it real? She passed away 4 years ago, and I really miss her.
Advanced Client Statement 3
[Fear of embarrassment] I had this moment where I totally forgot I had a body, and then I had the weirdest thought—"What if I piss my pants and these nice people have to clean me up? That would be so embarrassing."
Advanced Client Statement 4
[Self-acceptance] I was sitting at a big table and there were five of me, all representing different aspects of me and different times in my life. And they were all talking to each other, having this profound conversation. There were things my older, wiser self wanted to tell my restless headstrong self.

Assess and adjust the difficulty here (see Step 3 in the exercise instructions). If appropriate, follow the instructions to make the exercise even more challenging (see Appendix A).

Example Therapist Responses: Making Sense of the Experience: Integration I

Remember: Trainees should attempt to improvise their own responses before reading the example responses. **Do not read the following responses verbatim unless you are having trouble coming up with your own responses!**

EXAMPLE RESPONSES TO BEGINNER-LEVEL CLIENT STATEMENTS FOR EXERCISE 10
Example Response to Beginner Client Statement 1
I hear from you how meaningful yesterday felt; I think it makes great sense to take your time to unpack some of what you explored, and what was revealed to you during your experience. (Criterion 1) I also understand that it feels complex and also difficult to know where to start. Perhaps just begin with wherever you may find yourself today. If there are any parts of the experience that you feel drawn to putting words to, or where there is a curiosity or an urgency, you might start in any of those places. (Criterion 2)
Example Response to Beginner Client Statement 2
That sounds really difficult, and also really powerful. (Criterion 1) I appreciate you being willing to share that with me. Could we talk more about those feelings that came up for you? (Criterion 2)
Example Response to Beginner Client Statement 3
This sounds like a really important and sad moment. (Criterion 1) I'm curious about how you are making meaning from the experience. What did it help you understand? (Criterion 2)
Example Response to Beginner Client Statement 4
This sounds like a powerful insight! Sometimes the relationships in our day-to-day life become our teachers, showing us an opportunity to heal a past wound. (Criterion 1) With this new awareness, when your boss walks in and you notice your body falling into a familiar fear pattern, how might you speak to the younger part of yourself that is coming up for healing? (Criterion 2)
Example Response to Beginner Client Statement 5
Sounds like that experience of letting go was really hard. Then when you let go, something changed. (Criterion 1) I'm curious to hear more about the experience, and I'm wondering how it might be showing up in your life now? (Criterion 2)

EXAMPLE RESPONSES TO INTERMEDIATE-LEVEL
CLIENT STATEMENTS FOR EXERCISE 10

Example Response to Intermediate Client Statement 1

Yeah, thank you for bringing that up. It seemed like such a powerful dialogue you were having with yourself. (Criterion 1) Can you put a little more language to what that part of the experience was like for you, and what impact that experience might have on your life moving forward? (Criterion 2)

Example Response to Intermediate Client Statement 2

Oh, that sounds scary, I can understand why the memory and felt sense of it would continue to jar you. (Criterion 1) Sometimes the medicine sessions shine a light on patterns and belief systems that inform our behaviors and relationships but might be harder to see and feel in our day-to-day life. In this case, I wonder how this sense of being "trapped" is showing up in your day-to-day life? (Criterion 2)

Example Response to Intermediate Client Statement 3

Yeah, we were right there in the room with you and that visit from a younger part seemed to color the whole session. It was really moving to witness the experience. (Criterion 1) I wonder what it would be like to continue to cultivate your relationship with that part of yourself, after we're done working together. Or to make a practice out of communicating with that part of you. What do you think? (Criterion 2)

Example Response to Intermediate Client Statement 4

When I hear about you seeing your own beauty, I can't help but smile. It sounds like what might have been an idea in the past is becoming a "knowing" in your body. I can also understand how such knowing is hard in retrospect. (Criterion 1) I wonder if this newfound knowledge of your inherent beauty and worthiness could be applied to you, as you are, without condition. What might it look like for you to accept and have compassion for your past self—that you didn't know what you didn't know, and that you were doing the best you could with the knowledge and resources you had? (Criterion 2)

Example Response to Intermediate Client Statement 5

That sounds like a really important experience. (Criterion 1) If that older version of yourself was here right now, what do you think they would be telling you about how you're living your life? What do you think this version of you would say should be different? (Criterion 2)

EXAMPLE RESPONSES TO ADVANCED-LEVEL CLIENT STATEMENTS FOR EXERCISE 10
Example Response to Advanced Client Statement 1
Wow, that's a really powerful experience. I appreciate you sharing that with me. (Criterion 1) How was it for you to both be able to appreciate your son's depression but also feel responsible for it? (Criterion 2)
Example Response to Advanced Client Statement 2
Your experience sounds pretty real to me. It seems like there were some parallels in the life course of you and your grandmother. (Criterion 1) It also sounds like she had something important she wanted you to know. I wonder how this experience is impacting your life now? (Criterion 2)
Example Response to Advanced Client Statement 3
I appreciate you sharing that with me. Being in that state requires a lot of letting go of control, sometimes even of our bodily functions. (Criterion 1) I don't think you were actually incontinent, so that wasn't an issue, but what would it have been like if it were? (Criterion 2)
Example Response to Advanced Client Statement 4
Wow, it must have been so powerful to be so present and accepting of these various ages and versions of yourself. (Criterion 1) What insights are you taking with you from this experience? (Criterion 2)

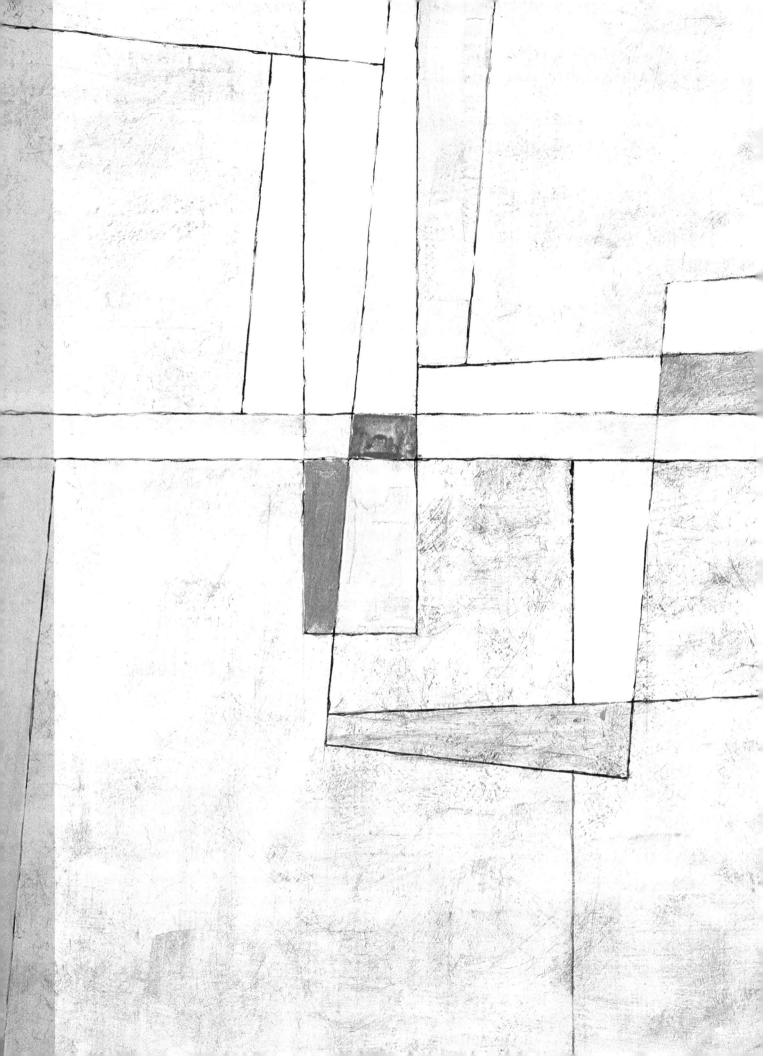

Working With Disappointment:
Integration II

Preparations for Exercise 11

1. Read the instructions in Chapter 2.

2. Download the Deliberate Practice Reaction Form and the Deliberate Practice Diary Form at https://www.apa.org/pubs/books/deliberate-practice-psychedelic-assisted-therapy (see the "Clinician and Practitioner Resources" tab; also available in Appendixes A and B, respectively).

Skill Description

Skill Difficulty Level: Advanced

Clients' expectations play a major role in any psychotherapy process and its outcomes (Frank & Frank, 1991; Kirsch, 1990). Similar to other treatments, clients can have expectations for psychedelic therapy that are not realistic or achievable in a single session (Fadiman, 2011). This can result in clients feeling disappointed after psychedelic medicine sessions. This tension and disappointment can signal a transition from a trusting therapeutic bond into the client, understandably, gripping for control of the treatment process (Safran & Muran, 2000). It is important to remember that a client's disappointment is often a marker for deeper fears that need to be validated and collaboratively explored. This exercise will help therapists do just that.

There are three main tasks that can help clients reestablish trust in the psychedelic therapy process:

- **Shift client expectations and focus from therapy outcomes to intentions.** Control of outcomes is often an illusion, and it's important to bring this illusion to conscious awareness. We cannot control the thoughts, feelings, and behaviors of others, and often, we cannot control these things in ourselves either! Many of our and others'

https://doi.org/10.1037/0000399-013

Deliberate Practice in Psychedelic-Assisted Therapy, by S. Dames, A. Penn, M. Williams, J. A. Zamaria, T. Rousmaniere, and A. Vaz

behaviors do not involve conscious choice at all—they are often unconscious reactions to perceived threats. This shift helps transform disappointment to awareness of resistance, reminding clients that all they can truly control is how they choose to engage in the process (in psychedelic therapy and in life), which then influences the outcomes. This is where the practice of surrender comes in because an intention and ability to surrender to the process is a powerful antidote to disappointment.

- **Notice when the client is gripping for control.** When you notice the client is ruminating, and especially when an emotional charge presents with the ruminating, it's a good sign that they are gripping for control. This is their edge. Notice it. Encourage a pause. What is on the surface is generally a small piece of the story. What lies beneath is the fear that is fueling the gripping. Like we practiced in Exercise 9 (Navigating Strong Emotions), encourage the client to turn to the emotion to seek understanding. Leaning in with curiosity and self-compassion can help them identify and name the source of the fear that is causing them to grip for control.

- **Gain perspective.** Expectations fester in the dark. If the client is gripping for control or having thought rumination, often accompanied by a stress response, they have likely lost perspective. Encourage the client to speak clearly about any disappointment they feel. Doing so, while in connection with a trusted other, brings an objective light to the subjective feelings. From this place, a shift in perspective becomes possible, enabling the client to focus on what can be controlled and to practice letting go of what they cannot control.

The therapist should improvise a response to each client statement following these skill criteria:

1. **Acknowledge and validate the client's disappointment.** Acknowledge and validate the suffering associated with disappointment, without the need to reassure excessively or find a silver lining.

2. **Tend to the emotion beneath the disappointment.** Disappointment is an important signal, often pointing to a fear that is unresolved. Without dismissing the experience of disappointment, in this step, we attempt to explore its deeper meaning. Here, cultivate curiosity for the fears and insecurities that may be driving the disappointment. The therapist can explore what it feels like to notice these fears and the often unpredictable nature of the psychedelic process itself.

SKILL CRITERIA FOR EXERCISE 11
1. Acknowledge and validate the client's disappointment.
2. Tend to the emotion beneath the disappointment.

Examples of Working With Disappointment: Integration II

Example 1

CLIENT: [*disappointed*] I didn't feel anything. This isn't working.

THERAPIST: It's disappointing that you're not feeling what you expected to feel. (Criterion 1) Can you share a little more about your fears and worries that this treatment won't work for you? (Criterion 2)

Example 2

CLIENT: [*disappointed*] I really thought that all my cravings for alcohol were going to be gone after the session, but yesterday, I was really craving a drink.

THERAPIST: You were hoping that the medicine session was going to make those cravings go away. (Criterion 1) I'm wondering what it feels like to sense that the medicine may not resolve these urges, at least not in any predictable way? (Criterion 2)

Example 3

CLIENT: [*disappointed*] I thought you were going to keep me safe, and I didn't really feel safe after the medicine trip.

THERAPIST: I appreciate you sharing your feelings with me, and I understand you felt unsafe. I'm also hearing that you feel let down. (Criterion 1) Of course we want you to feel as safe as possible here. And, at the same time, it is unlikely that we'll be able to control the medicine process entirely. I'd like to explore this more with you. What is it like to notice that this process might come with some unpredictable highs and lows? (Criterion 2)

INSTRUCTIONS FOR EXERCISE 11

Step 1: Role-Play and Feedback

- The client says the first beginner client statement. The therapist **improvises** a response based on the skill criteria.
- The trainer (or, if not available, the client) provides **brief** feedback based on the skill criteria.
- The client then repeats the same statement, and the therapist again improvises a response. The trainer (or client) again provides brief feedback.

Step 2: Repeat

- Repeat Step 1 for all the statements **in the current difficulty level** (beginner, intermediate, or advanced).

Step 3: Assess and Adjust Difficulty

- The therapist completes the Deliberate Practice Reaction Form (see Appendix A) and decides whether to make the exercise easier or harder or to repeat the same difficulty level.

Step 4: Repeat for Approximately 15 Minutes

- Repeat Steps 1 to 3 for at least 15 minutes.
- The trainees then switch therapist and client roles and start over.

Now it's your turn! Follow Steps 1 and 2 from the exercise instructions.

Remember: The goal of the role-play is for trainees to practice improvising responses to the client statements in a manner that (a) uses the skill criteria and (b) feels authentic for the trainee. **Example therapist responses for each client statement are provided at the end of this exercise. Trainees should attempt to improvise their own responses before reading the example responses.**

BEGINNER-LEVEL CLIENT STATEMENTS FOR EXERCISE 11
Beginner Client Statement 1
[Disappointed] I cried the whole time and didn't enjoy any of it. It felt so dark. I thought at least some of it would be fun.
Beginner Client Statement 2
[Disappointed] I didn't feel anything. This isn't working.
Beginner Client Statement 3
[Disappointed] I really thought that all my cravings for alcohol were going to be gone after the session, but yesterday I was really craving a drink.
Beginner Client Statement 4
[Disappointed] I thought this would help me with my anxiety, but it's worse than ever.
Beginner Client Statement 5
[Disappointed] When I saw my father in the medicine session, I was able to forgive him for what he did, and it felt really good to release it. But now that I'm back in my regular state of mind, I'm still angry with him.

 Assess and adjust the difficulty before moving to the next difficulty level (see Step 3 in the exercise instructions).

INTERMEDIATE-LEVEL CLIENT STATEMENTS FOR EXERCISE 11

Intermediate Client Statement 1

[Disappointed] I totally thought I was going to have visions and see all these colors and patterns people talk about. But it was just dark and cold inside.

Intermediate Client Statement 2

[Disappointed] I just became too consumed with what I was experiencing physically—my nausea, feeling like I had to run to the bathroom, feeling dizzy—that I didn't feel like there was mental space for me to process my trauma. I'm really upset about this because I feel like I missed out on my chance to get some momentum and actually talk through my memories and past experiences.

Intermediate Client Statement 3

[Disappointed] All I felt for hours was a bottomless pit of darkness. It felt lonely and hopeless. Who would want to go through that again?

Intermediate Client Statement 4

[Disappointed] I know, it sounds silly, but I kinda thought I was going to meet God during the medicine session. All I saw was some swirling shapes and colors.

Intermediate Client Statement 5

[Disappointed] During my psychedelic journey, I realized I caused so much pain for my husband and our kids. I just couldn't see it before, and I am not sure what to do with that now. That's not what I was expecting.

 Assess and adjust the difficulty before moving to the next difficulty level (see Step 3 in the exercise instructions).

ADVANCED-LEVEL CLIENT STATEMENTS FOR EXERCISE 11

Advanced Client Statement 1

[Disappointed] I thought you were going to keep me safe, and I didn't really feel safe after the medicine trip.

Advanced Client Statement 2

[Disappointed] I know this sounds kind of, I don't know, unappreciative? But I was really kind of bored lying here yesterday. I know I said I'd stay all day, but after about 3 hours, I just wanted to go home.

Advanced Client Statement 3

[Disappointed] My experience was fun and silly. It was a great break from my usual day. But I didn't get any insight whatsoever into my depression. I feel as depressed as ever. The experience was a nice relief but nothing else. I feel like I'll never be free of this depression.

Advanced Client Statement 4

[Disappointed] I am pretty sure I fell asleep during the session. I was told by a friend that couldn't happen, so I let myself go with it. I feel like I was misinformed, and now all that time and money is wasted.

Advanced Client Statement 5

[Disappointed] Things really started to take off for me, and then the fire alarm went off, and we all had to go outside for 20 minutes. I just couldn't get back into the process after that.

✋ **Assess and adjust the difficulty here (see Step 3 in the exercise instructions). If appropriate, follow the instructions to make the exercise even more challenging (see Appendix A).**

Example Therapist Responses: Working With Disappointment: Integration II

Remember: Trainees should attempt to improvise their own responses before reading the example responses. **Do not read the following responses verbatim unless you are having trouble coming up with your own responses!**

EXAMPLE RESPONSES TO BEGINNER-LEVEL CLIENT STATEMENTS FOR EXERCISE 11
Example Response to Beginner Client Statement 1
I am sorry to hear that was a difficult journey. It sounds like you feel disappointed in your experience. Often we have to go through a dark tunnel before we can emerge into the light on the other side. (Criterion 1) When you think back to the experience, can you get in touch with any specific fears or worries you have around this dark place you encountered? (Criterion 2)
Example Response to Beginner Client Statement 2
It's disappointing that you're not feeling what you expected to feel. (Criterion 1) Can you share a little more about your fears and worries that this treatment won't work for you? (Criterion 2)
Example Response to Beginner Client Statement 3
You were hoping that the medicine session was going to make those cravings go away? (Criterion 1) I'm wondering what it feels like to sense that the medicine may not resolve these urges, at least not in any predictable way? (Criterion 2)
Example Response to Beginner Client Statement 4
Hoping for a break from the anxiety and then not receiving it sounds pretty disappointing. While these "in-between" spaces are part of meaningful change, I understand it can feel really discombobulating! (Criterion 1) In the days after these sessions, these emotions are important parts of your integration process. How do you feel about checking what other, vulnerable emotions might be lurking underneath the anxiety? (Criterion 2)
Example Response to Beginner Client Statement 5
So in that moment, you were able to release those hurt feelings, but now they're back? I can see why that would feel like a setback. (Criterion 1) Maybe the feeling you had in the session was not an end point, but some kind of teaching or instruction of sorts that showed you what you were moving toward. How does it feel to notice the unpredictable nature of this change process you're going through? (Criterion 2)

EXAMPLE RESPONSES TO INTERMEDIATE-LEVEL CLIENT STATEMENTS FOR EXERCISE 11

Example Response to Intermediate Client Statement 1

Yeah, a lot of people talk about the visions and patterns, but what you describe is pretty common, too. I'm aware you sound disappointed with the experience you had. (Criterion 1) I'm curious to hear if you'd be willing to explore that a little further. What was it like to find yourself in that dark, cold place? (Criterion 2)

Example Response to Intermediate Client Statement 2

I saw how physically uncomfortable you were, and it looked really difficult. I understand that you're disappointed that you didn't feel able to process your trauma. (Criterion 1) Can you say more about your disappointment? In particular, what fears came up for you after this experience? (Criterion 2)

Example Response to Intermediate Client Statement 3

It sounds like you are feeling a sense of disappointment about your experience. I can understand why you wouldn't want to do it again. Ultimately, the decision to have another session is yours. Even, and perhaps especially, the difficult sessions provide important teachings for us. They can illuminate the more subtle emotions and belief systems that tend to color our day-to-day experience. (Criterion 1) From this vantage point, I'd like to tend to the experience of darkness and loneliness that you described earlier. How do you feel about us going back to the darkness together, so we can explore and make sense of it? (Criterion 2)

Example Response to Intermediate Client Statement 4

So it sounds like you were hoping this experience was going to be really important, and it wasn't what you imagined it would be. (Criterion 1) We don't really know what or who we'll find during our psychedelic sessions. I understand surrendering to that unknown can be tough. What does the unpredictability of this process bring up for you? (Criterion 2)

Example Response to Intermediate Client Statement 5

That sounds like such a hard thing to experience and understand. (Criterion 1) I know that is not what you were expecting, and I am wondering how you are making sense of this. (Criterion 2)

EXAMPLE RESPONSES TO ADVANCED-LEVEL **CLIENT STATEMENTS FOR EXERCISE 11**
Example Response to Advanced Client Statement 1
I appreciate you sharing your feelings with me, and I understand you felt unsafe. I'm also hearing that you feel let down. (Criterion 1) Of course we want you to feel as safe as possible here. And, at the same time, it is unlikely that we'll be able to control the medicine process entirely. I'd like to explore this more with you. What is it like to notice that this process might come with some unpredictable highs and lows? (Criterion 2)
Example Response to Advanced Client Statement 2
That actually makes a lot of sense. (Criterion 1) Most of us don't take a whole day to lie on a couch and reflect, psychedelics or no, and it can be an unfamiliar and uncomfortable feeling to spend that time inward. Can you tell me more about any fears or worries you're having after this experience? (Criterion 2)
Example Response to Advanced Client Statement 3
I hear the disappointment in your voice. It sounds like you experienced some of the relief you've been hoping for in the session, but perhaps this relief still feels hard to find in your day-to-day life. (Criterion 1) When you think about the fear of not "getting free of depression," where does it show up in your body? Perhaps you can put some words to your fear about not getting well, about your depression persisting? (Criterion 2)
Example Response to Advanced Client Statement 4
I can totally understand why you would feel frustrated. It sounds like you're dealing with some disappointment that I'd be happy to explore further with you. (Criterion 1) I'm also curious how the psychedelic experience has been unfolding since the session. What's been coming up for you since? (Criterion 2)
Example Response to Advanced Client Statement 5
That was so unfortunate and so jarring for everyone, and I felt sad that your process was interrupted like that. Sometimes things happen that are outside of everyone's control. (Criterion 1) Hopefully, that particular unpredictability won't happen again. But the psychedelic process itself is, in my experience, full of unpredictability. Do you notice any fears or worries around that? (Criterion 2)

Embodying Insights: Integration III

Preparations for Exercise 12

1. Read the instructions in Chapter 2.

2. Download the Deliberate Practice Reaction Form and the Deliberate Practice Diary Form at https://www.apa.org/pubs/books/deliberate-practice-psychedelic-assisted-therapy (see the "Clinician and Practitioner Resources" tab; also available in Appendixes A and B, respectively).

Skill Description

Skill Difficulty Level: Advanced

Psychedelic experiences are often hard to articulate. Integration can be seen as essentially knowledge translation between the mind and the body. To promote integration, it can be helpful to encourage clients not just to make sense of their psychedelic experience (Exercise 10) but also nudge them to take what they have learned into their daily lives. As clients move about their daily activities, it's important that they continue to focus on the felt sense of their lived experience and staying present in the body, which ensures insights are felt and actualized in the body.

Because it is common for resistant and avoidant patterns to emerge when difficult emotions arise, it is important to have strategies ready for when they do. It is perfectly normal for people to experience temporary setbacks or moments of forgetting. The goal is to shorten the time between the misstep and the time it takes to repair and come back into conscious awareness. After all, habits take time to develop. New ways of being and doing take practice and repetition, enabling them to move from conscious effort to unconscious ease.

https://doi.org/10.1037/0000399-014

Deliberate Practice in Psychedelic-Assisted Therapy, by S. Dames, A. Penn, M. Williams, J. A. Zamaria, T. Rousmaniere, and A. Vaz

The therapist should improvise a response to each client statement following these skill criteria:

1. **Name what the client is integrating.** What insight is coming up to integrate? In this first step, the therapist highlights the insight that is coming forward from the client. Use your active listening skills to consider if there is a deeper meaning, which is not always explicitly stated by clients. This first step is essential because it ensures that you have adequately understood the crux of the client's insight.

2. **Encourage actions to promote further integration.** The next step is to invite the client to consider how they might take a significant action that is aligned with the insight. Much like Exercise 3 (Exploring Intentions and Expectations), it's important to focus on process over outcome in the determination of the significant action. The outcome provides the north star—meaning and motivation—and the process represents the steps on the pathway there. The client cannot control the outcome, but they can take the next step.

SKILL CRITERIA FOR EXERCISE 12
1. Name what the client is integrating.
2. Encourage actions to promote further integration.

Examples of Therapists Embodying Insights: Integration III

Example 1

CLIENT: [*confident*] I finally realized that I don't need to be sorry for who I am anymore.

THERAPIST: Wow. What a powerful realization, not needing to be sorry for who you are! (Criterion 1) What do you think this suggests about how you live your life after our work here is done? What practice will help you integrate this realization and remember it, moving forward? (Criterion 2)

Example 2

CLIENT: [*joyful*] I didn't realize that joy was within me. When I was able to drop into a sense of peace in my body, there it was! I'm afraid I'll forget how that feels, or I won't be able to access it again.

THERAPIST: It makes me smile to imagine you being surprised that joy is within you when you have the opportunity to drop fully into your inner world—what a gift! I'm also hearing your fear of losing sight of it. (Criterion 1) It sounds like the joy came when you were able to drop into a sense of peace in your body. How might you support your body to be regulated and relaxed enough to experience this sense of peace in your daily life? (Criterion 2)

Example 3

CLIENT: [*accepting*] You know, when I was in the session, I kept seeing scenes from my childhood coming up where I was bullied and I thought, "Why did I let them do that to me?" And it made me feel really angry at myself.

THERAPIST: So it sounds like you spent a bit of time with that younger self and weren't too happy with how that younger you dealt with those people who bullied you? (Criterion 1) Would you be open to exploring what was happening for you then, so that perhaps we might better understand how you can best support your needs today? (Criterion 2)

INSTRUCTIONS FOR EXERCISE 12

Step 1: Role-Play and Feedback

- The client says the first beginner client statement. The therapist **improvises** a response based on the skill criteria.
- The trainer (or, if not available, the client) provides **brief** feedback based on the skill criteria.
- The client then repeats the same statement, and the therapist again improvises a response. The trainer (or client) again provides brief feedback.

Step 2: Repeat

- Repeat Step 1 for all the statements **in the current difficulty level** (beginner, intermediate, or advanced).

Step 3: Assess and Adjust Difficulty

- The therapist completes the Deliberate Practice Reaction Form (see Appendix A) and decides whether to make the exercise easier or harder or to repeat the same difficulty level.

Step 4: Repeat for Approximately 15 Minutes

- Repeat Steps 1 to 3 for at least 15 minutes.
- The trainees then switch therapist and client roles and start over.

Now it's your turn! Follow Steps 1 and 2 from the exercise instructions.

Remember: The goal of the role-play is for trainees to practice improvising responses to the client statements in a manner that (a) uses the skill criteria and (b) feels authentic for the trainee. **Example therapist responses for each client statement are provided at the end of this exercise. Trainees should attempt to improvise their own responses before reading the example responses.**

BEGINNER-LEVEL CLIENT STATEMENTS FOR EXERCISE 12
Beginner Client Statement 1
[Confident] I finally realized that I don't need to be sorry for who I am anymore.
Beginner Client Statement 2
[Grounded] Connecting to nature in that way reminded me that it's a resource that's really important for me.
Beginner Client Statement 3
[Sadness] Remember that part of my journey where I was seeing that beautiful landscape? As I came back into the room, I felt this real sadness because I realized that I spend most of my life looking at a computer screen.
Beginner Client Statement 4
[Self-compassion] You know, when I was coming back into my body, I found myself repeating in my head, "You have to take care of the vessel," and I realized that even though we're all going to die, we only get to be in this body for a little while.
Beginner Client Statement 5
[Self-compassion] I realized how hard I've been on myself my whole life.

 Assess and adjust the difficulty before moving to the next difficulty level (see Step 3 in the exercise instructions).

INTERMEDIATE-LEVEL CLIENT STATEMENTS FOR EXERCISE 12

Intermediate Client Statement 1

[Joy] I didn't realize that joy was within me. When I was able to drop into a sense of peace in my body, there it was! I'm afraid I'll forget how that feels, or I won't be able to access it again.

Intermediate Client Statement 2

[Acceptance] I was always so self-conscious about my body because it doesn't fit into these "ideal" standards that you see in the media. But now, I really appreciate the body God gave me—I am healthy, it works well, and I am okay with that.

Intermediate Client Statement 3

[Joy] I'm still trying to make sense of yesterday. But one of the things that stood out to me was how vibrant the plants and flowers in the space were. They were stunning. It just made me think about how years ago, I used to do these seemingly little things that would make me happy. One of them was putting beautiful plants and fresh cut flowers in my home. I haven't done that in so many years.

Intermediate Client Statement 4

[Relief] I just got this realization that I've been staying sad about when my dad died because if I didn't it would be disrespecting his memory. But when I saw him in the session, I realized I don't need to do that anymore.

Intermediate Client Statement 5

[Playful] I could really see, for the first time, how I'd kept that child part of me locked up. And that's been stifling my creativity my whole adult life. Now I feel an urge to start writing and painting again.

 Assess and adjust the difficulty before moving to the next difficulty level (see Step 3 in the exercise instructions).

ADVANCED-LEVEL CLIENT STATEMENTS FOR EXERCISE 12
Advanced Client Statement 1
[Accepting] You know, when I was in the session, I kept seeing scenes from my childhood coming up where I was bullied and I thought, "Why did I let them do that to me?" and it made me feel really angry at myself.
Advanced Client Statement 2
[Self-compassion] I realized that the anger I'm carrying is hurting me more than it hurts him. I've always thought that forgiving him would be letting him off the hook, but now I'm seeing that it's me I need to let off the hook.
Advanced Client Statement 3
[Shame] I realized the shame I've been carrying my whole life was his, not mine.
Advanced Client Statement 4
[Self-compassion] I finally understood that I don't need to stay in that abusive work situation anymore. A recruiter called me this morning, and instead of hanging up, like I usually do, I was like, hey, let me hear what he has to say.
Advanced Client Statement 5
[Acceptance] I could see clearly how my bad marriage is affecting the kids. I wanted to stay together with them, but now I realize I need to make a change for all of us.

 Assess and adjust the difficulty here (see Step 3 in the exercise instructions). If appropriate, follow the instructions to make the exercise even more challenging (see Appendix A).

Example Therapist Responses: Embodying Insights: Integration III

Remember: Trainees should attempt to improvise their own responses before reading the example responses. **Do not read the following responses verbatim unless you are having trouble coming up with your own responses!**

EXAMPLE RESPONSES TO BEGINNER-LEVEL CLIENT STATEMENTS FOR EXERCISE 12
Example Response to Beginner Client Statement 1
Wow. What a powerful realization! (Criterion 1) What do you think this suggests about how you live your life after our work here is done? What practice will help you integrate this realization and remember it, moving forward? (Criterion 2)
Example Response to Beginner Client Statement 2
What a great insight. It sounds like incorporating nature into your life could provide some real benefits for you. (Criterion 1) What could it look like for you to incorporate nature more in your day-to-day life? (Criterion 2)
Example Response to Beginner Client Statement 3
Sounds like you were really noticing a contrast between what you saw during the medicine session and how you're spending your time now. (Criterion 1) Does that get you thinking about how you might like things to be different? (Criterion 2)
Example Response to Beginner Client Statement 4
So that realization of taking care of your body was really important to you? (Criterion 1) What would "taking care of the vessel" look like in day-to-day life? (Criterion 2)
Example Response to Beginner Client Statement 5
Yeah, I saw you explore those areas of judgment and self-criticism. It seems like it was painful, but useful, to take a look at those aspects of yourself. (Criterion 1) What did you glean from that exploration? What would you like your life to look like, moving forward, now that you realize how hard you have been on yourself? What actions would you like to take to honor this realization? (Criterion 2)

EXAMPLE RESPONSES TO INTERMEDIATE-LEVEL CLIENT STATEMENTS FOR EXERCISE 12

Example Response to Intermediate Client Statement 1

It makes me smile to imagine you being surprised that joy is within you when you have the opportunity to fully drop into your inner world—what a gift! I'm also hearing your fear of losing sight of it. (Criterion 1) It sounds like the joy came when you were able to drop into a sense of peace in your body. How might you support your body to be regulated and relaxed enough to experience this sense of peace in your daily life? (Criterion 2)

Example Response to Intermediate Client Statement 2

It's so important that we feel comfortable about the skin we're in, and I'm so happy to hear that you are at this new place in your self-perception. (Criterion 1) How does this change how you feel and what you do around others? (Criterion 2)

Example Response to Intermediate Client Statement 3

You're lighting up right now, talking about that. It sounds like these small but meaningful gestures of care that you expressed toward yourself made you feel alive. (Criterion 1) What would it be like to return to that practice of furnishing your place with plants and flowers? (Criterion 2)

Example Response to Intermediate Client Statement 4

So seeing your dad in the therapy session was a really important moment for your healing. (Criterion 1) Could we talk more about what you realized when you saw your dad in that part of the session? Maybe there's something important there to take with you into your daily life. (Criterion 2)

Example Response to Intermediate Client Statement 5

It's wonderful to hear how you are reconnecting with a part of yourself that has been locked away. (Criterion 1) When and how are you going to restart these creative activities? (Criterion 2)

EXAMPLE RESPONSES TO ADVANCED-LEVEL CLIENT STATEMENTS FOR EXERCISE 12

Example Response to Advanced Client Statement 1

So it sounds like you spent a bit of time with that younger self and weren't too happy with how that younger you dealt with those people who bullied you? (Criterion 1) Would you be open to exploring what was happening for you then so that perhaps we might better understand how you can best support your needs today? (Criterion 2)

Example Response to Advanced Client Statement 2

Wow, what a powerful and perhaps liberating insight! When you referred to the anger as something you carry, and then the idea of letting it go, I felt a lightness in my chest. (Criterion 1) Sometimes forgiveness happens over time, which may mean getting comfortable with a practice that helps you let go of the anger each time it comes up. When you imagine your future self grappling with anger, what would it look like to "let yourself off the hook" in that moment? (Criterion 2)

Example Response to Advanced Client Statement 3

That's a really important realization. So what I think I'm hearing is that there are feelings that you've had about yourself that were actually about the person who abused you? (Criterion 1) Maybe there's some insight there that is important to carry into your daily life. Would you be willing to describe what it feels like to not have that be your emotion to carry? (Criterion 2)

Example Response to Advanced Client Statement 4

It sounds like you have come to understand that you deserve to feel safe, and to be in places where people will appreciate and respect you. (Criterion 1) It sounds like you are playing with the potential for something new, and allowing some time and space before you make any major decisions. When you imagine yourself in a different place, what feels different for you? (Criterion 2)

Example Response to Advanced Client Statement 5

It sounds like you've had some powerful insights. Sometimes this is just the sort of insight we need to choose a new path. (Criterion 1) As we spoke about before beginning these sessions, sometimes more clarity comes with time, providing more insight into next steps. For now, without any pressure to act, what would a change of direction look like for you? (Criterion 2)

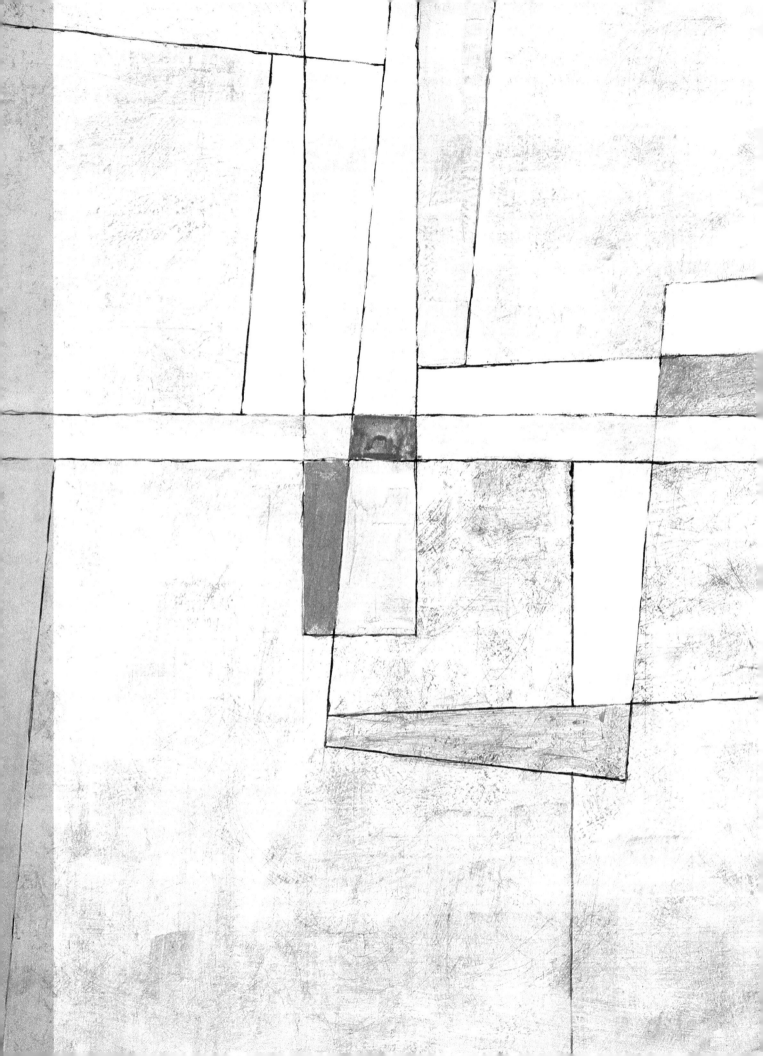

Annotated Psychedelic-Assisted Therapy Practice Session Transcript

It is now time to put all the skills you have learned together! This exercise presents a transcript from a typical psychedelic-assisted therapy (PAT) integration session. Each therapist statement is annotated to indicate which PAT skill from Exercises 1 through 12 is used. This transcript provides an example of how therapists can interweave many skills in response to clients.

Instructions

As in the previous exercises, one trainee can play the client while the other plays the therapist. As much as possible, the trainee who plays the client should try to adopt an authentic emotional tone as if they are a real client. The first time through, both partners can read verbatim from the transcript. After one complete run-through, try it again. This time, the client can read from the script while the therapist can improvise to the degree that they feel comfortable. At this point, you may also want to reflect on it with a supervisor and go through it again. Before you start, it is recommended that both therapist and client read the entire transcript through on their own, until the end. The purpose of the sample transcript is to give trainees the opportunity to try out what it is like to offer the responses in a sequence that mimics live therapy sessions. This transcript also provides an opportunity for trainees to explore their reactions to the strong emotional content often present in PAT (Shulgin, 2019).

https://doi.org/10.1037/0000399-015

Deliberate Practice in Psychedelic-Assisted Therapy, by S. Dames, A. Penn, M. Williams, J. A. Zamaria, T. Rousmaniere, and A. Vaz

> **Note to Therapists**
>
> Remember to be aware of your vocal quality. Match your tone to the client's presentation. Thus, if the client presents vulnerable, soft emotions behind their words, soften your tone to be soothing and calm. On the other hand, if the client presents as aggressive and angry, match your tone to be firm and solid, while remaining calm and nonthreatening. If you choose responses that are prompting client exploration, such as Exercise 3: Exploring Intentions and Expectations, remember to adopt a more querying, exploratory tone of voice.

Note to trainers and trainees who are acting as the client: Although not included in the 12 exercises explicitly, self-awareness is an important therapeutic skill for PAT (e.g., Shulgin, 2019). This skill can be practiced as you role-play the annotated transcript. The person playing the role of the client will be most effective if they can access authentic emotional states at least to some degree, making for a more meaningful experience for both parties.

Annotated Psychedelic-Assisted Therapy Transcript

THERAPIST 1: Hello, it's good to see you again. I've been thinking about you since the psychedelic medicine session and have been looking forward to supporting you in your integration process. I thought we'd start this first session by talking about what you're hoping for in our time together. (Skill 3: Exploring Intentions and Expectations)

CLIENT 1: After my psychedelic experience, I've been struggling to make sense of what I went through. It was so profound and surreal, and I'm having difficulty integrating it into my everyday life.

THERAPIST 2: I hear you, and it's common for the psychedelic experience to be deeply transformative and challenging to integrate. Making sense of the experience is an important part of the integration process. We can explore the themes, emotions, and insights that emerged during your journey and find ways to connect them with your daily life. It may involve reflecting on the symbolism, exploring the meaning behind certain experiences, or identifying any shifts in your perspectives and beliefs. By engaging in this process, we can help you find a sense of coherence and meaning from your psychedelic experience. I'm curious what's been surfacing for you. Are there any specific topics and processes that you would like to discuss in this integration process? (Skill 10: Making Sense of the Experience: Integration I)

CLIENT 2: Well, the most prominent feeling is disappointment. I had high hopes for profound changes after the session, but it seems like some of my old patterns and struggles are still present. I'm not sure how to deal with this disappointment.

THERAPIST 3: As I hear you talk about some old patterns and struggles surfacing, I can feel a sense of tightness right here in my chest. It sounds like you were hoping they would be gone for good, and I can imagine from that frame, it must feel pretty frustrating to have them resurface. When you imagine the hopes you had coming into the PAT session, and the disappointment you are feeling now, how is that showing up in your body? (Skill 11: Working With Disappointment: Integration II)

CLIENT 3: Oh, that. I don't like feeling that. It feels dark. Scary. Like something must be terribly wrong with me . . . shame—that's what it is. Shame.

THERAPIST 4: Thank you for sharing that with me. It takes a lot of courage to be vulnerable like this, and it's really normal for it to feel pretty scared. Can you describe what the sensation of "shame" feels like in your body right now? (Skill 1: Redirecting to the Body)

CLIENT 4: I don't know. A few moments ago, it felt like nausea, but now, I don't seem to feel anything at all anymore. I just got all numb.

THERAPIST 5: That's understandable. It's normal for feelings to lead to overwhelm. Sometimes they can feel too threatening to feel for long. Let's take a few deep breaths together and just pay attention to what it feels like to breathe space into your body. What are you noticing in your body now? (Skill 9: Navigating Strong Emotions)

CLIENT 5: It's mixed. It feels like constricting heaviness on my chest. Right here. [The client points to their chest.] It feels like a ball of something that is getting tighter and tighter, and then around the pressure is a heaviness.

THERAPIST 6: As I hear you share your experience, I'm feeling tension in my chest, like an elastic band that is being pulled two directions. I wonder if you are sensing any emotions associated with them? (Skill 2: Compassionately Witnessing Strong Emotions)

CLIENT 6: Yeah, it feels like fear, and despair. It's familiar. I have been struggling with depression and anxiety most of my adult life, I'd say from about my early 20s on. . . . I am 52 now.

THERAPIST 7: Mm hmm. It sounds like you've been managing two challenging emotions for a long time. When I imagine what that must be like, I feel a sense of fatigue and overwhelm all at once. I can imagine it must be confusing at times. I'd like to make space for both experiences that you're having. To clarify, it sounds like your intention for our time together is to experience some relief from these feelings. When I say that, how does it land in your body? (Skill 7: Working With the Client's Internal Conflict)

CLIENT 7: [*sighs*] Yeah, that's exactly right. The fear is the worst. It always feels like a shoe is going to drop, but I never know why or when. I just want some peace.

THERAPIST 8: Mm hmmm. It must be hard to enjoy the moment when you're on high alert like that. Let's start by making some space for that fear, but this time, I'm going to sit here with you, and help you hold it. How does that feel to you? (Skill 9: Navigating Strong Emotions)

CLIENT 8: It feels comforting in part, and I feel the fear with me right now too.

THERAPIST 9: Yeah, I get that. It's common for parts of ourselves to conflict with one another, and it can be exhausting to navigate two opposing emotions. If you feel like you need a break at any time, just let me know. It's important that you feel in control of this process. We can only move at the pace of trust, and no faster. Perhaps a good place to start is to take a moment to explore what lies beneath the fear you are feeling. We could start some of that today if you feel ready. How does this sound to you? (Skill 7: Working With the Client's Internal Conflict)

CLIENT 9: Yes. Yeah. I'm ready. I guess this is what I came for.

THERAPIST 10: Okay! Before we jump in, I'd like to say a few things that I'm hoping will help you feel in control of our process together. Again, please pay attention to your body. Ideally, your body will inform our pace. Throughout our time together, you will find that

I often refer to what you are feeling in your body. I do this because the roots and wounds that lie beneath our fear and anxiety are found there. In order to heal, these feelings and sensations need to come into the light, so we can tend to them, and nurture them. In a way, it's like digesting our food. If the digestion process doesn't complete, we can start to feel ill. As you notice a sense of "ill" in your body, there can be an opportunity to help the digestion process complete. If you feel overwhelmed at any point, it's a good opportunity to practice speaking from the cues your body is giving you. As you do, trust develops, and that, too, is an important part of our healing journey.

I'd also like to acknowledge the courage it took for you to take the steps that got you here today. As I hear you speak, and I witness your honesty and commitment to continue on this path you're on, I feel humbled and honored to be here with you. (Skill 1: Redirecting to the Body)

CLIENT 10: This process is making me realize how disconnected from my body I've been. I think I've been living pretty cut off for a long time. There is so much happening in there, it feels really uncomfortable to spend much time in my body.

THERAPIST 11: When there is a lot happening there, it's totally understandable that it can feel overwhelming. I want you to know that we'll work at a pace that feels safe for you and that if at any time it's starting to feel like it's too much, you can ask for a break. This can be a great way to practice self-compassion, which will help you feel safer and develop the trust necessary to move through some of the trickier moments. I'm here to support your process, but ultimately, it's really important that the pace we move and the depths we go to move at the pace of trust. (Skill 5: Boundaries and Informed Consent)

CLIENT 11: It's overwhelming to think about diving into the depths of my emotions. I've been avoiding them for so long, and I'm afraid of what I might uncover. It feels safer to keep them locked away.

THERAPIST 12: I hear your concerns and understand that diving into emotions can feel overwhelming. It's important to honor your readiness and pace throughout this process. Let's take a moment to witness any strong emotions that arise compassionately as we explore this fear. When I hear you talk about the fear of what might be uncovered, I feel a pinch in my lower stomach. It feels like I'm waiting for a shoe to drop. By acknowledging and giving space to these emotions, we can gradually work toward understanding and integrating them. (Skill 2: Compassionately Witnessing Strong Emotions)

CLIENT 12: Another thing I'd like to address in our time together is the impact of my cultural background on how I respond to the world, and how it informs my healing journey. It feels like an important piece to consider.

THERAPIST 13: I appreciate your recognition of the impact of your cultural background. Cultural considerations are essential in our work together, and it feels really important to me that we create a space that respects and honors your unique experiences. Let's take the time to delve into how your cultural background intersects with your healing journey. By exploring this aspect, we can gain a deeper understanding of how it influences your experiences and integration process. I wonder if there is anything surfacing for you right now in this regard? (Skill 4: Cultural Considerations: Racially and Ethnically Diverse Communities)

CLIENT 13: Yes, definitely. One thing that comes up for me is the pressure to be strong and self-reliant. In my culture, there is a lot of emphasis on resilience and pushing through challenges without showing vulnerability. It's been ingrained in me to hide my struggles and emotions, which has made it difficult for me to seek help or express my needs.

THERAPIST 14: Thank you for sharing that cultural perspective. The pressure to be strong and self-reliant can create barriers to seeking support and expressing vulnerability. I want you to know that in this therapeutic space, it's okay to be vulnerable and ask for help. We can work together to create a safe environment where you can explore and express your emotions without judgment. If there comes a time when I say something that doesn't feel good for you, I'm hoping you will feel safe enough in our relationship to bring it forward. Being upfront in this way and working through tensions as they come up is a really important part of the therapy process. How does that resonate with you? (Skill 4: Cultural Considerations: Racially and Ethnically Diverse Communities)

CLIENT 14: That sounds reassuring. I appreciate the understanding and support. Another aspect is the spiritual beliefs and practices in my culture. They are deeply intertwined with my identity and worldview. I'm curious how psychedelic therapy can integrate and respect those beliefs.

THERAPIST 15: Absolutely, your spiritual beliefs and practices are significant and deserve respect in the therapeutic process. Psychedelic therapy can be adaptable to incorporate your cultural and spiritual framework. It's important for us to explore and discuss how we can integrate your beliefs into the therapeutic experience. By doing so, we can ensure that your spiritual identity is honored and can contribute positively to your healing journey. I invite you to share more about your spiritual beliefs and practices as you feel inspired, and let's explore together how they can be integrated into our work. (Skill 4: Cultural Considerations: Racially and Ethnically Diverse Communities)

CLIENT 15: I feel like I'm really rambling now. Didn't realize this was so big for me. I come from a community where mental health is often stigmatized, and seeking therapy is seen as a sign of weakness. It's challenging for me to break free from that mindset and prioritize my own well-being.

THERAPIST 16: I hear you, and it's important to acknowledge the cultural stigma surrounding mental health in your community. The fear of being perceived as weak or facing judgment can create significant barriers to seeking therapy. It takes courage to challenge these beliefs and prioritize your well-being. I want to assure you that by engaging in this therapeutic process, you are demonstrating strength and resilience. Together, we can navigate the cultural stigma and work towards your healing goals. How can we best support you in breaking free from this mindset and embracing your own well-being? (Skill 4: Cultural Considerations: Racially and Ethnically Diverse Communities)

CLIENT 16: Thanks, this is helpful. Another fear I have is that my family or friends will find out that I'm doing this and judge me.

THERAPIST 17: I completely understand your need for a safe and confidential space. Confidentiality is a fundamental aspect of therapy, and you can trust that your privacy will be respected. In terms of potential backlash or criticism from your community, we can work together to develop coping strategies and explore ways to navigate those challenges. It's important to have a support system in place that can provide understanding and validation, whether it's within your community or outside of it. (Skill 4: Cultural Considerations: Racially and Ethnically Diverse Communities)

CLIENT 17: Thanks. I will admit, I came in with some serious trust issues. I want to get the most from these sessions, but I sometimes feel uncertain about what I can share and how much to disclose.

THERAPIST 18: Thank you for sharing your concern about boundaries. Establishing clear boundaries and informed consent is crucial for our therapeutic relationship. I want you to feel safe and supported. Let's take a moment to discuss any concerns or questions you have about the boundaries of therapy. By openly addressing these issues, we can create a space that promotes trust and allows for a deeper level of engagement in the process. (Skill 5: Boundaries and Informed Consent)

CLIENT 18: Well, speaking to trust issues, I'd like to bring up something that's been sticking with me since the psychedelic medicine session. After the session, when I was emotional, I felt like you got impatient with me at one point. It left me feeling disconnected. I'm not sure how to move forward from that.

THERAPIST 19: I feel really honored that you feel safe enough with me to bring this up today. Thank you for your courage! When I hear about this sense of disconnection that came from my response to your emotions, I feel a heaviness in my chest. I apologize if you felt misunderstood; it was not my intention. I remember feeling like I needed to use the bathroom at one point and didn't want to leave your side at such a pivotal moment. Your experience reminds me that I need to tend to my body as well—for the good of us both! Your feelings and experiences are valid, and while in that moment it may have felt otherwise, I want you to know that I welcome your emotions. Just that fact that you brought this up today is a phenomenal act of trust. By openly discussing and understanding the rupture, we can work toward healing and rebuilding our therapeutic alliance. (Skill 6: Responding to Relational Ruptures)

CLIENT 19: It's a bit embarrassing to admit this, but to be honest, I also have very positive feelings about you. It's almost like you become this figure that I look up to and seek approval from. I'm not sure why this happens, but it feels intense at times.

THERAPIST 20: It's not uncommon for clients to develop feelings of attachment toward their therapists, and it can be a significant aspect of the therapeutic process. This phenomenon is called transference, where feelings and dynamics from past relationships are unconsciously transferred onto the therapist. It can provide valuable insights into underlying patterns and emotions. Let's explore this further together. How does it feel for you to bring up these feelings of attachment? (Skill 8: Addressing Transference)

CLIENT 20: It feels vulnerable, but also relieving to acknowledge it. I think it stems from my past experiences where I sought validation and approval from authority figures. It's like I'm projecting those needs onto you.

THERAPIST 21: It's understandable that past experiences can influence our current dynamics and relationships. Recognizing the origins of these feelings of attachment can help us gain a deeper understanding of your emotional needs and patterns. By exploring this transference, we can work together to provide the support and validation you're seeking in a healthy and therapeutic way. When you imagine this more vulnerable part of yourself seeking approval, what words might you offer yourself in those moments? (Skill 8: Addressing Transference)

CLIENT 21: I think I would sound something like, "You are enough. As you are. No performing necessary. You've got nothing to prove." I'm not sure I believe all that. But I want to. On that note, I'd like to dig into some of the images that stood out during my journey. There were moments of deep connection with nature and a sense of security and oneness that I struggle to put into words, but I want to hold onto the feeling.

THERAPIST 22: That sounds like a good starting point. So often we rely on words, but integration is often more about the felt sense of the experience. In this way, we come to embody (in the body) the insights that come to us as the medicine unfolds within us. We often say, "It's a time-released experience," meaning that so often finding language and meaning unfolds over the hours, days, and sometimes even years after a healing experience. In this way, we don't need to make the effort for understanding everything all at once. Rather, we simply notice what is arising within the body, and listen deeply to the subtle messages available as we do. How does it feel to begin this exploration? (Skill 10: Making Sense of the Experience: Integration I)

CLIENT 22: Yeah, I had some powerful insights during my psychedelic journey, but it's challenging to embody them in my daily life. It's like I understand them intellectually, but putting them into practice feels overwhelming. It brings me some comfort to hear that these things can unfold over time because it feels pretty fuzzy right now.

THERAPIST 23: I appreciate your honesty about the difficulty of embodying the insights you gained. Integration involves not only understanding the insights intellectually but also embodying them on an experiential level. It can take time and practice to fully integrate these changes into your daily life. We can explore different strategies to support you in embodying these insights, such as mindfulness exercises, somatic practices, or creating rituals or reminders that help anchor the insights in your body and behavior. By engaging in these practices, we can bridge the gap between intellectual understanding and embodied transformation. Let's start by exploring the specific insights you gained during your psychedelic journey. What are the key messages or realizations that stand out to you? (Skill 10: Making Sense of the Experience: Integration I)

CLIENT 23: One of the main insights I had was the importance of self-compassion and self-care. I realized that I've been neglecting my own well-being and constantly prioritizing others' needs. But when it comes to implementing self-compassion in my daily life, I struggle to prioritize myself.

THERAPIST 24: That's a powerful realization. Self-compassion and self-care are crucial aspects of personal growth and well-being. To embody these insights, we can explore practical ways to integrate self-compassion into your routines. It could involve setting aside dedicated time for self-care activities, practicing self-compassionate self-talk, or seeking support from loved ones. Together, we can develop a personalized plan that aligns with your values and helps you prioritize your own needs. How does the idea of having some reminders to practice self-compassion sound to you? (Skill 12: Embodying Insights: Integration III)

CLIENT 24: It resonates deeply with me, and I understand its importance. However, I often feel guilty or selfish when I prioritize myself. It's like I have this internal resistance that holds me back.

THERAPIST 25: I can certainly relate to that feeling. It's common to experience internal resistance when making shifts toward self-compassion and prioritizing oneself. This resistance can stem from deeply ingrained beliefs or conditioning. In our sessions, I'd like to explore the underlying sources of this resistance and how we might reframe these beliefs. We can also incorporate somatic practices and mindfulness techniques to help you connect with your body and cultivate self-compassion from a place of your embodied wisdom. Remember, this process is about progress, not perfection, and we can move at a pace that feels comfortable for you. How does this approach feel for you? (Skill 12: Embodying Insights: Integration III)

CLIENT 25: I appreciate your understanding and support in this process. It's challenging to change long-held patterns, but I'm ready to try something new. I need to try something new.

THERAPIST 26: It takes courage to challenge ingrained patterns and to create space for new ways of being. As we practice mirroring compassion in our relationship, and in the relationships you have in your day-to-day life, it can be a great way to learn how to direct that same compassion inwardly (Skill 12: Embodying Insights: Integration III)

CLIENT 26: I've never thought about the idea of receiving compassion and directing inwardly. In fact, I think I typically repel it! This sounds like something I'd like to pay more attention to—receiving and directing inwardly. . . . I'm grateful to have your guidance and support throughout this journey.

THERAPIST 27: I feel honored to accompany you on this path of growth and self-discovery. As you leave our time together, my greatest hope is that you remember to be gentle with yourself and celebrate each step forward, no matter how small. Progress is rarely linear. If it were linear, we wouldn't have nearly as many opportunities to exercise our self-compassion muscles! Our next integration session will provide another opportunity to deepen our exploration and develop further strategies for integration. Until then, take care and be kind to yourself. You are so worthy of that.

CLIENT 27: Thank you. I'll do my best. See you next time.

THERAPIST 28: Take care and see you soon!

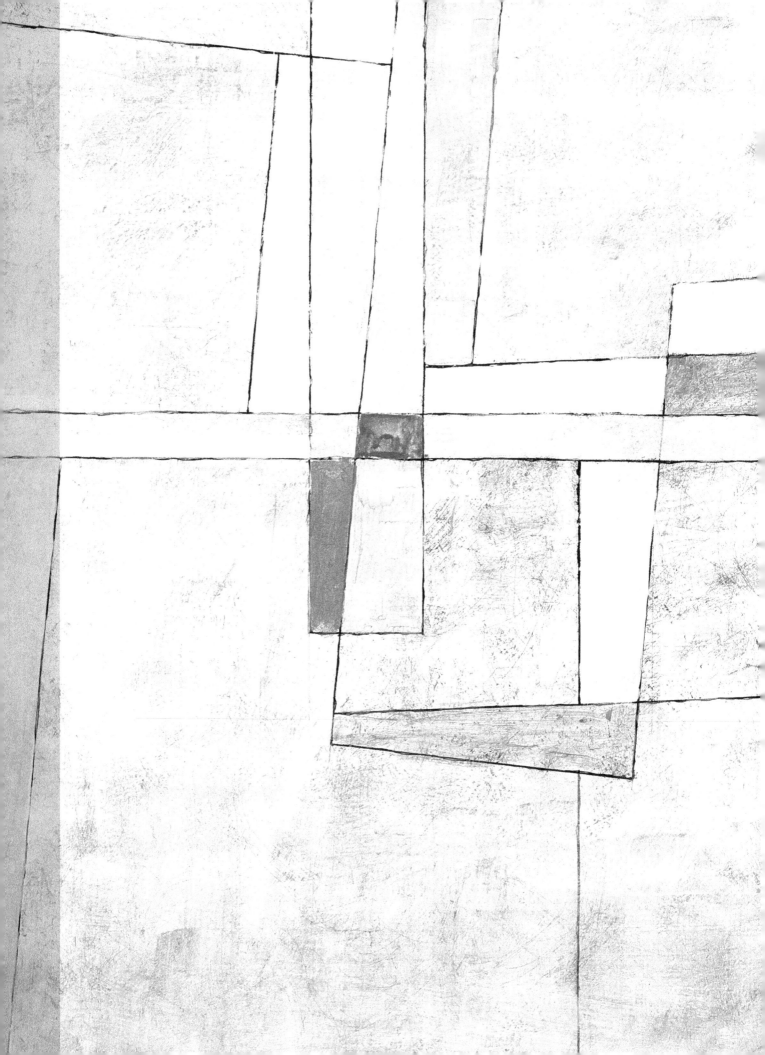

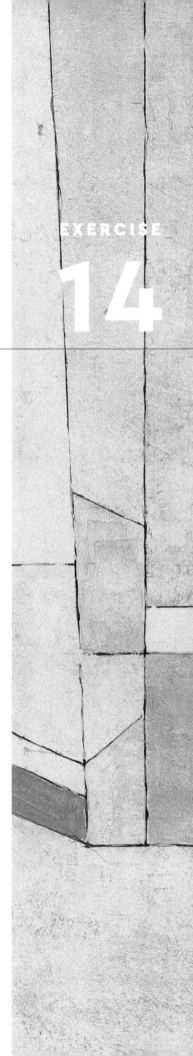

Mock Psychedelic-Assisted Therapy Sessions

In contrast to highly structured and repetitive deliberate practice exercises, a mock psychedelic-assisted therapy (PAT) session is an unstructured and improvised role-play therapy session. Like a jazz rehearsal, mock sessions let you practice the art and science of *appropriate responsiveness* (Hatcher, 2015; Stiles & Horvath, 2017), putting your psychotherapy skills together in a way that is helpful to your mock client. This exercise outlines the procedure for conducting a mock PAT session. It offers different client profiles you may choose to adopt when role-playing as the client.

Mock sessions are an opportunity for trainees to practice the following:

- using psychotherapy skills responsively
- navigating challenging choice-points in therapy
- choosing which interventions to use
- tracking the arc of a therapy session and the overall big-picture therapy treatment
- guiding treatment in the context of the client's preferences
- determining realistic goals for therapy in the context of the client's capacities
- knowing how to proceed when the therapist is unsure, lost, or confused
- recognizing and recovering from therapeutic errors
- discovering your personal therapeutic style
- building endurance for working with real clients

Mock Psychedelic-Assisted Therapy Session Overview

For the mock session, **you will perform a role-play of an integration therapy session**. As is true with the exercises to build individual skills, the role-play involves three people: One trainee role-plays the therapist, another trainee role-plays the client, and a trainer (a professor or a supervisor) observes and provides feedback. Alternatively, if a supervisor is not available, a peer feedback process is used instead. This is an open-ended role-play, as is commonly done in training. However, this differs in two important ways

https://doi.org/10.1037/0000399-016

Deliberate Practice in Psychedelic-Assisted Therapy, by S. Dames, A. Penn, M. Williams, J. A. Zamaria, T. Rousmaniere, and A. Vaz

from the role-plays used in more traditional training. First, the therapist will use their hand to indicate how difficult the role-play feels. Second, the client will attempt to make the role-play easier or harder to ensure the therapist is practicing at the right difficulty level.

Preparation

1. Download the Deliberate Practice Reaction Form and Deliberate Practice Diary Form from the "Clinician and Practitioner Resources" tab at https://www.apa.org/pubs/books/deliberate-practice-psychedelic-assisted-therapy (also available in Appendixes A and B, respectively). Every student will need their own copy of the Deliberate Practice Reaction Form on a separate piece of paper so they can access it quickly.

2. Designate one student to role-play the therapist and one student to role-play the client. The trainer will observe and provide corrective feedback.

Mock Psychedelic-Assisted Therapy Session Procedure

1. The trainees will role-play an integration session. The trainee role-playing the client selects a client profile from the end of this exercise.

2. Before beginning the role-play, the therapist raises their hand to their side, at the level of their chair seat (see Figure E14.1). They will use this hand throughout the whole role-play to indicate how challenging it feels to them to help the client. Their starting hand

FIGURE E14.1. Ongoing Difficulty Assessment Through Hand Level

Note. Left: Start of role-play. Right: Role-play is too difficult. From *Deliberate Practice in Emotion-Focused Therapy* (p. 156), by R. N. Goldman, A. Vaz, and T. Rousmaniere, 2021, American Psychological Association (https://doi.org/10.1037/0000227-000). Copyright 2021 by the American Psychological Association.

level (chair seat) indicates that the role-play feels easy. By raising their hand, the therapist indicates that the difficulty is rising. If their hand rises above their neck level, it indicates that the role-play is too difficult.

3. The therapist begins the role-play. The therapist and client should engage in the role-play in an improvised manner, as they would engage in a real therapy session. The therapist keeps their hand out at their side throughout this process. (This may feel strange at first!)

4. Whenever the therapist feels that the difficulty of the role-play has changed significantly, they should move their hand up if it feels more difficult and down if it feels easier. If the therapist's hand drops below the seat of their chair, the client should make the role-play more challenging; if the therapist's hand rises above their neck level, the client should make the role-play easier. Instructions for adjusting the difficulty of the role-play are described in the "Varying the Level of Challenge" section later in the exercise.

Note to Therapists

Remember to be aware of your vocal quality. Match your tone to the client's presentation. Thus, if the clients present vulnerable, soft emotions behind their words, soften your tone to be soothing and calm. If clients, on the other hand, are aggressive and angry, match your tone to be firm and solid yet calm. If you choose responses that are prompting client exploration, such as in Exercise 3, Exploring Intentions and Expectations, remember to adopt a more querying, exploratory tone of voice.

5. The role-play continues for at least 15 minutes. The trainer may provide corrective feedback during this process if the therapist gets significantly off track. However, trainers should exercise restraint and keep feedback as short and tight as possible because this will allow the therapist more opportunity for experiential training.

6. After the role-play is finished, the therapist and client switch roles and begin a new mock session.

7. After both trainees have completed the mock session as a therapist, the trainees and the trainer discuss the experience.

Varying the Level of Challenge

If the therapist indicates that the mock session is too easy, the person enacting the role of the client can use the following modifications to make it more challenging (see also Appendix A):

- The client can improvise with topics that are more evocative or make the therapist uncomfortable, such as expressing currently held strong feelings (see Figure A.2).
- The client can use a distressed voice (e.g., angry, sad, sarcastic) or unpleasant facial expression. This increases the emotional tone.
- The client can lend complex mixtures of opposing feelings (e.g., love and rage).

- The client can become confrontational, questioning the purpose of therapy or the therapist's fitness for the role.

  If the therapist indicates that the mock session is too hard:

- The client can be guided by Figure A.2 to
  - present topics that are less evocative,
  - present material on any topic but without expressing feelings, or
  - present material concerning the future or the past or events outside therapy.
- The client can ask the questions in a soft voice or with a smile. This softens the emotional stimulus.
- The therapist can take short breaks during the role-play.
- The trainer can expand the "feedback phase" by discussing the application of PAT or psychotherapy theory.

Mock Session Client Profiles

Following are six client profiles for trainees to use during mock sessions, presented in order of difficulty. The choice of client profile may be determined by the trainee playing the therapist, the trainee playing the client, or assigned by the trainer.

The most important aspect of role-plays is for trainees to convey the emotional tone indicated by the client profile (e.g., "angry" or "sad"). The demographics of the client (e.g., age, gender) and specific content of the client profiles are not important. Thus, trainees should adjust the client profile to be most comfortable and easy for the trainee to role-play. For example, a trainee may change the client profile from female to male, from 45 to 22 years old, and so on.

Beginner Profile: Processing Grief With a Receptive Client

Laura is a 28-year-old, who identifies as Latinx and works as a waitress. Her mother died from cancer about 6 months ago. Laura has been experiencing sadness about losing her mother. Laura's grief is complicated by feelings of anger she has about her mother not being very attentive or loving during Laura's childhood. Laura's mother was very busy when she was growing up, caring for the family while trying to hold multiple jobs; however, Laura still feels her mother was hard on her. Laura also misses her two siblings who were forced to go back to Mexico because they were undocumented.

In the PAT session, Laura was able to see how hard her mother worked to support her and her sisters, with little outside help. She was also able to see how the anger she felt for her mother hindered their relationship and led to some lost opportunities while she was alive. Since the session, she no longer feels angry, but in its place, she finds herself feeling a sense of overwhelming grief.

- **Symptoms:** Grief, anger, and loneliness

- **Client's integration goals after a PAT session:** Laura understands that feeling the grief is a normal part of moving through it. She is identifying ways to sit with the strong emotions without getting overwhelmed by them. She is realizing that reconnecting with her siblings is an important part of her grieving and healing process.

- **Attitude toward therapy:** Laura had good experiences in therapy previously when she was in high school and is optimistic about therapy helping again.

- **Strengths:** Laura is very motivated for therapy and is emotionally open with the therapist. She understands that part of the overwhelm she is experiencing in her grieving process revolves around the loss of closeness with her siblings in addition to the loss of her mother.

Beginner Profile: Addressing Loneliness With an Engaged Client

Susan, age 25 years, identifies as Black and queer and works as an accountant who recently moved across the country for a new job. While she loves her new job, she has had trouble making friends. She is coming to therapy because she is feeling lonely. Susan has been starting to date more frequently but is disappointed by the outcomes. She's worried that there may be something wrong with her and that if she continues to feel disappointed, she will stop trying to make new friends and be destined to live a lonely life.

In a recent PAT session, for the first time in Susan's memory, she felt an overwhelming sense of love and appreciation for herself. She was also able to recognize how she continues to seek relationships that remind her of a broken relationship with her mother, from whom she always longed for approval but never felt "good enough." In this realization, she felt immense relief in the idea that perhaps there is nothing "wrong" with her but rather that she is enacting old relational patterns that end in the same predictable outcomes. With this new insight, she feels empowered to seek out friends and partners who can see and accept her for who she is.

- **Symptoms:** Loneliness, sadness, and demoralization

- **Client's integration goals after a PAT session:** Susan wants to build greater awareness of the relational patterns that continue to end in the same disappointing outcomes and to seek out individuals that are able to accept her for who she is. She is feeling inspired to reach out to a few new people at work that she has been feeling curious about and who feel safe to her.

- **Attitude toward therapy:** Susan has had positive experiences in therapy before. She is hopeful that this therapy will help as well.

- **Strengths:** Susan is emotionally open and motivated to engage in the therapy tasks.

Intermediate Profile: Addressing Anxiety With a Nervous Client

Bob is 35 years old, identifies as White, and works as an electrician. He suffers from extreme anxiety, panic attacks, and shame. He's always felt different from others, which led to bullying in high school. He has this enduring feeling that he has been a "loser" his whole life and thinks that people will always see him this way. He tries to avoid contact with people except through online computer games. He was referred to therapy by his boss, who noticed that although Bob has exceptional talents in his role, he often isolates himself and would sometimes not show up for work or leave work early. Bob has trouble identifying any of his feelings except anxiety. Furthermore, Bob recently learned that he is likely on the autism spectrum and is grappling with how to integrate this new knowledge of self.

In a recent PAT session, Bob was able to see himself from a different angle, one that wasn't colored by the voices he grew up with. He saw how his atypical neurology has provided him with brilliance in areas that are rare and that in some ways are a superpower that others lack. He also developed a sense of understanding, compassion, and acceptance for the social challenges on the other side of his neurology. For the first time, he was able to hold both the benefits and the challenges with more acceptance, compassion, and even pride.

- **Symptoms:** Shame, anxiety, panic attacks, and social isolation

- **Client's integration goals after a PAT session:** With a renewed understanding and compassion for himself, Bob wants to learn how to be more up-front about his neurotype, shaking off the shame of "feeling different" and stepping into the benefits of being unique. As he learns to "come out of the shadows" of who he isn't and into integrity with who he is, he aims to be able to engage in work more reliably.

- **Attitude toward therapy:** Initially, Bob didn't want to come to therapy because he felt nervous about it and thought that the therapist would judge him. Bob's boss convinced him to try it. After experiencing a PAT session, he is seeing the benefits of continuing on this path of self-discovery.

- **Strengths:** Underneath his anxiety and shame, Bob really wants to be seen and accepted for who he is and to connect with other people, including the therapist.

Intermediate Profile: Helping a Sarcastic and Skeptical Client

Jeff is a 45-year-old who identifies as Asian, works as an engineer, and was referred to therapy by his employer because he has been getting angry at work. He is very smart and gets frustrated quickly when his colleagues do not understand his decisions. When he gets frustrated, Jeff is sarcastic or mean. Jeff understands that this is a problem and wants to be more friendly, but he has been unable to change his behavior. He knows that his colleagues do not like him and has recently been formally written up for creating a hostile work environment.

After a PAT session, Jeff came to realize that the way he is treating his colleagues is a reflection of the messaging he received from his parents growing up. Unrealistically high standards led to a belief system that anything less than perfect was unacceptable. The relentlessly high standards for himself are also applied to those around him. These insights helped him understand the source of his daily frustration and gave him a sense of hope for a different way forward.

- **Symptoms:** Outbursts of sarcasm and meanness that cover loneliness and social isolation

- **Client's integration goals after a PAT session:** Jeff wants to learn how to be more patient and relate better to his colleagues. He has come to understand that if he can learn to have more compassion and grace for himself, he will be more able to provide the same for those around him. He aims to notice when he is self-critical and to practice speaking to himself with more compassion and grace, working with mistakes as an opportunity to practice rather than seeing them as a threat to his survival.

- **Attitude toward therapy:** Jeff has never been in therapy before and is skeptical whether it will help. He came to therapy because his employer asked him to. He is beginning to see that there may be something here for him.

- **Strengths:** Jeff honestly wants to be more prosocial and to develop friendships at work.

Advanced Profile: Helping a Very Distrustful Client

Betty is a 27-year-old who identifies as an Indigenous graduate student at law school. She wants to become a public defender when she graduates. Betty is the oldest of four siblings. Betty and her siblings were sexually and physically abused by her father when she was a child. Her father also beat her mother frequently (her father is currently in prison for the physical and sexual abuse). She also feels she has been very hurt and traumatized by systematic racism and discrimination. She has fought very hard to achieve her current status. She does not generally trust the system because she does not feel her interests have been prioritized or protected. Betty feels a lot of anger toward her father, but also toward her mother for not protecting her and her siblings. Betty's youngest sister recently died of an overdose, which she feels is related to her need to cope with the abuse. Betty feels guilty about not protecting her siblings from her father.

In a recent PAT session, Betty realized that the anger she feels for her father is preventing her from developing intimacy in her relationships and is draining energy that is already in short supply. For years, she felt justified for holding onto the anger but is now seeing that by holding on to the anger, she remains a victim of the past. She also saw her father in a different light. She saw him as a child, enduring hardship and abuse himself, and becoming buried under layers of trauma that he continues to be trapped under.

- **Symptoms:** Anger at parents, guilt about not protecting siblings, and grief about her sister's recent death

- **Client's integration goals after a PAT session:** Betty wants to resolve her guilt about her sister. She is developing self-efficacy and coming to understand how impossible it can feel when stuck in a survival cycle. In this way, she is developing compassion for herself and her capacity to "save" her sister. While she doesn't feel ready to forgive her father, she is starting to understand that there is more to the story and is becoming more open to understand him, beyond the harmful behaviors.

- **Attitude toward therapy:** Betty went to therapy in grade school but had a bad experience: When she told her therapist about her father's abuse, the therapist didn't believe her and told the father what Betty had said. (Betty found out later that the therapist was a friend of the father.) Thus, Betty is very distrustful of therapists, particularly non-Indigenous therapists.

- **Strengths:** Betty is focused and dedicated to improving her mental health. Betty is extremely resilient. She has strong convictions about social justice. She is fiercely loyal to her friends and family.

Advanced Profile: Helping a Client With Mood Lability and Self-Harm

Jane is a 20-year-old who identifies as White and is a college student. She is having problems in her relationship, in which she cycles between being deeply in love with her boyfriend and then hating him when he does something that disappoints her, like forgetting her birthday. When Jane is disappointed by her boyfriend, she feels betrayed and abandoned, gets very angry and depressed, and cuts herself. Jane has a similar pattern with her family and friends, where she cycles between liking them a lot and then feeling betrayed and abandoned when they disappoint her.

In a recent PAT session, Jane was able to understand that despite how she seems so quick to push people away, in reality, her deepest longing is to connect with her loved ones. She was able to connect with the younger version of herself and to see the wound that formed in her childhood, which prevents her from trusting those close to her. She could see how this wounded part of herself reacts in anger in her day-to-day life, but underneath the anger, there is a sea of hurt. The cutting began to make sense as she understood that it helped her release the intensity of the pain she feels when her emotional pain overwhelms her.

- **Symptoms:** Mood lability, self-harm (cutting), and relationship instability

- **Client's integration goals after the PAT session:** Jane wants to find stability in herself and her relationships as an end goal but understands that the path to get there is to tend to the wound that is causing her to push her loved ones away. Her intention is to allow the anger to come and, before she reacts or externalizes, to take a breath or pause, and ask the anger what it is protecting her from.

- **Attitude toward therapy:** Jane was in therapy before, which was helpful until the therapist disappointed Jane by missing a session, after which Jane felt betrayed and abandoned and quit therapy. Jane is worried that you (her new therapist) may betray or abandon her. She is starting to understand that if she can cultivate trust with her therapist, she may be able to transfer this same trust to other relationships in her life.

- **Strengths:** Jane is very open to what the therapist says (when she feels safe in therapy).

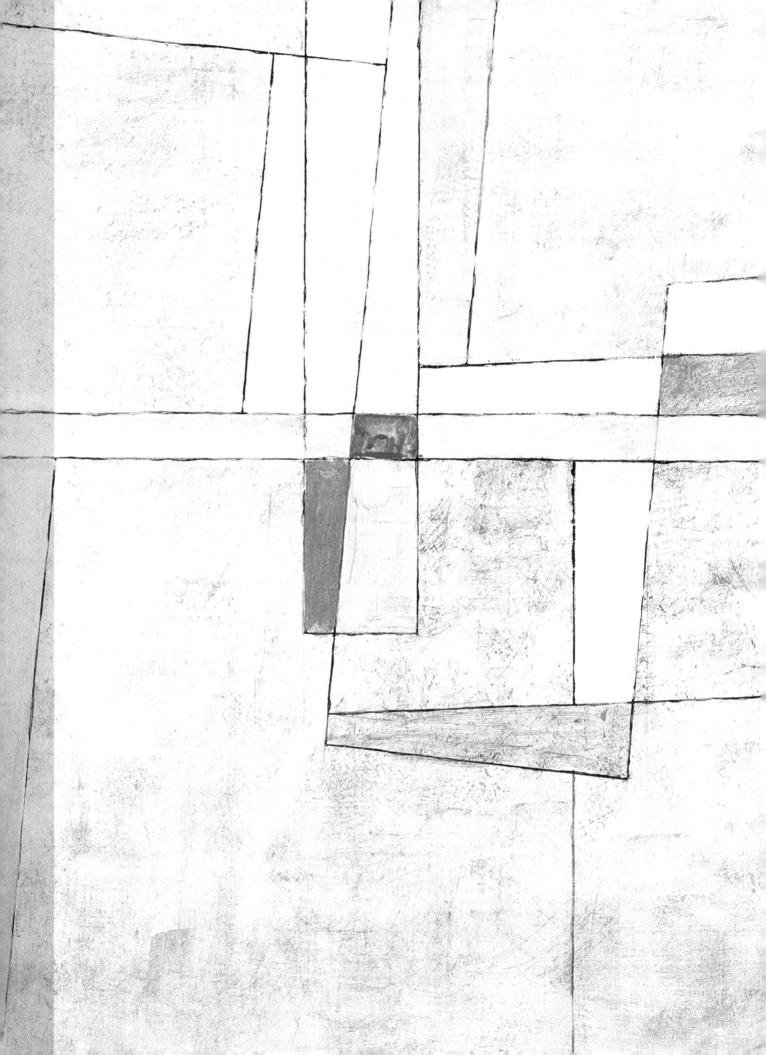

Strategies for Enhancing the Deliberate Practice Exercises

Part III consists of one chapter, Chapter 3, that provides additional advice and instructions for trainers and trainees so that they can reap more benefits from the deliberate practice exercises in Part II. Chapter 3 offers six key points for getting the most out of deliberate practice, guidelines for practicing appropriately responsive treatment, evaluation strategies, methods for ensuring trainee well-being and respecting their privacy, and advice for monitoring the trainer–trainee relationship.

How to Get the Most Out of Deliberate Practice: Additional Guidance for Trainers and Trainees

In Chapter 2 and in the exercises themselves, we provide instructions for completing the deliberate practice exercises. This chapter provides guidance on big-picture topics that trainers will need to integrate deliberate practice successfully into their training program. This guidance is based on relevant research and the experiences and feedback from trainers at more than a dozen psychotherapy training programs who volunteered to test the deliberate practice exercises in this book. We cover topics including evaluation, getting the most from deliberate practice, trainee well-being, respecting trainee privacy, trainer self-evaluation, responsive treatment, and the trainee–trainer alliance.

The use of psychoactive substances for healing and wellness is deeply rooted in Indigenous cultures, where extensive training and supervision, often spanning 15 to 20 years, are required to facilitate medicine-assisted ceremonies. Likewise, becoming an expert in psychedelic-assisted therapy (PAT) takes many years of practice, self- and peer assessment, and formal mentorship. It is imperative that trainees understand that completing a training program and practicing basic PAT skills does not equate to practice competency or readiness. Rather, these activities provide an orientation to the field, an opportunity to understand one's skillfulness, the core safety aspects that must be adhered to, and an ongoing skill development path to gain proficiency over time. To help set realistic expectations and to set trainees up for ongoing learning and skill development, we recommend trainees develop a continuous education and mentorship plan as a component of their PAT training program.

Six Key Points for Getting the Most From Deliberate Practice

Following are six key points of advice for trainers and trainees to get the most benefit from the PAT deliberate practice exercises. The following advice is gleaned from experiences vetting and practicing the exercises, sometimes in different languages, with many trainees, across many countries.

https://doi.org/10.1037/0000399-017

Deliberate Practice in Psychedelic-Assisted Therapy, by S. Dames, A. Penn, M. Williams, J. A. Zamaria, T. Rousmaniere, and A. Vaz

Key Point 1: Create Realistic Emotional Stimuli

A key component of deliberate practice is using stimuli that provoke similar reactions to challenging real-life work settings. For example, pilots train with flight simulators that present mechanical failures and dangerous weather conditions; surgeons practice with surgical simulators that present medical complications with only seconds to respond. Training with challenging stimuli will increase trainees' capacity to perform therapy effectively under stress, for example with clients they find challenging. The stimuli used for PAT deliberate practice exercises are role-plays of challenging client statements in therapy. **It is important that the trainee who is role-playing the client performs the script with appropriate emotional expression and maintains eye contact with the therapist.** For example, if the client statement calls for sad emotion, the trainee should try to express sadness eye-to-eye with the therapist. We offer these suggestions regarding emotional expressiveness:

1. The emotional tone of the role-play matters more than the exact words of each script. Trainees role-playing the client should feel free to improvise and change the words if it will help them be more emotionally expressive. Trainees do not need to stick 100% exactly to the script. In fact, to read off the script during the exercise can sound flat and prohibit eye contact. Rather, trainees in the client role should first read the client statement silently to themselves, then, when ready, say it in an emotional manner while looking directly at the trainee playing the therapist. This will help the experience feel more real and engaging for the therapist.

2. Trainees whose first language isn't English may particularly benefit from reviewing and changing the words in the client statement script before each role-play so that they can find words that feel congruent and facilitate emotional expression.

3. Trainees role-playing the client should try to use tonal and nonverbal expressions of feelings. For example, if a script calls for anger, the trainee can speak with an angry voice and make fists with their hands; if a script calls for shame or guilt, the trainee could hunch over and wince; if a script calls for sadness, the trainee could speak in a soft or deflated voice.

4. If trainees are having persistent difficulties acting believably when following a particular script in the role of client, it may help to first do a "demo round" by reading directly from the paper, and then, immediately after, dropping the paper to make eye contact and repeating the same client statement from memory. Some trainees reported this helped them "become available as real clients" and made the role-play feel less artificial. Some trainees did three or four demo rounds to get fully into their role as a client.

Key Point 2: Customize the Exercises to Fit Your Unique Training Circumstances

Deliberate practice is less about adhering to specific rules than it is about using training principles. Every trainer has their own individual teaching style and every trainee their own learning process. Thus, the exercises in this book are designed to be flexibly customized by trainers across different training contexts within different cultures. Trainees and trainers are encouraged to adjust exercises continually to optimize their practice. The most effective training will occur when deliberate practice exercises are customized to fit the learning needs of each trainee and culture of each training site. In our experience with numerous trainers and trainees across many countries, we found that everyone spontaneously customized the exercises for their unique training circumstances. No two trainers followed the exact same procedure. Following are a few examples.

- One supervisor used the exercises with a trainee who found all the client statements to be too hard, including the "beginner" stimuli. This trainee had multiple reactions in the "too hard" category, including nausea, severe shame, and self-doubt. The trainee disclosed to the supervisor that she had experienced extremely harsh learning environments earlier in her life and found the role-plays to be highly evocative. To help, the supervisor followed the suggestions offered in Appendix A to make the stimuli progressively easier until the trainee reported feeling "good challenge" on the Deliberate Practice Reaction Form. Over many weeks of practice, the trainee developed a sense of safety and was able to practice with more difficult client statements. (Note that if the supervisor had proceeded at the too hard difficulty level, the trainee might have complied while hiding her negative reactions, become emotionally flooded and overwhelmed, leading to withdrawal and thus prohibiting her skill development and risking dropout from training.)

- Supervisors of trainees for whom English was not their first language adjusted the client statements to their own primary language.

- One supervisor used the exercises with a trainee who found all the stimuli to be too easy, including the advanced client statements. This supervisor quickly moved to improvising more challenging client statements from scratch by following the instructions in Appendix A on how to make client statements more challenging.

Key Point 3: Discover Your Own Unique Personal Therapeutic Style

Deliberate practice in psychotherapy can be likened to the process of learning to play jazz music. Every jazz musician prides themselves in their skillful improvisations, and the process of "finding your own voice" is a prerequisite for expertise in jazz musicianship. Yet improvisations are not a collection of random notes but the culmination of extensive deliberate practice over time. Indeed, the ability to improvise is built on many hours of dedicated practice of scales, melodies, harmonies, and so on. In much the same way, psychotherapy trainees are encouraged to experience the scripted interventions in this book not as ends in themselves but as a means to promote skill in a systematic fashion. Over time, effective therapeutic creativity can be aided, instead of constrained, by dedicated practice in these therapeutic "melodies."

Key Point 4: Engage in a Sufficient Amount of Rehearsal

Deliberate practice uses rehearsal to move skills into procedural memory, which helps trainees maintain access to skills even when working with challenging clients. This only works if trainees engage in many repetitions of the exercises. Think of a challenging sport or musical instrument you learned: How many rehearsals would a professional need to feel confident performing a new skill? Psychotherapy is no easier than those other fields!

Key Point 5: Continually Adjust Difficulty

A crucial element of deliberate practice is training at an optimal difficulty level: neither too easy nor too hard. To achieve this, do difficulty assessments and adjustments with the Deliberate Practice Reaction Form in Appendix A. **Do not skip this step!** If trainees don't feel any of the "good challenge" reactions at the bottom of the Deliberate Practice Reaction Form, then the exercise is probably too easy; if they feel any of the "too hard" reactions, then the exercise could be too difficult for the trainee to benefit.

Advanced trainees and therapists may find all the client statements too easy. If so, they should follow the instructions in Appendix A on making client statements harder to make the role-plays sufficiently challenging.

Key Point 6: Putting It All Together

Some trainees may seek greater contextualization of the individual therapy responses associated with each skill, feeling the need to integrate the disparate pieces of their training in a more coherent manner with a simulation that mimics a real therapy session. The annotated transcript in Exercise 13 and the mock therapy sessions in Exercise 14 give trainees this opportunity, allowing them to practice delivering different responses sequentially in a more realistic therapeutic encounter.

Responsive Treatment

The exercises in this book are designed not only to help trainees acquire specific skills of PAT but also to use them in ways that are responsive to each individual client. Across the psychotherapy literature, this stance has been referred to as *appropriate responsiveness*, wherein the therapists exercise flexible judgment, based in their perception of the client's emotional state, needs, and goals, and integrates techniques and other interpersonal skills in pursuit of optimal client outcomes (Hatcher, 2015; Stiles et al., 1998). The effective therapist is responsive to the emerging context. As Stiles and Horvath (2017) argued, therapists are effective because they are appropriately responsive. Doing the "right thing" may be different each time and means providing each client with an individually tailored response.

Appropriate responsiveness counters a misconception that deliberate practice rehearsal is designed to promote robotic repetition of therapy techniques. Psychotherapy researchers have shown that over-adherence to a particular model while neglecting client preferences reduces therapy effectiveness (e.g., Castonguay et al., 1996; Henry et al., 1993; Owen & Hilsenroth, 2014). Therapist flexibility, on the other hand, has been shown to improve outcomes (e.g., Bugatti & Boswell, 2016; Kendall & Beidas, 2007; Kendall & Frank, 2018). It is important, therefore, that trainees practice their newly learned skills in a manner that is flexible and responsive to the unique needs of a diverse range of clients (Hatcher, 2015; Hill & Knox, 2013). It is thus of paramount importance for trainees to develop the necessary perceptual skills to be able to attune to what the client is experiencing in the moment and form their response based on the client moment-by-moment context.

The supervisor must help the supervisee to specifically attune themselves to the unique and specific needs of the clients during sessions. Process supervision (Greenberg & Tomescu, 2017), the practice of supervisor and supervisee listening to tapes, stopping at particular poignant moments and considering client's feelings and meanings, lends itself to teaching appropriate responsiveness. The supervisor can stop the recording, ask the supervisee to reflect upon client's current feelings and meanings, and help the supervisee consider which response would be best in that moment. By enacting responsiveness with the supervisee, the supervisor can demonstrate its value and make it more explicit. In these ways, attention can be given to the larger picture of appropriate responsiveness. Here the trainee and supervisor can work together to help the trainee master not just the techniques, but how therapists can use their judgment to put the techniques together to foster positive change. Helping trainees keep this overarching goal in mind while reviewing therapy process is a valuable feature of supervision that is difficult to obtain otherwise (Hatcher, 2015).

It is also important that deliberate practice occurs within a context of wider PAT learning. As noted in Chapter 1, training should be combined with supervision of actual therapy recordings, theoretical learning, observation of competent PAT therapists, and personal therapeutic work. When the trainer or trainee determines that the trainee is having difficulty acquiring PAT skills, it is important to assess carefully what is missing or needed. Assessment should then lead to the appropriate remedy, as the trainer and trainee collaboratively determine what is needed.

Being Mindful of Trainee Well-Being

Although negative effects that some clients experience in psychotherapy have been well documented (Barlow, 2010), negative effects of training and supervision on trainees have received less attention (Ellis et al., 2014). PAT requires intuitive development over years of practice and mentorship. From this vantage point, it's important that trainees understand that becoming skillful often means we are practicing in unskillful ways. Stumbling is a normal part of the development process. Furthermore, while the importance of self-compassion is intuitively applied in the client's healing and development process, in the same way, practicing self-compassion will improve the trainee's ability to receive feedback, and even welcome it as an important tool in their ongoing growth process. In keeping with the transpersonal tradition, the supervisory and training relationship is built on a somatic approach, establishing a therapeutic alliance, a safe set and setting, and promoting a sense of agency in the client's inner healing intelligence.

To support strong self-efficacy, trainers must ensure that trainees are practicing at a correct difficulty level. The exercises in this book feature guidance for frequently assessing and adjusting the difficulty level, so that trainees can rehearse at a level that targets their personal skill threshold precisely. Trainers and supervisors must be mindful to provide an appropriate challenge. One risk to trainees that is particularly pertinent to this book occurs when using role-plays that are too difficult. The Deliberate Practice Reaction Form in Appendix A is provided to help trainers ensure that role-plays are done at an appropriate challenge level. Trainers or trainees may be tempted to skip the difficulty assessments and adjustments out of a motivation to focus on rehearsal and thus make fast progress and acquire skills quickly. But across all our test sites, we found that skipping the difficulty assessments and adjustments caused more problems and hindered skill acquisition more than any other error. Thus, trainers are advised to remember that **one of their most important responsibilities is to remind trainees to do the difficulty assessments and adjustments.**

Additionally, the Deliberate Practice Reaction Form serves a dual purpose of helping trainees develop the important skills of self-monitoring and self-awareness (Bennett-Levy, 2019). This will help trainees adopt a positive and empowered stance regarding their own self-care and should facilitate career-long professional development.

Respecting Trainee Privacy

The deliberate practice exercises in this book may stir up complex or uncomfortable personal reactions within trainees, including, for example, memories of past traumas. Exploring psychological and emotional reactions may make some trainees feel vulnerable.

Therapists of every career stage, from trainees to seasoned therapists with decades of experience, commonly experience shame, embarrassment, and self-doubt in this process. Although these experiences can be valuable for building trainees' self-awareness, it is important that training remains focused on professional skill development and not blur into personal therapy (e.g., Ellis et al., 2014). Therefore, one trainer role is to remind trainees to maintain appropriate boundaries.

Trainees must have the final say about what to disclose or not disclose to their trainer. Trainees should keep in mind that the goal is for the trainee to expand their own self-awareness and psychological capacity to stay active and helpful while experiencing uncomfortable reactions. The trainer does not need to know the specific details about the trainee's inner world for this to happen.

Trainees should be instructed only to disclose personal information that they feel comfortable sharing. The Deliberate Practice Reaction Form and difficulty assessment process is designed to help trainees build their self-awareness while retaining control over their privacy. Trainees can be reminded that the goal is for them to learn about their own inner world. They do not necessarily have to share that information with trainers or peers (Bennett-Levy & Finlay-Jones, 2018). Likewise, trainees should be instructed to respect the confidentiality of their peers.

Trainer Self-Evaluation

The exercises in this book were tested at a wide range of training sites around the world, including graduate courses, practicum sites, and private practice offices. Although trainers reported that the exercises were highly effective for training, some also said that they felt disoriented by how different deliberate practice feels compared with their traditional methods of clinical education. Many felt comfortable evaluating their trainees' performance but were less sure about their own performance as trainers.

The most common concern we heard from trainers was "My trainees are doing great, but I'm not sure if I am doing this correctly!" To address this concern, we recommend trainers perform periodic self-evaluations along the following five criteria:

1. Observe trainees' work performance.
2. Provide continual corrective feedback.
3. Ensure rehearsal of specific skills is just beyond the trainees' current ability.
4. Ensure that the trainee is practicing at the right difficulty level (neither too easy nor too challenging).
5. Continuously assess trainee performance with real clients.

Criterion 1: Observe Trainees' Work Performance

Determining how well we are doing as trainers means first having valid information about how well trainees are responding to training. This requires that we directly observe trainees practicing skills to provide corrective feedback and evaluation. One risk of deliberate practice is that trainees gain competence in performing therapy skills in role-plays but those skills do not transfer to trainees' work with real clients. Thus, trainers will ideally also have the opportunity to observe samples of trainees' work with real clients, either live or via recorded video. Supervisors and consultants rely heavily—and, too often, exclusively—on supervisees' and consultees' narrative accounts of their work with clients (Goodyear & Nelson, 1997). Haggerty and Hilsenroth (2011) described this challenge:

Suppose a loved one has to undergo surgery and you need to choose between two surgeons, one of whom has never been directly observed by an experienced surgeon while performing any surgery. He or she would perform the surgery and return to his or her attending physician and try to recall, sometimes incompletely or inaccurately, the intricate steps of the surgery they just performed. It is hard to imagine that anyone, given a choice, would prefer this over a professional who has been routinely observed in the practice of their craft. (p. 193)

Criterion 2: Provide Continual Corrective Feedback

Trainees need corrective feedback to learn what they are doing well and doing poorly and how to improve their skills. Feedback should be as specific and incremental as possible. Ideally, trainees become adept at providing this feedback to one another, so that once they complete their time with the trainer, they have an ongoing practice to support their continued growth. Examples of specific feedback are, "Your voice sounds rushed. Try slowing down by pausing for a few seconds between your statements to the client" and "You're doing an excellent job at making eye contact with the client." Examples of vague and nonspecific feedback are "Try to build better rapport with the client" and "Try to be more open to the client's feelings."

Criterion 3: Specific Skill Rehearsal Just Beyond the Trainees' Current Ability (Zone of Proximal Development)

Deliberate practice emphasizes skill acquisition via behavioral rehearsal. Trainers should endeavor not to get caught up in client conceptualization at the expense of focusing on skills. For many trainers, this requires significant discipline and self-restraint. It is simply more enjoyable to talk about psychotherapy theory (e.g., case conceptualization, treatment planning, nuances of psychotherapy models, similar cases the supervisor has had) than watch trainees rehearse skills. Trainees have many questions, and supervisors have an abundance of experience; the allotted supervision time can easily be filled by sharing knowledge. The supervisor gets to sound smart, while the trainee doesn't have to struggle with acquiring skills at their learning edge. Although answering questions is important, trainees' intellectual knowledge about psychotherapy can quickly surpass their procedural ability to perform psychotherapy, particularly with clients they find challenging. Here's a simple rule of thumb: The trainer provides the knowledge, but the behavioral rehearsal provides the skill (Rousmaniere, 2019).

Criterion 4: Practice at the Right Difficulty Level (Neither Too Easy nor Too Challenging)

Deliberate practice involves *optimal strain*: practicing skills just beyond the trainee's current skill threshold so that they can learn incrementally without becoming overwhelmed (Ericsson, 2006).

Trainers should use difficulty assessments and adjustments throughout deliberate practice to ensure that trainees are practicing at the right difficulty level. Note that some trainees are surprised by their unpleasant reactions to exercises (e.g., disassociation, nausea, blanking out), and may be tempted to "push through" exercises that are too hard. This can happen out of fear of failing a course, fear of being judged as incompetent, or negative self-impressions by the trainee (e.g., "This shouldn't be so hard"). Trainers should normalize the fact that there will be wide variation in perceived difficulty of the exercises and encourage trainees to respect their own personal training process.

Criterion 5: Continuously Assess Trainee Performance With Real Clients

The goal of deliberately practicing psychotherapy skills is to improve trainees' effectiveness at helping real clients. One of the risks in deliberate practice training is that the benefits will not generalize: Trainees' acquired competence in specific skills may not translate into work with real clients. Thus, it is important that trainers assess the impact of deliberate practice on trainees' work with real clients. Ideally, this is done through triangulation of multiple data points:

1. client data (verbal self-report and routine outcome monitoring data)
2. supervisor's report (optional peer feedback report)
3. trainee's self-report

If the trainee's effectiveness with real clients is not improving after deliberate practice, the trainer should do a careful assessment of the difficulty. If the supervisor or trainer feels it is a skill acquisition issue, they may want to consider adjusting the deliberate practice routine to better suit the trainee's learning needs or style.

Therapists have traditionally been evaluated from a lens of *process accountability* (Markman & Tetlock, 2000; see also Goodyear, 2015), which focuses on demonstrating specific behaviors (e.g., fidelity to a treatment model) without regard to the impact on clients. We propose that clinical effectiveness is better assessed through a lens tightly focused on client outcomes and that learning objectives shift from performing behaviors that experts have decided are effective (i.e., the competence model) to highly individualized behavioral goals tailored to each trainee's zone of proximal development and performance feedback. This model of assessment has been termed *outcome accountability* (Goodyear, 2015), which focuses on client changes, rather than therapist competence, independent of how the therapist might be performing expected tasks.

Guidance for Trainees

The central theme of this book has been that skill rehearsal is not automatically helpful. Deliberate practice must be done well for trainees to benefit (Ericsson & Pool, 2016). In this chapter and in the exercises, we offer guidance for effective deliberate practice. We would also like to provide additional advice specifically for trainees. That advice is drawn from what we have learned at our volunteer deliberate practice test sites around the world. We cover how to discover your own training process, active effort, playfulness and taking breaks during deliberate practice, your right to control your self-disclosure to trainers, monitoring training results, monitoring complex reactions toward the trainer, and your own personal therapy.

Individualized PAT Training: Finding Your Zone of Proximal Development

Deliberate practice works best when training targets each trainee's personal skill thresholds. Also termed the *zone of proximal development*, a term first coined by Vygotsky in reference to developmental learning theory (Zaretskii, 2009), this is the area just beyond the trainee's current ability but that is possible to reach with the assistance of a teacher or coach (Wass & Golding, 2014). **If a deliberate practice exercise is either too easy or too hard, the trainee will not benefit.** To maximize training productivity, elite performers follow a "challenging but not overwhelming" principle: Tasks that are too far beyond their capacity will prove ineffective and even harmful, and it is equally true that mindlessly repeating what they can already do confidently will prove equally fruitless. Because of this, deliberate practice requires ongoing assessment of the trainee's current skill and concurrent difficulty adjustment to consistently target a "good enough" challenge. Thus, if you are practicing Exercise 7 ("Working With the Client's Internal Conflict") and it just feels too difficult, consider moving back to a more comfortable skill such as Exercise 1 ("Redirecting to the Body") that you may feel you have already mastered.

Active Effort

It is important for trainees to maintain an active and sustained effort, while doing the deliberate practice exercises in this book. Deliberate practice really helps when trainees push themselves up to and past their current ability. This is best achieved when trainees take ownership of their own practice by guiding their training partners to adjust role-plays to be as high on the difficulty scale as possible without hurting themselves. This will look different for every trainee. While it can feel uncomfortable or even frightening, this is the zone of proximal development where the most gains can be made. Simply reading and repeating the written scripts will provide little or no benefit. Trainees are advised to remember that their effort from training should lead to more confidence and comfort in session with real clients.

Stay the Course: Effort Versus Flow

Deliberate practice only works if trainees push themselves hard enough to break out of their old patterns of performance, which then permits growth of new skills (Ericsson & Pool, 2016). Because deliberate practice constantly focuses on the current edge of one's performance capacity, it is inevitably a straining endeavor. Indeed, professionals are unlikely to make lasting performance improvements unless there is sufficient engagement in tasks that are just at the edge of one's current capacity (Ericsson, 2003, 2006). From athletics or fitness training, many of us are familiar with this process of being pushed out of our comfort zones followed by adaptation. The same process applies to our mental and emotional abilities.

Many trainees might be surprised to discover that deliberate practice for PAT feels harder than psychotherapy with a real client. This may be because when working with a real client a therapist can get into a state of *flow* (Csikszentmihalyi, 1997), where work feels effortless. Furthermore, some therapists come with many years of experience in one skill area but are lacking in others. For instance, a PAT therapist in training may feel proficiency and ease navigating strong emotions with clients, but engaging a somatic approach by compassionately witnessing strong emotions may be new territory, making it more effortful at first. PAT therapists in training may find it difficult to focus continually on one or two skills in their response to client statements, feeling they "are just repeating themselves" or have captured the experience as best as they can and are ready to move forward. In such cases, therapists may want to move back to offering response formats with which they are more familiar and feel more proficient and try those for a short time, in part to increase a sense of confidence and mastery.

Discover Your Own Training Process

The effectiveness of deliberate practice is directly related to the effort and ownership trainees exert while doing the exercises. Trainers can provide guidance, but it is important for trainees to learn about their own idiosyncratic training processes over time. This will let them become masters of their own training and prepare for a career-long process of professional development. The following are a few examples of personal training processes that trainees discovered while engaging in deliberate practice:

- One trainee noticed that she is good at persisting while an exercise is challenging, but also that she requires more rehearsal than other trainees to feel comfortable with a new skill. This trainee focused on developing patience with her own pace of progress.

- One trainee noticed that he could acquire new skills rather quickly, with only a few repetitions. However, he also noticed that his reactions to evocative client statements could jump very quickly and unpredictably from the "good challenge" to "too hard" categories, so he needs to attend carefully to the reactions listed in the Deliberate Practice Reaction Form.

- One trainee described herself as "perfectionistic" and felt a strong urge to "push through" an exercise even when she had anxiety reactions in the "too hard" category, such as nausea and dissociation. This caused the trainee to not benefit from the exercises and risk getting demoralized. This trainee focused on going slower, developing self-compassion regarding her anxiety reactions, and asking her training partners to make role-plays less challenging.

Trainees are encouraged to reflect deeply on their own experiences using the exercises to learn the most about themselves and their personal learning processes.

Playfulness and Taking Breaks

Psychotherapy is serious work that often involves painful feelings. However, practicing psychotherapy can be playful and fun (Scott Miller, personal communication, 2017). Trainees should remember that one of the main goals of deliberate practice is to experiment with different approaches and styles of therapy. If deliberate practice ever feels rote, boring, or routine, it probably isn't going to help advance trainees' skill. In this case, trainees should try to liven it up. A good way to do this is to introduce an atmosphere of playfulness. For example, trainees can try the following:

- Use different vocal tones, speech pacing, body gestures, or other languages. This can expand trainees' communication range.

- Practice while simulating being blind (with a blindfold). This can increase sensitivity in the other senses.

- Practice while standing up or walking around outside. This can help trainees get new perspectives on the process of therapy.

The supervisor can also ask trainees if they would like to take a 5- to 10-minute break between questions, particularly if the trainees are dealing with difficult emotions and are feeling stressed out.

Additional Deliberate Practice Opportunities

This book focuses on deliberate practice methods that involve active, live engagement between trainees and a supervisor. Importantly, deliberate practice can extend beyond these focused training sessions as be used for homework. For example, a trainee might read the client stimuli quietly or aloud and practice their responses independently between sessions with a supervisor. In such cases, it is important for the trainee to say their therapist responses aloud, rather than rehearse silently in one's head. Alternatively, two trainees can practice as a pair, without the supervisor. Although the absence of a supervisor limits one source of feedback, the peer trainee who is playing the client can serve this role, as they can when a supervisor is present. These additional deliberate practice opportunities are intended to take place between focused training sessions with a supervisor. To optimize the quality of the deliberate practice when conducted independently or without a supervisor, we have developed a Deliberate Practice Diary Form that can be found in Appendix B or downloaded from https://www.apa.org/pubs/books/deliberate-practice-psychedelic-assisted-therapy (see the "Clinician and Practitioner Resources" tab). This form provides a template for the trainee to record their experience of the deliberate practice activity, and, ideally, it will aid in the consolidation of learning. This form can be used as part of the evaluation process with the supervisor but is not necessarily intended for that purpose, and trainees are certainly welcome to bring their experience with the independent practice into the next meeting with the supervisor.

Monitoring Training Results

While trainers will evaluate trainees using a competency-focused model, trainees are also encouraged to take ownership of their own training process and look for results of deliberate practice themselves. Trainees should experience the results of deliberate practice within a few training sessions. A lack of results can be demoralizing for trainees and result in them applying less effort and focus in deliberate practice. Trainees who are not seeing results should openly discuss this problem with their trainer and experiment with adjusting their deliberate practice process. Results can include client outcomes and improving the trainee's own work as a therapist, their personal development, and their overall training.

Client Outcomes

The most important result of deliberate practice is an improvement in trainees' client outcomes. This can be assessed via routine outcome measurement (Lambert, 2010; Prescott et al., 2017), qualitative data (McLeod, 2017), and informal discussions with clients. However, trainees should note that an improvement in client outcome due to deliberate practice can sometimes be challenging to achieve quickly, given that the largest amount of variance in client outcome is due to client variables (Bohart & Wade, 2013). For example, a client with severe chronic symptoms may not respond quickly to any treatment, regardless of how effectively a trainee practices. For some clients, an increase in patience and self-compassion regarding their symptoms may be a sign of progress, rather than an immediate decrease in symptoms. Thus, trainees are advised to keep their expectations for client change realistic in the context of their client's symptoms, history, and presentation. It is important that trainees do not try to force their clients to improve in therapy in order for the trainee to feel like they are making progress in their training (Rousmaniere, 2016).

Trainee's Work as a Therapist

One important result of deliberate practice is change within the trainee regarding their work with clients. For example, trainees at test sites reported feeling more comfortable sitting with evocative clients, more confident addressing uncomfortable topics in therapy, and more responsive to a broader range of clients.

Trainee's Personal Development

Another important result of deliberate practice is personal growth within the trainee. For example, trainees at test sites reported becoming more in touch with their own feelings, increased self-compassion, and enhanced motivation to work with a broader range of clients.

Trainee's Training Process

Another valuable result of deliberate practice is improvement in the trainees' training process. For example, trainees at test sites reported becoming more aware of their personal training style, preferences, strengths, and challenges. Over time, trainees should grow to feel more ownership of their training process. It is also recommended that training to become a psychotherapist is a complex process that occurs over many years. Experienced, expert therapists still report continuing to grow well beyond their graduate school years (Orlinsky et al., 2005). Furthermore, training is not a linear process. As we practice, and attain feedback on our practice, we develop more confidence and ease in our process; however, the path forward is not always linear. It is perfectly normal to feel like we are making good progress one day and to find ourselves grappling with a setback the next. As noted earlier, normalizing stumbles as a necessary component of learning and improving and practicing self-compassion in the process is not only important for our own growth and development but also one more way that we can "walk our talk" as therapists.

The Trainee–Trainer Alliance: Monitoring Complex Reactions Toward the Trainer

Trainees who engage in hard deliberate practice often report experiencing complex feelings toward their trainer. For example, one trainee said, "I know this is helping, but I also don't look forward to it!" Another trainee reported feeling appreciation and frustration toward her trainer simultaneously. Trainees are advised to remember intensive training they have done in other fields, such as athletics or music. When a coach pushes a trainee to the edge of their ability, it is common for trainees to have complex reactions toward them.

This does not necessarily mean that the trainer is doing anything wrong. In fact, intensive training inevitably stirs up reactions toward the trainer, such as frustration, annoyance, disappointment, or anger, that coexist with the appreciations they feel. In fact, if trainees do not experience complex reactions, it is worth considering if the deliberate practice is sufficiently challenging. But what we asserted earlier about rights to privacy apply here as well. Because professional mental health training is hierarchical, and evaluative, trainers should not require or even expect trainees to share complex reactions they may be experiencing toward them. Trainers should stay open to their sharing, but the choice always remains with the trainee.

Trainee's Own Therapy

When engaging in deliberate practice, many trainees discover aspects of their inner world that may benefit from attending their own psychotherapy. For example, one trainee discovered that her clients' anger stirred up her own painful memories of abuse, another trainee found himself disassociating while practicing empathy skills, and another experienced overwhelming shame and self-judgment when she couldn't master skills after just a few repetitions.

Although these discoveries were unnerving at first, they ultimately were very beneficial because they motivated the trainees to seek out their own therapy. Many therapists attend their own therapy. In fact, Norcross and Guy (2005) found in their review of 17 studies that about 75% of the more than 8,000 therapist participants have attended their own therapy. Orlinsky et al. (2005) found that more than 90% of therapists who attended their own therapy reported it as helpful.

QUESTIONS FOR TRAINEES

1. Are you balancing the effort to improve your skills with patience and self-compassion for your learning process?
2. Are you attending to any shame or self-judgment that is arising from training?
3. Are you being mindful of your personal boundaries and also respecting any complex feelings you may have toward your trainers?

Difficulty Assessments
and Adjustments

Deliberate practice works best if the exercises are performed at a good challenge that is neither too hard nor too easy. To ensure that they are practicing at the correct difficulty, trainees should do a difficulty assessment and adjustment after each level of client statement is completed (beginner, intermediate, and advanced). To do this, use the following instructions and the Deliberate Practice Reaction Form (Figure A.1), which is also available in the "Clinician and Practitioner Resources" tab online (https://www.apa.org/pubs/books/deliberate-practice-psychedelic-assisted-therapy). **Do not skip this process!**

How to Assess Difficulty

The therapist completes the Deliberate Practice Reaction Form (Figure A.1). If they

- rate the difficulty of the exercise above an 8 or had any of the reactions in the "Too Hard" column, follow the instructions to make the exercise easier;

- rate the difficulty of the exercise below a 4 or didn't have any of the reactions in the "Good Challenge" column, proceed to the next level of harder client statements or follow the instructions to make exercise harder; or

- rate the difficulty of the exercise between 4 and 8 and have at least one reaction in the "Good Challenge" column, do not proceed to the harder client statements but rather repeat the same level.

Making Client Statements Easier

If the therapist ever rates the difficulty of the exercise above an 8 or has any of the reactions in the "Too Hard" column, use the next level easier client statements (e.g., if you were using advanced client statements, switch to intermediate). But if you already were using beginner client statements, use the following methods to make the client statements even easier:

- The person playing the client can use the same beginner client statements but this time in a softer, calmer voice and with a smile. This softens the emotional tone.

FIGURE A.1. Deliberate Practice Reaction Form

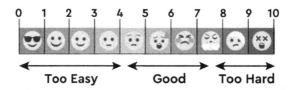

| **Question 1: How challenging was it to fulfill the skill criteria for this exercise?** |

Question 2: Did you have any reactions in "good challenge" or "too hard" categories? (yes/no)

Good Challenge			Too Hard		
Emotions and Thoughts	Body Reactions	Urges	Emotions and Thoughts	Body Reactions	Urges
Manageable shame, self-judgment, irritation, anger, sadness, etc.	Body tension, sighs, shallow breathing, increased heart rate, warmth, dry mouth	Looking away, withdrawing, changing focus	Severe or overwhelming shame, self-judgment, rage, grief, guilt, etc.	Migraines, dizziness, foggy thinking, diarrhea, disassociation, numbness, blanking out, nausea, etc.	Shutting down, giving up

Too Easy	Good Challenge	Too Hard
⬇	⬇	⬇
Proceed to next difficulty level	Repeat the same difficulty level	Go back to previous difficulty level

Note. From *Deliberate Practice in Emotion-Focused Therapy* (p. 180), by R. N. Goldman, A. Vaz, and T. Rousmaniere, 2021, American Psychological Association (https://doi.org/10.1037/0000227-000). Copyright 2021 by the American Psychological Association.

- The client can improvise with topics that are less evocative or make the therapist more comfortable, such as talking about topics without expressing feelings, the future or past (avoiding the here and now), or any topic outside therapy (see Figure A.2).

- The therapist can take a short break (5–10 minutes) between questions.

- The trainer can expand the "feedback phase" by discussing psychedelic-assisted therapy or psychotherapy theory and research. This should shift the trainees' focus toward more detached or intellectual topics and reduce the emotional intensity.

Making Client Statements Harder

If the therapist rates the difficulty of the exercise below a 4 or didn't have any of the reactions in the "Good Challenge" column, proceed to next-level harder client statements. If you were already using the advanced client statements, the client should make the exercise even harder, using the following guidelines:

FIGURE A.2. How to Make Client Statements Easier or Harder in Role-Plays

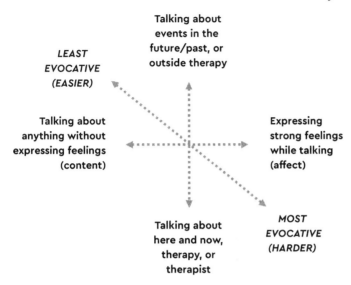

Note. Figure created by Jason Whipple, PhD.

- The person playing the client can use the advanced client statements again with a more distressed voice (e.g., very angry, sad, sarcastic) or unpleasant facial expression. This should increase the emotional tone.

- The client can improvise new client statements with topics that are more evocative or make the therapist uncomfortable, such as expressing strong feelings or talking about the here and now, therapy, or the therapist (see Figure A.2).

> *Note.* The purpose of a deliberate practice session is not to get through all the client statements and therapist responses but rather to spend as much time as possible practicing at the correct difficulty level. This may mean that trainees repeat the same statements/responses many times, which is okay, as long as the difficulty remains at the "Good Challenge" level.

Deliberate Practice Diary Form

This book focuses on deliberate practice methods that involve active, live engagement between trainees and a supervisor. Importantly, deliberate practice can extend beyond these focused training sessions. For example, a trainee might read the client stimuli quietly or aloud and practice their responses independently between sessions with a supervisor. In such cases, it is important for the trainee to speak aloud rather than rehearse silently in one's head. Alternatively, two trainees can practice without the supervisor. Although the absence of a supervisor limits one source of feedback, the peer trainee who is playing the client can serve this role, as they can when a supervisor is present. Importantly, these additional deliberate practice opportunities are intended to take place between focused training sessions with a supervisor. To optimize the quality of the deliberate practice when conducted independently or without a supervisor, we have developed a Deliberate Practice Diary Form that can also be downloaded from the "Clinician and Practitioner Resources" tab online (https://www.apa.org/pubs/books/deliberate-practice-psychedelic-assisted-therapy). This form provides a template for the trainee to record their experience of the deliberate practice activity and, ideally, will aid in the consolidation of learning. This form can also be used as part of the evaluation process with the supervisor but is not necessarily intended for that purpose, and trainees are certainly welcome to bring their experience with the independent practice into the next meeting with the supervisor.

Deliberate Practice Diary Form

Use this form to consolidate learnings from the deliberate practice exercises. Please protect your personal boundaries by only sharing information that you are comfortable disclosing.

Name:_____ Date:_____

Exercise: _____

Question 1. What was helpful or worked well this deliberate practice session? In what way?

Question 2. What was unhelpful or didn't go well this deliberate practice session? In what way?

Question 3. What did you learn about yourself, your current skills, and skills you'd like to keep improving? Feel free to share any details, but only those you are comfortable disclosing.

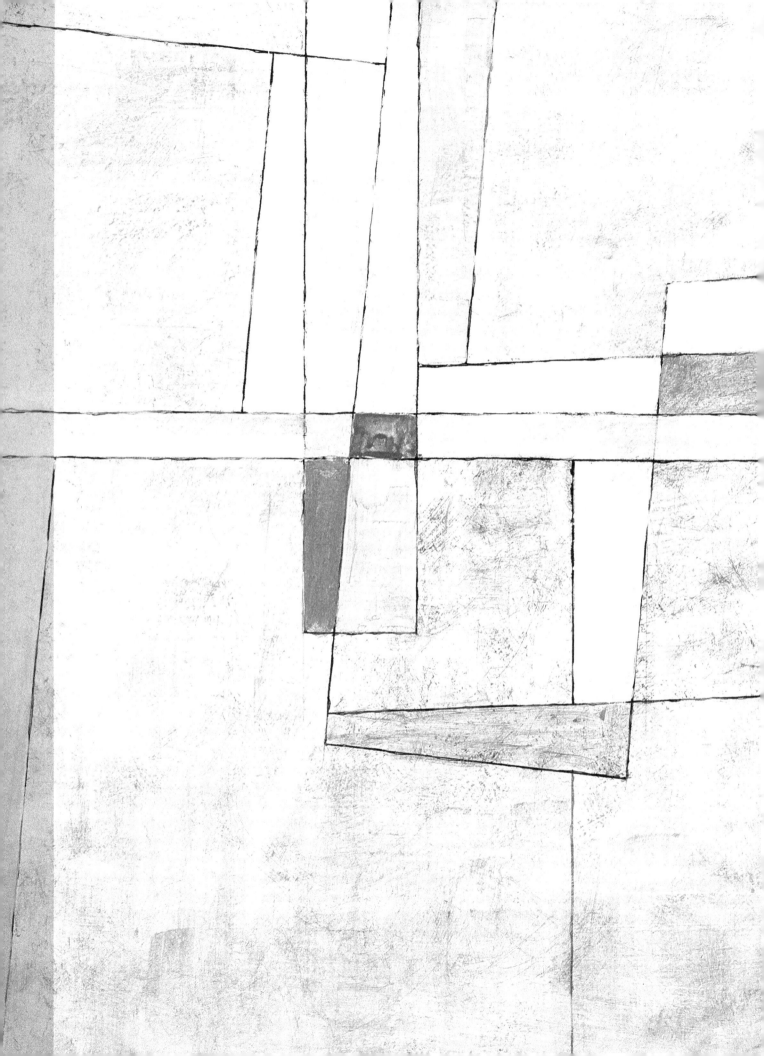

Sample Psychedelic-Assisted Therapy Syllabus With Embedded Deliberate Practice Exercises

This appendix provides a sample one-semester, three-unit course dedicated to teaching the application component of psychedelic-assisted therapy (PAT).

This course aims to orient learners to the field of psychedelic medicine and provide participants with an introduction to the theoretical foundations and practical applications of PAT. Drawing from current research and clinical experiences, the course will explore the integration of various therapeutic modalities and psychedelic substances to optimize treatment outcomes. Participants will engage in a combination of lectures, experiential exercises, case studies, and group discussions to bridge the gap between theory and practice in this emerging field.

In addition to this course, students should also complete foundational coursework informed by theory, research, and cultural considerations. Foundational coursework includes the landscape of relevant psychedelic and entheogenic approaches, a comprehensive review of therapeutic models and theoretical frameworks that pertain to PAT, the historical landscape that PAT is emerging from, regulatory requirements, cultural considerations in depth, review of the various international approaches to PAT, harm reduction approaches, ethical standards, and emerging best practices in PAT. When a strong theoretical base is achieved, students will be ready to begin applying theory to practice.

This course is appropriate for graduate students (master's and doctoral) at all levels of training. We present it as a model that can be adapted to a specific program's contexts and needs. For example, instructors may borrow portions of it to use in other courses, practica, didactic training events at externships and internships, workshops, and continuing education for postgraduate therapists. It is important to note that to become an expert in PAT takes many years of practice, self-assessment, peer assessment, and formal mentorship. It is essential for trainees to understand that completing a training program and acquiring basic PAT skills does not equate to practice competency or readiness. Instead, these activities provide an introduction to the field, an opportunity to assess one's skill level, a foundation in core safety aspects, and a path for ongoing skill development to gain proficiency over time. To set realistic expectations and support trainees in continuous learning and skill development, we strongly recommend the development of a comprehensive plan for continuous education and mentorship as an integral component of their PAT training program. In most Indigenous cultures, individuals aspiring to facilitate psychedelic medicine–assisted healing undergo extensive, years-long mentorship to attain competency.

Course Title: Psychedelic-Assisted Therapy

Course Description

Psychedelic substances, with their long-standing history in healing traditions, are now gaining recognition for their potential therapeutic benefits in treating various mental illnesses and substance use disorders and in enhancing emotional well-being. This course provides an introductory overview to the field of PAT.

Course Objectives

Students who complete this course will be able to

1. articulate how PAT theory and research apply to the practice of PAT.
2. apply the principles of deliberate practice to PAT skill exercises.
3. translate and address critical issues in PAT.
4. articulate how empirically supported psychotherapeutic treatment approaches interweave in the practice of PAT.
5. apply knowledge of key ethical issues and concerns surrounding PAT and practice enacting appropriate mitigation strategies.
6. describe and begin to practice developing competencies in processes related to preparation for and integration of PAT.
7. develop a peer feedback practice, continuing education plan, and mentorship pathway to support one's continued development of PAT competencies.

Although students will have a chance to practice core skills, they will not be ready to work with real clients upon completion of this course. Rather, this course serves as a basic orientation to PAT practice. To navigate the many complexities in PAT safely, students will need further knowledge and supervised practice in the following areas:

- Practitioner's capacity to provide safe care relates to their capacity for secure attachment, awareness of transference, projections, self-regulation, relational attunement, empathy, and access to one's intuitive capacities

- Pharmacological and pharmacokinetics of each psychedelic medicine

- Group-based models versus individual applications: considerations, risks, and benefits of each

- Pathways to enhance cultural awareness, humility, and inclusivity—holding paradox and complexity—awareness of traditional healing practices, honoring ceremonial aspects, and remaining tethered to research-informed practice/biomedical aspects

- Preventing and navigating power abuse and transgression

- Making decisions in regulatory gray areas in the delivery of PAT

- The role and application of music in the delivery of PAT

- PAT team development—promoting safety by ensuring a client's needs are holistically addressed by an interdisciplinary team

- Working within one's scope of practice in the delivery of PAT

- Ensuring continuity of care in the before, during, and after PAT: receiving referrals, intake, eligibility, suitability, charting aspects, consultation with wider care team, and post-PAT referrals

Date	Lecture and Discussion	Skills Lab	Homework (for next class)
Week 1	Review of psychedelic-assisted therapy (PAT) history and research: • Historical context • Psychedelic research • Therapeutic approaches for PAT in general Orientation to course process: • Applying and integrating deliberate practice scenarios • Case studies • Small group discussions	The history and principles of PAT theory, deliberate practice, and the first way of research; deliberate practice research Review deliberate practice preparation material (Chapters 1–3)	**Required** Costandi (2014); Luoma et al. (2020); Naranjo (1973/2013); Rush et al. (2022); Strauss et al. (2021) **Supplemental** Dubus (2020); Nutt et al. (2013); Passie (2018)
Week 2	Mechanisms of PAT medicines and the application of somatic approaches and attachment theory: • Refresher of mechanisms and neurobiological aspects of PAT • The role of attachment and attunement • Therapeutic alliance • Brief overview of the principles of transpersonal and somatic therapy approaches	Exercise 1: Redirecting to the Body	**Required** Banks et al. (2021); Constantino et al. (2010); de Vos et al. (2021); Kuhfuß et al. (2021); Swift & Greenberg (2015); Vollenweider & Kometer (2010) **Supplemental** López-Giménez & González-Maeso (2017); Lu et al. (2021); Mendes et al. (2022); Rønberg (2019)
Week 3	Developing a PAT working alliance; establishing treatment goals; inner healing intelligence principles: • Purpose and practice of compassionate witnessing in the process of "holding space" • Team compositions that satisfy regulatory requirements	Case study: practice establishing treatment goals Exercise 2: Compassionately Witnessing Strong Emotions	**Required** Kirst (2022); Murphy et al. (2022); Safran & Muran (2000); Talia et al. (2020); Vaid & Walker (2022); Weingarten (2003) **Supplemental** Haijen et al. (2018); Halstead et al. (2021)
Week 4	**Case study debrief from previous week** Ethical and therapeutic foundations: • Development of a code of ethics for the class • Establishing boundaries and providing informed and ongoing consent • Intentions and expectations • Boundaries	Small group: case study Exercise 3: Exploring Intentions and Expectations Contribute to a cocreated code of ethics	**Required** Carlin & Scheld (2019); Celidwen et al. (2023); Danforth (2009); Neitzke-Spruill (2020); Rochester et al. (2022); Ryan & Bennett (2020) **Supplemental** Brennan et al. (2021); McLane et al. (2021); Uthaug et al. (2021)
Week 5	**Case study debrief from previous week** Cultural considerations and diversity in psychedelic therapy: • Recognizing and addressing cultural biases and disparities • Adapting therapeutic approaches to diverse populations • Incorporating inclusivity and equity in psychedelic therapy practice • Overview of the role of one's awareness of culture and past lineage: application to one's perspective, biases, and application to PAT • Working with emotions	Small group: case study Exercise 4: Cultural Considerations: Racially and Ethnically Diverse Communities	**Required** Ching (2020); Fogg et al. (2021); Michaels et al. (2018); Rea & Wallace (2021); M. L. Williams et al. (2021); M. T. Williams et al. (2020) **Supplemental** Eriacho (2020); Hays (2009); Hook et al. (2017); D. T. Smith et al. (2022)
Week 6	**Case study debrief from previous week** Brief overview of PAT medicines: access, mechanisms, cultural considerations: • Ketamine • MDMA • Psilocybin • LSD • Ayahuasca • Peyote • In the context of legal options, what medicines are appropriate for what persons? • Components of suitability assessments • Components of informed and ongoing consent • The role of agreements and boundaries related to PAT	Small group: case study Exercise 5: Boundaries and Informed Consent	**Required** Dames et al. (2022); Diament et al. (2021); Dore et al. (2019); Dyck (2016); Little (2020); Roseman et al. (2018); Sloshower et al. (2020); Wießner et al. (2023) **Supplemental** Argento et al. (2019); Wolfson (2019)
Week 7	**Case study debrief from previous week** Relational ruptures as an important integration pathway: • Promoting acceptance and flexibility • Overview of nonviolent communication, and application to PAT • Leveraging ruptures	Small group: case study Exercise 6: Responding to Relational Ruptures	**Required** Eubanks et al. (2018); Walser et al. (2019); Watts & Luoma (2020); Wolff et al. (2020)

Date	Lecture and Discussion	Skills Lab	Homework (for next class)
Week 8	**Case study debrief from previous week** Interweaving somatic approaches with multiplicity of parts theory, and understanding context: • Systems theory • Validating conflicting parts of self	Small group: case study Exercise 7: Working With the Client's Internal Conflict	**Required** Carhart-Harris et al. (2018); Goodwin et al. (2018); Rousseau (2015); Whitfield (2021) **Supplemental** Redfern (2023)
Week 9	Supervised practice via mock sessions	Record and (self- and peer-) evaluate mock sessions) Midterm knowledge consolidation assignment due Midterm knowledge mobilization assignment due	
Week 10	**Case study debrief from previous week** Overview of transference and countertransference and the role of ritual and ceremony in PAT: • Developing self-awareness • Leveraging transference for therapeutic benefit	Small group: case study Exercise 8: Addressing Transference	**Required** Goldpaugh (2022); Prasko et al. (2022); Suszek et al. (2015)
Week 11	**Case study debrief from previous week** Self- and other regulation and trauma-informed practice: • Trauma-informed practice applications • Expanding the window of tolerance	Small group: case study Exercise 9: Navigating Strong Emotions	**Required** Corrigan et al. (2011); Knight (2019); Teixeira et al. (2022) **Supplemental** J. Fisher (2019)
Week 12	**Case study debrief from previous week** Integration and aftercare: • The role of integration in maximizing therapeutic benefits • Techniques for supporting clients in integrating insights into daily life • Designing comprehensive aftercare plans and follow-up sessions • Overview of integration theory and practice principles • Promoting meaning making of PAT experiences	Small group: case study Exercise 10: Making Sense of the Experience: Integration I	**Required** Amada & Shane (2022); Bathje et al. (2022); Frymann et al. (2022); Walsh & Thiessen (2018)
Week 13	**Case study debrief from previous week** Decision making amid uncertainty: • Risk reduction and harm reduction • Navigating gray areas (making decisions amid a lack of regulatory guidance) • Navigating disappointment, managing expectations, and exploring reflective patterns between what arises in PAT experiences and everyday life challenges	Small group: case study Exercise 11: Working With Disappointment: Integration II	**Required** Gorman et al. (2021); Pilecki et al. (2021); Watts & Luoma (2020); M. L. Williams et al. (2021)
Week 14	**Case study debrief from previous week** Integration: • Expanding the capacity by expanding the liminal space • Emotional regulation within liminal spaces • Promoting security within liminal spaces • Normalizing expansion and contraction	Small group: case study Exercise 12: Embodying Insights: Integration III	**Required** Grof (2008); Lutkajtis & Evans (2023) **Supplemental** A-Tjak et al. (2015)
Week 15	**Case study debrief from previous week** Review of ongoing learning planning Small group wrap-up	Final knowledge consolidation assignment due (demonstrating adequate knowledge acquisition) Final knowledge mobilization assignment due (demonstrating leadership in the field) Final deliberate practice exercises (via video or direct supervision), self- and peer assessments due (demonstrating understanding of core PAT skills) Sign a cocreated code of ethics	None

Format of Class

Classes are 3 hours long. Course time is split evenly among learning PAT theory, integrating the material in a small-group format, reviewing case studies, and acquiring PAT skills.

Lecture/Discussion Class: Each week, there will be one Lecture/Discussion class for 1.5 hours focusing on PAT theory and related research, followed by 1.5 hours in a small group or lab setting.

Psychedelic-Assisted Therapy Skills Lab: Each week, please plan to spend an additional 1.5 hours practicing skills on your own time. Skills labs are for practicing PAT skills using the exercises in this book. The exercises use therapy simulations (role-plays) with the following goals:

1. Build trainees' skill and confidence for using PAT skills with real clients.
2. Provide a safe space for experimenting with different therapeutic interventions, without fear of making mistakes.
3. Provide plenty of opportunity to explore and "try on" different styles of therapy, so trainees can ultimately discover their own personal, unique therapy style.

Mock Sessions: Twice in the semester (weeks 9 and 15), trainees will do a psychotherapy mock session in the PAT skills lab. In contrast to highly structured and repetitive deliberate practice exercises, a psychotherapy mock session is an unstructured and improvised role-played therapy session. Mock sessions let trainees:

1. Practice using PAT skills responsively.
2. Experiment with clinical decision making in an unscripted context.
3. Discover their personal therapeutic style.
4. Build endurance for working with real clients.

Homework

Homework will be assigned each week and will include reading, 1 hour of skills practice with an assigned practice partner, and occasional writing assignments. For the skills practice homework, trainees will repeat the exercise they did for that week's PAT skills lab. Because the instructor will not be there to evaluate performance, trainees should instead complete the Deliberate Practice Reaction Form, as well as the Deliberate Practice Diary Form, for themselves as a self-evaluation. Furthermore, it is important that students get in the practice of giving and receiving peer feedback, with the goal of developing a career-long habit of the same.

Assignments

Students are to complete a knowledge consolidation and translation assignment: one due at midterm and one due at the last day of class. In the spirit of cultural inclusivity and honoring a variety of ways of knowing and sharing knowledge, for the consolidation component, students have three options: They may submit an article suitable for publication, they can provide a recorded presentation, or they can compile a protocol and documentation package that will guide and document their practice. Some possible topics for the article or presentation forms of the assignment are as follows:

- Exploration of one aspect of PAT theory, research, or technique
- A partial transcript of one of the trainees' therapy cases with a real client, with discussion from a psychedelic-assisted therapy perspective

Multicultural Orientation

This course is taught in a multicultural context, defined as "how the cultural worldviews, values, and beliefs of the client and therapist interact and influence each another to co-create a relational experience that is in the spirit of healing" (Davis et al., 2018, p. 3). Core features of the multicultural orientation include cultural comfort, humility, and responding to cultural opportunities (or previously missed opportunities). Throughout this course, students are encouraged to reflect on their own cultural identity and improve their ability to attune with their clients' cultural identities (Hook et al., 2017). For further guidance on this topic and deliberate practice exercises to improve multicultural skills, see the book *Deliberate Practice in Multicultural Therapy* (J. Harris et al., 2024).

Vulnerability, Privacy, and Boundaries

This course is aimed at developing PAT skills, self-awareness, and interpersonal skills in an experiential framework and as relevant to clinical work. This course is not psychotherapy or a substitute for psychotherapy. Students should interact at a level of self-disclosure that is personally comfortable and helpful to their own learning. Although becoming aware of internal emotional and psychological processes is necessary for a therapist's development, it is not necessary to reveal all that information to the trainer. It is important for students to sense their own level of safety and privacy. Students are not evaluated on the level of material that they choose to reveal in the class.

In accordance with the *Ethical Principles of Psychologists and Code of Conduct* (American Psychological Association, 2017), students are **not required to disclose personal information.** Because this class is about developing both interpersonal and PAT competence, the following are some important points so that students are fully informed as they make choices to self-disclose:

- Students choose how much, when, and what to disclose. Students are not penalized for the choice not to share personal information.

- The learning environment is susceptible to group dynamics much like any other group space, and therefore students may be asked to share their observations and experiences of the class environment with the singular goal of fostering a more inclusive and productive learning environment.

Confidentiality

To create a safe learning environment that is respectful of client and therapist information and diversity and to foster open and vulnerable conversation in class, students are required to agree to strict confidentiality within and outside of the instruction setting.

Evaluation

Self-Evaluation: At the end of the semester (Week 15), trainees will perform a self-evaluation. This will help trainees track their progress and identify areas for further development. The "Guidance for Trainees" section in Chapter 3 of this book highlights potential areas of focus for self-evaluation.

Peer Evaluation: Between classes students will be paired up to practice with the deliberate practice exercises. Before you switch roles in the role-play, please provide feedback for your peer (who was acting in the role of a therapist)—for instance, speaking to body language, tone of voice, what felt effortful/challenging, what inspired you, and what might be said differently (quality improvement components).

Grading Criteria

As designed, students would be accountable for the level and quality of their performance in the following:

- facilitation and contribution to small group discussions,
- the skills lab (exercises and mock sessions),
- homework,
- midterm assignments (consolidating and translating knowledge), and
- a final exam (consolidating and translating knowledge).

Required Readings

Amada, N., & Shane, J. (2022). Self-actualization and the integration of psychedelic experience: The mediating role of perceived benefits to narrative self-functioning. *The Journal of Humanistic Psychology*. Advance online publication. https://doi.org/10.1177/00221678221099680

Banks, M. I., Zahid, Z., Jones, N. T., Sultan, Z. W., & Wenthur, C. J. (2021). Catalysts for change: The cellular neurobiology of psychedelics. *Molecular Biology of the Cell*, *32*(12), 1135–1144. https://doi.org/10.1091/MBC.E20-05-0340

Bathje, G. J., Majeski, E., & Kudowor, M. (2022). Psychedelic integration: An analysis of the concept and its practice. *Frontiers in Psychology*, *13*, Article 824077. https://doi.org/10.3389/fpsyg.2022.824077

Carhart-Harris, R. L., Roseman, L., Haijen, E., Erritzoe, D., Watts, R., Branchi, I., & Kaelen, M. (2018). Psychedelics and the essential importance of context. *Journal of Psychopharmacology*, *32*(7), 725–731. https://doi.org/10.1177/0269881118754710

Carlin, S. C., & Scheld, S. (2019, Spring). MAPS MDMA-Assisted Psychotherapy Code of Ethics [2021 update]. *Multidisciplinary Association of Psychedelic Studies Bulletin*, *29*(1). https://maps.org/news/bulletin/articles/436-maps-bulletin-spring-2019-vol-29,-no-1/7710-maps-mdma-assisted-psychotherapy-codeof-ethics-spring-2019

Celidwen, Y. Redvers, N., Githaiga, C., Calambás, J., Añaños, K., Evanjuanoy Chindoy, M., Vitale, R., Rojas, J. N., Mondragón, D., Vázquez Rosalío, Y., & Sacbajá, A. (2023). Ethical principles of traditional Indigenous medicine to guide western psychedelic research and practice. *The Lancet Regional Health—Americas*, *18*, Article 100410. https://doi.org/10.1016/j.lana.2022.100410

Ching, T. H. W. (2020). Intersectional insights from an MDMA-assisted psychotherapy training trial: An open letter to racial/ethnic and sexual/gender minorities. *Journal of Psychedelic Studies*, *4*(1) 61–68. https://doi.org/10.1556/2054.2019.017

Constantino, M. J., Castonguay, L. G., Zack, S., & DeGeorge, J. (2010). Engagement in psychotherapy: Factors contributing to the facilitation, demise, and restoration of the therapeutic alliance. In D. Castro-Blanco & M. S. Carver (Eds.), *Elusive alliance: Treatment engagement strategies with high-risk adolescents* (pp. 21–57). American Psychological Association. https://doi.org/10.1037/12139-001

Corrigan, F., Fisher, J., & Nutt, D. (2011). Autonomic dysregulation and the window of tolerance model of the effects of complex emotional trauma. *Journal of Psychopharmacology*, *25*(1), 17–25. https://doi.org/10.1177/0269881109354930

Costandi, M. (2014). A brief history of psychedelic psychiatry. *The Psychologist*, *27*(9), 714–715.

Dames, S., Kryskow, P., & Watler, C. (2022). A cohort-based case report: The impact of ketamine-assisted therapy embedded in a community of practice framework for healthcare providers with PTSD and depression. *Frontiers in Psychiatry*, *12*, Article 803279. https://doi.org/10.3389/fpsyt.2021.803279

Danforth, A. (2009). Focusing-oriented psychotherapy as a supplement to preparation for psychedelic therapy. *The Journal of Transpersonal Psychology*, *41*(2), 151–181.

de Vos, Cato M. H., Mason, N. L., & Kuypers, K. P. C. (2021). Psychedelics and neuroplasticity: A systematic review unraveling the biological underpinnings of psychedelics. *Frontiers in Psychiatry*, *12*, Article 724606. https://doi.org/10.3389/fpsyt.2021.724606

Diament, M., Gomes, B. R., Tófoli, L. F. (2021). Ayahuasca and psychotherapy: Beyond integration. In B. C. Labate & C. Cavnar (Eds.), *Ayahuasca healing and science*. Springer. https://doi.org/10.1007/978-3-030-55688-4_4

Dore, J., Turnipseed, B., Dwyer, S., Turnipseed, A., Andries, J., Ascani, G., Monnette, C., Huidekoper, A., Strauss, N., & Wolfson, P. (2019). Ketamine assisted psychotherapy (KAP): Patient demographics, clinical data and outcomes in three large practices administering ketamine with psychotherapy. *Journal of Psychoactive Drugs, 51*(2), 189–198. https://doi.org/10.1080/02791072.2019.1587556

Dyck, E. (2016). Peyote and psychedelics on the Canadian prairies. In B. C. Labate & C. Cavnar (Eds.), *Peyote: History, tradition, politics, and conservation* (pp. 151–170). Praeger/ABC-CLIO.

Eubanks, C. F., Muran, J. C., & Safran, J. D. (2018). Repairing alliance ruptures. In J. C. Norcross & B. E. Wampold (Eds.), *Psychotherapy relationships that work: Evidence-based responsiveness* (3rd ed., pp. 549–579). Oxford University Press.

Fogg, C., Michaels, T. I., de la Salle, S., Jahn, Z. W., & Williams, M. T. (2021). Ethnoracial health disparities and the ethnopsychopharmacology of psychedelic medicine. *Experimental and Clinical Psychopharmacology, 29*(5), 539–554. https://doi.org/10.1037/pha0000490

Frymann, T., Whitney, S., Yaden, D. B., & Lipson, J. (2022). The Psychedelic Integration Scales: Tools for measuring psychedelic integration behaviors and experiences. *Frontiers in Psychology, 13*, Article 863247. https://doi.org/10.3389/fpsyg.2022.863247

Goldpaugh, D. D. (2022). Finding the divine within: Exploring the role of the sacred in psychedelic integration therapy for sexual trauma and dysfunction. *Sexual and Relationship Therapy, 37*(3), 314–323. https://doi.org/10.1080/14681994.2021.1994138

Goodwin, B. J., Coyne, A. E., & Constantino, M. J. (2018). Extending the context-responsive psychotherapy integration framework to cultural processes in psychotherapy. *Psychotherapy, 55*(1), 3–8. https://doi.org/10.1037/pst0000143

Gorman, I., Nielson, E. M., Molinar, A., Cassidy, K., & Sabbagh, J. (2021). Psychedelic harm reduction and integration: A transtheoretical model for clinical practice. *Frontiers in Psychology, 12*, Article 645246. https://doi.org/10.3389/fpsyg.2021.645246

Grof, S. (2008). Brief history of transpersonal psychology. *International Journal of Transpersonal Studies, 27*(1), 46–54. https://doi.org/10.24972/ijts.2008.27.1.46

Kirst, P. F. (2022). Compassionate witnessing. *Psychological Perspectives, 65*(1), 1–4. https://doi.org/10.1080/00332925.2022.2081469

Knight, C. (2019). Trauma informed practice and care: Implications for field instruction. *Clinical Social Work Journal, 47*(1), 79–89. https://doi.org/10.1007/s10615-018-0661-x

Kuhfuβ, M., Maldei, T., Hetmanek, A., & Baumann, N. (2021). Somatic experiencing—Effectiveness and key factors of a body-oriented trauma therapy: A scoping literature review. *European Journal of Psychotraumatology, 12*(1), Article 1929023. https://doi.org/10.1080/20008198.2021.1929023

Little, R. (2020). Boundary applications and violations: Clinical interpretations in a transference-countertransference-focused psychotherapy. *Transactional Analysis Journal, 50*(3), 221–235. https://doi.org/10.1080/03621537.2020.1771031

Luoma, J. B., Chwyl, C., Bathje, G. J., Davis, A. K., & Lancelotta, R. (2020). A meta-analysis of placebo-controlled trials of psychedelic assisted therapy. *Journal of Psychoactive Drugs, 52*(4), 289–299. https://doi.org/10.1080/02791072.2020.1769878

Lutkajtis, A., & Evans, J. (2023). Psychedelic integration challenges: Participant experiences after a psilocybin truffle retreat in the Netherlands. *Journal of Psychedelic Studies, 6*(3), 211–221. https://doi.org/10.1556/2054.2022.00232

Michaels, T. I., Purdon, J., Collins, A., & Williams, M. T. (2018). Inclusion of people of color in psychedelic-assisted psychotherapy: A review of the literature. *BMC Psychiatry, 18*(245), Article 245. https://doi.org/10.1186/s12888-018-1824-6

Murphy, R., Kettner, H., Zeifman, R., Giribaldi, B., Kartner, L., Martell, J., Read, T., Murphy-Beiner, A., Baker-Jones, M., Nutt, D., Erritzoe, D., Watts, R., & Carhart-Harris, R. (2022). Therapeutic alliance and rapport modulate responses to psilocybin assisted therapy for depression. *Frontiers in Pharmacology, 12*, Article 788155. https://doi.org/10.3389/fphar.2021.788155

Naranjo, C. (1973/2013). *The healing journey: Pioneering approaches to psychedelic therapy* (2nd ed.). Multidisciplinary Association for Psychedelic Studies.

Neitzke-Spruill, L. (2020). Race as a component of set and setting: How experiences of race can influence psychedelic experiences. *Journal of Psychedelic Studies*, *1*(4), 51–60. https://doi.org/10.1556/2054.2019.022

Pilecki, B., Luoma, J. B., Bathje, G. J., Rhea, J., & Narloch, V. F. (2021). Ethical and legal issues in psychedelic harm reduction and integration therapy. *Harm Reduction Journal*, *18*(1), 40–40. https://doi.org/10.1186/s12954-021-00489-1

Prasko, J., Ociskova, M., Vanek, J., Burkauskas, J., Slepecky, M., Bite, I., Krone, I., Sollar, T., & Juskiene, A. (2022). Managing transference and countertransference in cognitive behavioral supervision: Theoretical framework and clinical application. *Psychology Research and Behavior Management*, *15*, 2129–2155. https://doi.org/10.2147/PRBM.S369294

Rea, K., & Wallace, B. (2021). Enhancing equity-oriented care in psychedelic medicine: Utilizing the EQUIP framework. *The International Journal of Drug Policy*, *98*, Article 103429. https://doi.org/10.1016/j.drugpo.2021.103429

Rochester, J., Vallely, A., Grof, P., Williams, M., Chang, H., & Caldwell, K. (2022). Entheogens and psychedelics in Canada: Proposal for a new paradigm. *Canadian Psychology*, *63*(3), 413–430. https://doi.org/10.1037/cap0000285

Roseman, L., Nutt, D. J., & Carhart-Harris, R. L. (2018). Quality of acute psychedelic experience predicts therapeutic efficacy of psilocybin for treatment-resistant depression. *Frontiers in Pharmacology*, *8*, Article 974. https://doi.org/10.3389/fphar.2017.00974

Rousseau, D. (2015). General systems theory: Its present and potential. *Systems Research and Behavioral Science*, *32*(5), 522–533. https://doi.org/10.1002/sres.2354

Rush, B., Marcus, O., Shore, R., Cunningham, L., Thompson, N., & Rideout, K. (2022). *Psychedelic medicine: A rapid review of therapeutic applications and implications for future research*. Homewood Research Institute. https://hriresearch.com/research/exploratoryresearch/research-reports/

Ryan, W., & Bennett, R. (2020). Ethical guidelines for ketamine clinicians. *The Journal of Psychedelic Psychiatry*, *2*(4), 19–23.

Safran, J. D., & Muran, J. C. (2000). *Negotiating the therapeutic alliance: A relational treatment guide*. Guilford Press.

Sloshower, J., Guss, J., Krause, R., Wallace, R. M., Williams, M. T., Reed, S., & Skinta, M. D. (2020). Psilocybin-assisted therapy of major depressive disorder using acceptance and commitment therapy as a therapeutic frame. *Journal of Contextual Behavioral Science*, *15*, 12–19. https://doi.org/10.1016/j.jcbs.2019.11.002

Strauss, D., de la Salle, S., Sloshower, J., & Williams, M. T. (2021). Research abuses against people of colour in psychedelic research. *Journal of Medical Ethics*. Advance online publication. https://doi.org/10.1136/medethics-2021-107262

Suszek, H., Wegner, E., & Maliszewski, N. (2015). Transference and its usefulness in psychotherapy in the light of empirical evidence. *Annals of Psychology*, *18*(3), 363–380.

Swift, J. K., & Greenberg, R. P. (2015). Foster the therapeutic alliance. In J. K. Swift & R. P. Greenberg (Eds.), *Premature termination in psychotherapy: Strategies for engaging clients and improving outcomes* (pp. 137–147). American Psychological Association. https://doi.org/10.1037/14469-010

Talia, A., Muzi, L., Lingiardi, V., & Taubner, S. (2020). How to be a secure base: Therapists' attachment representations and their link to attunement in psychotherapy. *Attachment & Human Development*, *22*(2), 189–206. https://doi.org/10.1080/14616734.2018.1534247

Teixeira, P. J., Johnson, M. W., Timmermann, C., Watts, R., Erritzoe, D., Douglass, H., Kettner, H., & Carhart-Harris, R. L. (2022). *Psychedelics and health behaviour change*. Sage Publications. https://doi.org/10.1177/02698811211008554

Vaid, G., & Walker, B. (2022). Psychedelic psychotherapy: Building wholeness through connection. *Global Advances in Health and Medicine*, *11*, Article 2164957X221081113. https://doi.org/10.1177/2164957X221081113

Vollenweider, F. X., & Kometer, M. (2010). The neurobiology of psychedelic drugs: Implications for the treatment of mood disorders. *Nature Reviews: Neuroscience*, *11*(9), 642–651. https://doi.org/10.1038/nrn2884

Walser, R. D., Coulter, C., Hayes, S. C., & O'Connell, M. (2019). *The heart of ACT: Developing a flexible, process-based, and client-centered practice using acceptance and commitment therapy*. Context Press.

Walsh, Z., & Thiessen, M. S. (2018). Psychedelics and the new behaviourism: Considering the integration of third-wave behaviour therapies with psychedelic-assisted therapy. *International Review of Psychiatry*, *30*(4), 343–349. https://doi.org/10.1080/09540261.2018.1474088

Watts, R., & Luoma, J. B. (2020). The use of the psychological flexibility model to support psychedelic assisted therapy. *Journal of Contextual Behavioral Science*, *15*, 92–102. https://doi.org/10.1016/j.jcbs.2019.12.004

Weingarten, K. (2003). *Compassionate witnessing and the transformation of societal violence: How individuals can make a difference*. https://www.humiliationstudies.org/documents/WeingartenCompassionateWitnessing.pdf

Whitfield, H. J. (2021). A spectrum of selves reinforced in multilevel coherence: A contextual behavioural response to the challenges of psychedelic-assisted therapy development. *Frontiers in Psychiatry*, *12*, Article 727572. https://doi.org/10.3389/fpsyt.2021.727572 [Erratum in *Frontiers in Psychiatry*, 2021, *12*, Article 832766]

Wießner, I., Falchi, M., Palhano-Fontes, F., Feilding, A., Ribeiro, S., & Tófoli, L. F. (2023). LSD, madness and healing: Mystical experiences as possible link between psychosis model and therapy model. *Psychological Medicine*, *53*(4), 1151–1165. https://doi.org/10.1017/S0033291721002531

Williams, M. L., Korevaar, D., Harvey, R., Fitzgerald, P. B., Liknaitzky, P., O'Carroll, S., Puspanathan, P., Ross, M., Strauss, N., & Bennett-Levy, J. (2021). Translating psychedelic therapies from clinical trials to community clinics: Building bridges and addressing potential challenges ahead. *Frontiers in Psychiatry*, *12*, Article 737738. https://doi.org/10.3389/fpsyt.2021.737738

Williams, M. T., Reed, S., & Aggarwal, R. (2020). Culturally informed research design issues in a study for MDMA-assisted psychotherapy for posttraumatic stress disorder. *Journal of Psychedelic Studies*, *4*(1), 40–50. https://doi.org/10.1556/2054.2019.016

Wolff, M., Evens, R., Mertens, L. J., Koslowski, M., Betzler, F., Gründer, G., & Jungaberle, H. (2020). Learning to let go: A cognitive-behavioral model of how psychedelic therapy promotes acceptance. *Frontiers in Psychiatry*, *11*, 5. https://doi.org/10.3389/fpsyt.2020.00005

Supplemental Readings

Argento, E., Capler, R., Gerald, T., Lucas, P., & Tupper, K. (2019). Exploring ayahuasca-assisted therapy for addiction: A qualitative analysis of preliminary findings among an Indigenous community in Canada. *Drug and Alcohol Review*, *38*(7), 781–789. https://doi.org/10.1111/dar.12985

A-Tjak, J. G. L., Davis, M. L., Morina, N., Powers, M. B., Smits, J. A., Emmelkamp, P. M. (2015). A meta-analysis of the efficacy of acceptance and commitment therapy for clinically relevant mental and physical health problems. *Psychotherapy and Psychosomatics*, *84*(1), 30–36. https://doi.org/10.1159/000365764

Brennan, W., Jackson, M. A., MacLean, K., & Ponterotto, J. G. (2021). A qualitative exploration of relational ethical challenges and practices in psychedelic healing. *Journal of Humanistic Psychology*. Advance online publication. https://doi.org/10.1177/00221678211045265

Castonguay, L. G., Constantino, M. J., Boswell, J. F., & Kraus, D. (2010). The therapeutic alliance: Research and theory. In L. Horowitz & S. Strack (Eds.), *Handbook of interpersonal psychology: Theory, research, assessment, and therapeutic interventions* (pp. 509–518). John Wiley & Sons.

Davis, D. E., DeBlaere, C., Owen, J., Hook, J. N., Rivera, D. P., Choe, E., Van Tongeren, D. R., Worthington, E. L., & Placeres, V. (2018). The multicultural orientation framework: A narrative review. *Psychotherapy*, *55*(1), 89–100. https://doi.org/10.1037/pst0000160

Dubus, Z. (2020). Using psychedelics to "cure" gay adolescents? Conversion therapy trial, France, 1960. *Annales Médico Psychologiques*, *178*(6), 650–656. https://doi.org/10.1016/j.amp.2020.04.009

Eriacho, B. (2020). Considerations for psychedelic therapists when working with Native American people and communities. *Journal of Psychedelic Studies*, *4*(1), 69–71. https://doi.org/10.1556/2054.2019.030

Eubanks, C. F., Burckell, L. A., & Goldfried, M. R. (2018). Clinical consensus strategies to repair ruptures in the therapeutic alliance. *Journal of Psychotherapy Integration, 28*(1), 60–76. https://doi.org/10.1037/int0000097

Fisher, J. (2019). Sensorimotor psychotherapy in the treatment of trauma. *Practice Innovations, 4*(3), 156–165. https://doi.org/10.1037/pri0000096

Haijen, E. C. H. M., Kaelen, M., Roseman, L., Timmermann, C., Kettner, H., Russ, S., Nutt, D., Daws, R. E., Hampshire, A. D. G., Lorenz, R., & Carhart-Harris, R. L. (2018). Predicting responses to psychedelics: A prospective study. *Frontiers in Pharmacology, 9*, 897. https://doi.org/10.3389/fphar.2018.00897

Halstead, M., Reed, S., Krause, R., & Williams, M. T. (2021). Ketamine-assisted psychotherapy for PTSD related to experiences of racial discrimination. *Clinical Case Studies, 20*(4), 310–330. https://doi.org/10.1177/1534650121990894

Hays, P. A. (2009). Integrating evidence-based practice, cognitive-behavior therapy, and multicultural therapy: Ten steps for culturally competent practice. *Professional Psychology: Research and Practice, 40*(4), 354–360. https://doi.org/10.1037/a0016250

Hook, J. N., Davis, D. D., Owen, J., & DeBlaere, C. (2017). *Cultural humility: Engaging diverse identities in therapy.* American Psychological Association. https://doi.org/10.1037/0000037-000

López-Giménez, J. F., & González-Maeso, J. (2017). Hallucinogens and serotonin 5-HT$_{2A}$ receptor-mediated signaling pathways. In Halberstadt, A. L., Vollenweider, F. X., Nichols, D. E. (Eds.), *Behavioral neurobiology of psychedelic drugs. Current Topics in Behavioral Neurosciences, 36*, 45–73. Springer. https://doi.org/10.1007/7854_2017_478

Lu, J., Tjia, M., Mullen, B., Cao, B., Lukasiewicz, K., Shah-Morales, S., Weiser, S., Cameron, L. P., Olson, D. E., Chen, L., & Zuo, Y. (2021). An analog of psychedelics restores functional neural circuits disrupted by unpredictable stress. *Molecular Psychiatry, 26*(11), 6237–6252. https://doi.org/10.1038/s41380-021-01159-1

McLane, H., Hutchison, C., Wikler, D., Howell, T., & Knighton, E. (2021, December 22). Respecting autonomy in altered states: Navigating ethical quandaries in psychedelic therapy. *Forum: Journal of Medical Ethics.* https://blogs.bmj.com/medical-ethics/2021/12/22/respecting-autonomy-in-altered-states-navigating-ethical-quandaries-in-psychedelic-therapy/

Mendes, F. R., Costa, C. dos S., Wiltenburg, V. D., Morales-Lima, G., Fernandes, J. A. B., & Filev, R. (2022). Classic and non-classic psychedelics for substance use disorder: A review of their historic, past and current research. *Addiction Neuroscience, 3*, Article 100025. https://doi.org/10.1016/J.ADDICN.2022.100025

Nutt, D. J., King, L. A., & Nichols, D. E. (2013). Effects of Schedule I drug laws on neuroscience research and treatment innovation. *Nature Reviews Neuroscience, 14*(8), 577–585. https://doi.org/10.1038/nrn3530

Passie, T. (2018). The early use of MDMA ("Ecstasy") in psychotherapy (1977–1985). *Drug Science, Policy and Law, 4*, 1–19. https://doi.org/10.1177/2050324518767442

Redfern, E. E. (2023). *Transitioning to internal family systems therapy: A companion for therapists and practitioners.* Taylor & Francis Group.

Rønberg, M. T. (2019). Depression: Out-of-tune embodiment, loss of bodily resonance, and body work. *Medical Anthropology, 38*(4), 399–411. https://doi.org/10.1080/01459740.2018.1550754

Smith, D. T., Faber, S. C., Buchanan, N. T., Foster, D. & Green, L. (2022). The need for psychedelic-assisted therapy in the Black community and the burdens of its provision. *Frontiers in Psychiatry, 12*, Article 774736. https://doi.org/10.3389/fpsyt.2021.774736

Uthaug, M., Mason, N., Toennes, S., Reckweg, J., de Sousa Fernandes Perna, E., Kuypers, K., van Oorsouw, Riba, K., & Ramaekers, J. (2021). A placebo-controlled study of the effects of ayahuasca, set and setting on mental health of participants in ayahuasca group retreats. *Psychopharmacology, 238*(7), 1899–1910. https://doi.org/10.1007/s00213-021-05817-8

Williams, M. T., Reed, S., & George, J. (2020). Culture and psychedelic psychotherapy: Ethnic and racial themes from three Black women therapists. *Journal of Psychedelic Studies, 4*(3), 125–138. https://doi.org/10.1556/2054.2020.00137

Wolfson, P. (2019). Ketamine assisted psychotherapy (KAP): Patient demographics, clinical data and outcomes in three large practices administering ketamine with psychotherapy. *Journal of Psychoactive Drugs, 51*(2), 189–198. https://doi.org/10.1080/0279

References

Amada, N., & Shane, J. (2022). Self-actualization and the integration of psychedelic experience: The mediating role of perceived benefits to narrative self-functioning. *The Journal of Humanistic Psychology*. Advance online publication. https://doi.org/10.1177/00221678221099680

American Psychological Association. (2017). *Ethical principles of psychologists and code of conduct* (2002, Amended June 1, 2010, and January 1, 2017). https://www.apa.org/ethics/code/

Anderson, T., Ogles, B. M., Patterson, C. L., Lambert, M. J., & Vermeersch, D. A. (2009). Therapist effects: Facilitative interpersonal skills as a predictor of therapist success. *Journal of Clinical Psychology, 65*(7), 755–768. https://doi.org/10.1002/jclp.20583

Aponte, H. J., & Kissil, K. (Eds.). (2016). *The person of the therapist training model: Mastering the use of self*. Routledge. https://doi.org/10.4324/9781315719030

Arntz, A., & Jacob, G. (2017). *Schema therapy in practice: An introductory guide to the schema mode approach*. John Wiley & Sons.

Bailey, R. J., & Ogles, B. M. (2019, August 1). Common factors as a therapeutic approach: What is required? *Practice Innovations, 4*(4), 241–254. https://doi.org/10.1037/pri0000100

Banks, M. I., Zahid, Z., Jones, N. T., Sultan, Z. W., & Wenthur, C. J. (2021). Catalysts for change: The cellular neurobiology of psychedelics. *Molecular Biology of the Cell, 32*(12), 1135–1144. https://doi.org/10.1091/MBC.E20-05-0340

Barlow, D. H. (2010). Negative effects from psychological treatments: A perspective. *American Psychologist, 65*(1), 13–20. https://doi.org/10.1037/a0015643

Bathje, G. J., Majeski, E., & Kudowor, M. (2022). Psychedelic integration: An analysis of the concept and its practice. *Frontiers in Psychology, 13*, Article 824077. https://doi.org/10.3389/fpsyg.2022.824077

Baum, D. (2016, April). Legalize it all. *Harper's Magazine*. https://harpers.org/archive/2016/04/legalize-it-all/

Benner, P. E. (1984). *From novice to expert: Excellence and power in clinical nursing practice*. Addison-Wesley Nursing Division. https://doi.org/10.1097/00000446-198412000-00027

Bennett-Levy, J. (2019). Why therapists should walk the talk: The theoretical and empirical case for personal practice in therapist training and professional development. *Journal of Behavior Therapy and Experimental Psychiatry, 62*, 133–145. https://doi.org/10.1016/j.jbtep.2018.08.004

Bennett-Levy, J., & Finlay-Jones, A. (2018). The role of personal practice in therapist skill development: A model to guide therapists, educators, supervisors and researchers. *Cognitive Behaviour Therapy, 47*(3), 185–205. https://doi.org/10.1080/16506073.2018.1434678

Bohart, A. C., & Wade, A. G. (2013). The client in psychotherapy. In M. J. Lambert (Ed.), *Bergin and Garfield's handbook of psychotherapy and behavior change* (5th ed., pp. 13–43). John Wiley & Sons.

Breeksema, J. J., Kuin, B. W., Kamphuis, J., van den Brink, W., Vermetten, E., & Schoevers, R. (2022). Adverse events in clinical treatments with serotonergic psychedelics and MDMA: A mixed-methods systematic review. *Journal of Psychopharmacology*, *36*(10), 1100–1117. https://doi.org/10.1177/02698811221116926

Bugatti, M., & Boswell, J. F. (2016). Clinical errors as a lack of context responsiveness. *Psychotherapy*, *53*(3), 262–267. https://doi.org/10.1037/pst0000080

Carhart-Harris, R. L., & Nutt, D. J. (2017). Serotonin and brain function: A tale of two receptors. *Journal of Psychopharmacology*, *31*(9), 1091–1120. https://doi.org/10.1177/0269881117725915

Carhart-Harris, R. L., Roseman, L., Haijen, E., Erritzoe, D., Watts, R., Branchi, I., & Kaelen, M. (2018). Psychedelics and the essential importance of context. *Journal of Psychopharmacology*, *32*(7), 725–731. https://doi.org/10.1177/0269881118754710

Carlin, S. C., & Scheld, S. (2019, Spring). MAPS MDMA-Assisted Psychotherapy Code of Ethics [2021 update]. *Multidisciplinary Association of Psychedelic Studies Bulletin*, *29*(1). https://maps.org/news/bulletin/articles/436-maps-bulletin-spring-2019-vol-29,-no-1/7710-maps-mdma-assisted-psychotherapy-codeof-ethics-spring-2019

Castonguay, L. G., Goldfried, M. R., Wiser, S., Raue, P. J., & Hayes, A. M. (1996). Predicting the effect of cognitive therapy for depression: A study of unique and common factors. *Journal of Consulting and Clinical Psychology*, *64*(3), 497–504. https://doi.org/10.1037/0022-006X.64.3.497

Celidwen, Y., Redvers, N., Githaiga, C., Calambás, J., Añaños, K., Evanjuanoy Chindoy, M., Vitale, R., Rojas, J. N., Mondragón, D., Vázquez Rosalío, Y., & Sacbajá, A. (2023). Ethical principles of traditional Indigenous medicine to guide western psychedelic research and practice. *The Lancet Regional Health—Americas*, *18*, Article 100410. https://doi.org/10.1016/j.lana.2022.100410

Ching, T. H. W. (2020). Intersectional insights from an MDMA-assisted psychotherapy training trial: An open letter to racial/ethnic and sexual/gender minorities. *Journal of Psychedelic Studies*, *4*(1) 61–68. https://doi.org/10.1556/2054.2019.017

Coker, J. (1990). *How to practice jazz*. Jamey Aebersold.

Constantine, M. (2007). Racial microaggression against African American clients in cross-racial counseling relationships. *Journal of Counseling Psychology*, *54*(1), 1–16. https://doi.org/10.1037/0022-0167.54.1.1

Constantino, M. J., Castonguay, L. G., Zack, S., & DeGeorge, J. (2010). Engagement in psychotherapy: Factors contributing to the facilitation, demise, and restoration of the therapeutic alliance. In D. Castro-Blanco & M. S. Carver (Eds.), *Elusive alliance: Treatment engagement strategies with high-risk adolescents* (pp. 21–57). American Psychological Association. https://doi.org/10.1037/12139-001

Constantino, M. J., Vîslă, A., Coyne, A. E., & Boswell, J. F. (2018). A meta-analysis of the association between patients' early treatment outcome expectation and their posttreatment outcomes. *Psychotherapy*, *55*(4), 473–485. https://doi.org/10.1037/pst0000169

Cook, R. (2005). *It's about that time: Miles Davis on and off record*. Atlantic Books.

Corrigan, F., Fisher, J., & Nutt, D. (2011). Autonomic dysregulation and the window of tolerance model of the effects of complex emotional trauma. *Journal of Psychopharmacology*, *25*(1), 17–25. https://doi.org/10.1177/0269881109354930

Costandi, M. (2014). A brief history of psychedelic psychiatry. *The Psychologist*, *27*(9), 714–715.

Crowley, M., & Shulgin, A. (2019). *Secret drugs of Buddhism: Psychedelic sacraments and the origins of the Vajrayana*. Synergetic Press.

Csikszentmihalyi, M. (1997). *Finding flow: The psychology of engagement with everyday life*. HarperCollins.

Dames, S., Kryskow, P., & Watler, C. (2022). A cohort-based case report: The impact of ketamine-assisted therapy embedded in a community of practice framework for healthcare providers with PTSD and depression. *Frontiers in Psychiatry*, *12*, Article 803279. https://doi.org/10.3389/fpsyt.2021.803279

Danforth, A. (2009). Focusing-oriented psychotherapy as a supplement to preparation for psychedelic therapy. *The Journal of Transpersonal Psychology*, *41*(2), 151–181.

Davis, D. E., DeBlaere, C., Owen, J., Hook, J. N., Rivera, D. P., Choe, E., Van Tongeren, D. R., Worthington, E. L., & Placeres, V. (2018). The multicultural orientation framework: A narrative review. *Psychotherapy*, *55*(1), 89–100. https://doi.org/10.1037/pst0000160

Desmond, T. (2015). *Self-compassion in psychotherapy: Mindfulness-based practices for healing and transformation*. W. W. Norton.

de Vos, C. M. H., Mason, N. L., & Kuypers, K. P. C. (2021). Psychedelics and neuroplasticity: A systematic review unraveling the biological underpinnings of psychedelics. *Frontiers in Psychiatry*, *12*, Article 724606. https://doi.org/10.3389/fpsyt.2021.724606

Diament, M., Gomes, B. R., & Tófoli, L. F. (2021). Ayahuasca and psychotherapy: Beyond integration. In B. C. Labate & C. Cavnar (Eds.), *Ayahuasca healing and science*. Springer. https://doi.org/10.1007/978-3-030-55688-4_4

Dore, J., Turnipseed, B., Dwyer, S., Turnipseed, A., Andries, J., Ascani, G., Monnette, C., Huidekoper, A., Strauss, N., & Wolfson, P. (2019). Ketamine assisted psychotherapy (KAP): Patient demographics, clinical data and outcomes in three large practices administering ketamine with psychotherapy. *Journal of Psychoactive Drugs*, *51*(2), 189–198. https://doi.org/10.1080/02791072.2019.1587556

Dos Santos, R. G., Bouso, J. C., & Hallak, J. E. C. (2017). Ayahuasca, dimethyltryptamine, and psychosis: A systematic review of human studies. *Therapeutic Advances in Psychopharmacology*, *7*(4), 141–157. https://doi.org/10.1177/2045125316689030

Dyck, E. (2016). Peyote and psychedelics on the Canadian prairies. In B. C. Labate & C. Cavnar (Eds.), *Peyote: History, tradition, politics, and conservation* (pp. 151–170). Praeger/ABC-CLIO.

Elliott, R., & Greenberg, L. S. (1997). Multiple voices in process-experiential therapy: Dialogues between aspects of the self. *Journal of Psychotherapy Integration*, *7*(3), 225–239. https://doi.org/10.1037/h0101127

Ellis, M. V., Berger, L., Hanus, A. E., Ayala, E. E., Swords, B. A., & Siembor, M. (2014). Inadequate and harmful clinical supervision: Testing a revised framework and assessing occurrence. *The Counseling Psychologist*, *42*(4), 434–472. https://doi.org/10.1177/0011000013508656

Ericsson, K. A. (2003). Development of elite performance and deliberate practice: An update from the perspective of the expert performance approach. In J. L. Starkes & K. A. Ericsson (Eds.), *Expert performance in sports: Advances in research on sport expertise* (pp. 49–83). Human Kinetics.

Ericsson, K. A. (2004). Deliberate practice and the acquisition and maintenance in medicine and related domains: Invited address. *Academic Medicine*, *79*(10), S70–S81. https://doi.org/10.1097/00001888-200410001-00022

Ericsson, K. A. (2006). The influence of experience and deliberate practice on the development of superior expert performance. In K. A. Ericsson, N. Charness, P. J. Feltovich, & R. R. Hoffman (Eds.), *The Cambridge handbook of expertise and expert performance* (pp. 683–703). Cambridge University Press. https://doi.org/10.1017/CBO9780511816796.038

Ericsson, K. A., Hoffman, R. R., Kozbelt, A., & Williams, A. M. (Eds.). (2018). *The Cambridge handbook of expertise and expert performance* (2nd ed.). Cambridge University Press. https://doi.org/10.1017/9781316480748

Ericsson, K. A., Krampe, R. T., & Tesch-Römer, C. (1993). The role of deliberate practice in the acquisition of expert performance. *Psychological Review*, *100*(3), 363–406. https://doi.org/10.1037/0033-295X.100.3.363

Ericsson, K. A., & Pool, R. (2016). *Peak: Secrets from the new science of expertise*. Houghton Mifflin Harcourt.

Eubanks, C. F., Muran, J. C., & Safran, J. D. (2018). Repairing alliance ruptures. In J. C. Norcross & B. E. Wampold (Eds.), *Psychotherapy relationships that work: Evidence-based responsiveness* (3rd ed., pp. 549–579). Oxford University Press.

Eubanks-Carter, C., Muran, J. C., & Safran, J. D. (2015). Alliance-focused training. *Psychotherapy*, *52*(2), 169–173. https://doi.org/10.1037/a0037596

Evans, J., Robinson, O., Ketzitzidou-Argyri, E., Suseelan, S., Murphy-Beiner, A., & McAlpine, R. (2023). *Extended difficulties following the use of psychedelic drugs: A mixed methods study*. https://papers.ssrn.com/sol3/papers.cfm?abstract_id=4505228

Fadiman, J. (2011). *The psychedelic explorer's guide: Safe, therapeutic, and sacred journeys*. Park Street Press.

Fisher, J. (2017). *Healing the fragmented selves of trauma survivors: Overcoming internal self-alienation.* Taylor & Francis. https://doi.org/10.4324/9781315886169

Fisher, R. P., & Craik, F. I. M. (1977). Interaction between encoding and retrieval operations in cued recall. *Journal of Experimental Psychology: Human Learning and Memory, 3*(6), 701–711. https://doi.org/10.1037/0278-7393.3.6.701

Fogg, C., Michaels, T. I., de la Salle, S., Jahn, Z. W., & Williams, M. T. (2021). Ethnoracial health disparities and the ethnopsychopharmacology of psychedelic medicine. *Experimental and Clinical Psychopharmacology, 29*(5), 539–554. https://doi.org/10.1037/pha0000490

Fosha, D., Thoma, N., & Yeung, D. (2019). Transforming emotional suffering into flourishing: Metatherapeutic processing of positive affect as a trans-theoretical vehicle for change. *Counselling Psychology Quarterly, 32*(3–4), 563–593. https://doi.org/10.1080/09515070.2019.1642852

Frank, J. D., & Frank, J. B. (1991). *Persuasion and healing: A comparative study of psychotherapy* (3rd ed.). Johns Hopkins Press. https://doi.org/10.56021/9780801840678

Frymann, T., Whitney, S., Yaden, D. B., & Lipson, J. (2022). The Psychedelic Integration Scales: Tools for measuring psychedelic integration behaviors and experiences. *Frontiers in Psychology, 13*, Article 863247. https://doi.org/10.3389/fpsyg.2022.863247

Gilbert, P. (2010). *Compassion focused therapy: Distinctive features.* Routledge. https://doi.org/10.4324/9780203851197

Gladwell, M. (2008). *Outliers: The story of success.* Little, Brown & Company.

Goldberg, S., Rousmaniere, T. G., Miller, S. D., Whipple, J., Nielsen, S. L., Hoyt, W., & Wampold, B. E. (2016). Do psychotherapists improve with time and experience? A longitudinal analysis of outcomes in a clinical setting. *Journal of Counseling Psychology, 63*(1), 1–11. https://doi.org/10.1037/cou0000131

Goldman, R. N., & Greenberg, L. S. (2015). *Case formulation in emotion-focused therapy: Co-creating clinical maps for change.* American Psychological Association. https://doi.org/10.1037/14523-000

Goldman, R. N., Vaz, A., & Rousmaniere, T. (2021). *Deliberate practice in emotion-focused therapy.* American Psychological Association. https://doi.org/10.1037/0000227-000

Goldpaugh, D. D. (2022). Finding the divine within: Exploring the role of the sacred in psychedelic integration therapy for sexual trauma and dysfunction. *Sexual and Relationship Therapy, 37*(3), 314–323. https://doi.org/10.1080/14681994.2021.1994138

Goodwin, B. J., Coyne, A. E., & Constantino, M. J. (2018). Extending the context-responsive psychotherapy integration framework to cultural processes in psychotherapy. *Psychotherapy, 55*(1), 3–8. https://doi.org/10.1037/pst0000143

Goodyear, R. K. (2015). Using accountability mechanisms more intentionally: A framework and its implications for training professional psychologists. *American Psychologist, 70*(8), 736–743. https://doi.org/10.1037/a0039828

Goodyear, R. K., & Nelson, M. L. (1997). The major formats of psychotherapy supervision. In C. E. Watkins, Jr. (Ed.), *Handbook of psychotherapy supervision* (pp. 328–334). John Wiley & Sons.

Gorman, I., Nielson, E. M., Molinar, A., Cassidy, K., & Sabbagh, J. (2021). Psychedelic harm reduction and integration: A transtheoretical model for clinical practice. *Frontiers in Psychology, 12*, Article 645246. https://doi.org/10.3389/fpsyg.2021.645246

Greenberg, L. S., & Goldman, R. L. (1988). Training in experiential therapy. *Journal of Consulting and Clinical Psychology, 56*(5), 696–702. https://doi.org/10.1037/0022-006X.56.5.696

Greenberg, L. S., & Paivio, S. C. (2003). *Working with emotions in psychotherapy.* Guilford Press.

Greenberg, L. S., & Tomescu, L. R. (2017). *Supervision essentials for emotion-focused therapy.* American Psychological Association. https://doi.org/10.1037/15966-000

Griffiths, R. R., Richards, W. A., McCann, U., & Jesse, R. (2006). Psilocybin can occasion mystical-type experiences having substantial and sustained personal meaning and spiritual significance. *Psychopharmacology, 187*(3), 268–283. https://doi.org/10.1007/s00213-006-0457-5

Grof, S. (2000). *Psychology of the future: Lessons from modern consciousness research*. State University of New York Press.

Grof, S. (2008). Brief history of transpersonal psychology. *International Journal of Transpersonal Studies, 27*(1), 46–54. https://doi.org/10.24972/ijts.2008.27.1.46

Grof, S. (2019). *The way of the psychonaut: Vols. 1 and 2. Encyclopedia for inner journeys.* Multidisciplinary Association for Psychedelic Studies.

Haggerty, G., & Hilsenroth, M. J. (2011). The use of video in psychotherapy supervision. *British Journal of Psychotherapy, 27*(2), 193–210. https://doi.org/10.1111/j.1752-0118.2011.01232.x

Harner, M. (1990). *The way of the shaman*. HarperOne.

Harris, J., Jin, J., Hoffman, S., Phan, S., Prout, T. A., Rousmaniere, T., & Vaz, A. (2024). *Deliberate practice in multicultural therapy*. American Psychological Association. https://doi.org/10.1037/0000357-000

Harris, R. (2017). *Listening to ayahuasca: New hope for depression, addiction, PTSD, and anxiety*. New World Library.

Hart, C. (2022). *Drug use for grown-ups: Chasing liberty in the land of fear*. Penguin.

Hatcher, R. L. (2015). Interpersonal competencies: Responsiveness, technique, and training in psychotherapy. *American Psychologist, 70*(8), 747–757. https://doi.org/10.1037/a0039803

Henry, W. P., Strupp, H. H., Butler, S. F., Schacht, T. E., & Binder, J. L. (1993). Effects of training in time-limited dynamic psychotherapy: Changes in therapist behavior. *Journal of Consulting and Clinical Psychology, 61*(3), 434–440. https://doi.org/10.1037/0022-006X.61.3.434

Hill, C. E., Kivlighan, D. M. I. I. I., Rousmaniere, T., Kivlighan, D. M., Jr., Gerstenblith, J., & Hillman, J. (2020). Deliberate practice for the skill of immediacy: A multiple case study of doctoral student therapists and clients. *Psychotherapy, 57*(4), 587–597. https://doi.org/10.1037/pst0000247

Hill, C. E., & Knox, S. (2013). Training and supervision in psychotherapy: Evidence for effective practice. In M. J. Lambert (Ed.), *Handbook of psychotherapy and behavior change* (6th ed., pp. 775–811). John Wiley & Sons.

Hook, J. N., Davis, D., Owen, J., & DeBlaere, C. (2017). *Cultural humility: Engaging diverse identities in therapy*. American Psychological Association. https://doi.org/10.1037/0000037-000

Hook, J. N., Davis, D. E., Owen, J., Worthington, E. L., Jr., & Utsey, S. O. (2013). Cultural humility: Measuring openness to culturally diverse clients. *Journal of Counseling Psychology, 60*(3), 353–366. https://doi.org/10.1037/a0032595

Horton, D. M., Morrison, B., & Schmidt, J. (2021). Systematized review of psychotherapeutic components of psilocybin-assisted psychotherapy. *American Journal of Psychotherapy, 74*(4), 140–149. https://doi.org/10.1176/appi.psychotherapy.20200055

Jung, C. (1979). *Aion: Researches into the phenomenology of the self*. Princeton University Press.

Kellogg, S., & Garcia Torres, A. (2021). Toward a chairwork psychotherapy: Using the four dialogues for healing and transformation. *Practice Innovations, 6*(3), 171–180. https://doi.org/10.1037/pri0000149

Kendall, P. C., & Beidas, R. S. (2007). Smoothing the trail for dissemination of evidence-based practices for youth: Flexibility within fidelity. *Professional Psychology, Research and Practice, 38*(1), 13–20. https://doi.org/10.1037/0735-7028.38.1.13

Kendall, P. C., & Frank, H. E. (2018). Implementing evidence-based treatment protocols: Flexibility within fidelity. *Clinical Psychology: Science and Practice, 25*(4), Article e12271. https://doi.org/10.1111/cpsp.12271

Kirsch, I. (1990). *Changing expectations: A key to effective psychotherapy*. Thomson Brooks/Cole Publishing Co.

Kirsch, I. (1997). Response expectancy theory and application: A decennial review. *Applied & Preventive Psychology, 6*(2), 69–79. https://doi.org/10.1016/S0962-1849(05)80012-5

Kirst, P. F. (2022). Compassionate witnessing. *Psychological Perspectives, 65*(1), 1–4. https://doi.org/10.1080/00332925.2022.2081469

Knight, C. (2019). Trauma informed practice and care: Implications for field instruction. *Clinical Social Work Journal*, *47*(1), 79–89. https://doi.org/10.1007/s10615-018-0661-x

Koziol, L. F., & Budding, D. E. (2012). Procedural learning. In N. M. Seel (Ed.), *Encyclopedia of the sciences of learning* (pp. 2694–2696). Springer. https://doi.org/10.1007/978-1-4419-1428-6_670

Kuhfuß, M., Maldei, T., Hetmanek, A., & Baumann, N. (2021). Somatic experiencing—Effectiveness and key factors of a body-oriented trauma therapy: A scoping literature review. *European Journal of Psychotraumatology*, *12*(1), 1929023. https://doi.org/10.1080/20008198.2021.1929023

Lambert, M. J. (2010). Yes, it is time for clinicians to monitor treatment outcome. In B. L. Duncan, S. C. Miller, B. E. Wampold, & M. A. Hubble (Eds.), *Heart and soul of change: Delivering what works in therapy* (2nd ed., pp. 239–266). American Psychological Association. https://doi.org/10.1037/12075-008

Lambert, M. J., & Ogles, B. M. (2004). The efficacy and effectiveness of psychotherapy. In M. J. Lambert (Ed.), *Bergin and Garfield's handbook of psychotherapy and behaviour change* (5th ed., pp. 139–193). John Wiley & Sons.

Levenson, H., Gay, V., & Binder, J. L. (2023). *Deliberate practice in psychodynamic psychotherapy*. American Psychological Association. https://doi.org/10.1037/0000351-000

Little, R. (2020). Boundary applications and violations: Clinical interpretations in a transference-countertransference-focused psychotherapy. *Transactional Analysis Journal*, *50*(3), 221–235. https://doi.org/10.1080/03621537.2020.1771031

Luoma, J. B., Chwyl, C., Bathje, G. J., Davis, A. K., & Lancelotta, R. (2020). A meta-analysis of placebo-controlled trials of psychedelic assisted therapy. *Journal of Psychoactive Drugs*, *52*(4), 289–299. https://doi.org/10.1080/02791072.2020.1769878

Lutkajtis, A., & Evans, J. (2023). Psychedelic integration challenges: Participant experiences after a psilocybin truffle retreat in the Netherlands. *Journal of Psychedelic Studies*, *6*(3), 211–221. https://doi.org/10.1556/2054.2022.00232

Malcolm, B., & Thomas, K. (2022). Serotonin toxicity of serotonergic psychedelics. *Psychopharmacology*, *239*(6), 1881–1891. https://doi.org/10.1007/s00213-021-05876-x

Mangini, M. (1998). Treatment of alcoholism using psychedelic drugs: A review of the program of research. *Journal of Psychoactive Drugs*, *30*(4), 381–418. https://doi.org/10.1080/02791072.1998.10399714

Mans, K., Kettner, H., Erritzoe, D., Haijen, E. C. H. M., Kaelen, M., & Carhart-Harris, R. L. (2021). Sustained, multifaceted improvements in mental well-being following psychedelic experiences in a prospective opportunity sample. *Frontiers in Psychiatry*, *12*, Article 647909. https://doi.org/10.3389/fpsyt.2021.647909

Markman, K. D., & Tetlock, P. E. (2000). Accountability and close-call counterfactuals: The loser who nearly won and the winner who nearly lost. *Personality and Social Psychology Bulletin*, *26*(10), 1213–1224. https://doi.org/10.1177/0146167200262004

Marks, M. (2021). A strategy for rescheduling psilocybin. *Scientific American*. https://www.scientificamerican.com/article/a-strategy-for-rescheduling-psilocybin/

Maté, G. (2011). *When the body says no: The cost of hidden stress*. Vintage Canada.

McConnaughy, E. A. (1987). The person of the therapist in psychotherapeutic practice. *Psychotherapy*, *24*(3), 303–314. https://doi.org/10.1037/h0085720

McGaghie, W. C., Issenberg, S. B., Barsuk, J. H., & Wayne, D. B. (2014). A critical review of simulation-based mastery learning with translational outcomes. *Medical Education*, *48*(4), 375–385. https://doi.org/10.1111/medu.12391

McKenna, T. (1993). *Food of the gods: The search for the original tree of knowledge a radical history of plants, drugs, and human evolution*. Bantam.

McLeod, J. (2017). Qualitative methods for routine outcome measurement. In T. Rousmaniere, R. Goodyear, S. D. Miller, & B. E. Wampold (Eds.), *The cycle of excellence: Using deliberate practice to improve supervision and training* (pp. 99–122). Wiley. https://doi.org/10.1002/9781119165590.ch5

McWilliams, N. (2004). *Psychoanalytic psychotherapy: A practitioner's guide*. Guilford Press.

Metzner, R. (2015). *Allies for awakening*. Regent Press.

Michaels, T. I., Purdon, J., Collins, A., & Williams, M. T. (2018). Inclusion of people of color in psychedelic-assisted psychotherapy: A review of the literature. *BMC Psychiatry*, *18*(245), Article 245. https://doi.org/10.1186/s12888-018-1824-6

Mithoefer, M. C., Grob, C. S., & Brewerton, T. D. (2016). Novel psychopharmacological therapies for psychiatric disorders: Psilocybin and MDMA. *The Lancet Psychiatry*, *3*(5), 481–488. https://doi.org/10.1016/S2215-0366(15)00576-3

Mohr, D. C. (1995). Negative outcome in psychotherapy: A critical review. *Clinical Psychology*, *2*(1), 1–27. https://doi.org/10.1111/j.1468-2850.1995.tb00022.x

Muraresku, B. C. (2020). *The immortality key: The secret history of the religion with no name*. St. Martin's Press.

Murphy, R., Kettner, H., Zeifman, R., Giribaldi, B., Kartner, L., Martell, J., Read, T., Murphy-Beiner, A., Baker-Jones, M., Nutt, D., Erritzoe, D., Watts, R., & Carhart-Harris, R. (2022). Therapeutic alliance and rapport modulate responses to psilocybin assisted therapy for depression. *Frontiers in Pharmacology*, *12*, Article 788155. https://doi.org/10.3389/fphar.2021.788155

Naranjo, C. (1973/2013). *The healing journey: Pioneering approaches to psychedelic therapy* (2nd ed.). Multidisciplinary Association for Psychedelic Studies.

Neff, K. (2011). *Self-compassion: The proven power of being kind to yourself*. Hachette UK.

Neitzke-Spruill, L. (2020). Race as a component of set and setting: How experiences of race can influence psychedelic experiences. *Journal of Psychedelic Studies*, *1*(4), 51–60. https://doi.org/10.1556/2054.2019.022

Nichols, D. E. (2016). Psychedelics. *Pharmacological Reviews*, *68*(2), 264–355. https://doi.org/10.1124/pr.115.011478

Nichols, D. E., Johnson, M. W., & Nichols, C. D. (2017). Psychedelics as medicines: An emerging new paradigm. *Clinical Pharmacology and Therapeutics*, *101*(2), 209–219. https://doi.org/10.1002/cpt.557

Nielson, E. M., & Guss, J. (2018). The influence of therapists' first-hand experience with psychedelics on psychedelic-assisted psychotherapy research and therapist training. *Journal of Psychedelic Studies*, *2*(2), 64–73. https://doi.org/10.1556/2054.2018.009

Norcross, J. C., & Guy, J. D. (2005). The prevalence and parameters of personal therapy in the United States. In J. D. Geller, J. C. Norcross, & D. E. Orlinsky (Eds.), *The psychotherapist's own psychotherapy: Patient and clinician perspectives* (pp. 165–176). Oxford University Press.

Norcross, J. C., Lambert, M. J., & Wampold, B. E. (2019). *Psychotherapy relationships that work* (3rd ed.). Oxford University Press.

Nutt, D. (2022). *Drugs without the hot air: Making sense of legal and illegal drugs*. Green Books.

Nutt, D., & Carhart-Harris, R. (2021). The current status of psychedelics in psychiatry. *JAMA Psychiatry*, *78*(2), 121–122. https://doi.org/10.1001/jamapsychiatry.2020.2171

Ogden, P., & Fisher, J. (2015). *Sensorimotor psychotherapy: Interventions for trauma and attachment*. W. W. Norton.

Oram, M. (2014). Efficacy and enlightenment: LSD psychotherapy and the Drug Amendments of 1962. *Journal of the History of Medicine and Allied Sciences*, *69*(2), 221–250. https://doi.org/10.1093/jhmas/jrs050

Oregon Psilocybin Evidence Review Writing Group. (2021). *Oregon Psilocybin Advisory Board rapid evidence review and recommendations*. https://www.oregon.gov/oha/PH/PREVENTIONWELLNESS/Documents/Psilocybin%20evidence%20report%20to%20OHA%206-30-21_Submitted.pdf

Orlinsky, D. E., Rønnestad, M. H., & Collaborative Research Network of the Society for Psychotherapy Research. (2005). *How psychotherapists develop: A study of therapeutic work and professional growth*. American Psychological Association. https://doi.org/10.1037/11157-000

Owen, J., & Hilsenroth, M. J. (2014). Treatment adherence: The importance of therapist flexibility in relation to therapy outcomes. *Journal of Counseling Psychology*, *61*(2), 280–288. https://doi.org/10.1037/a0035753

Pilecki, B., Luoma, J. B., Bathje, G. J., Rhea, J., & Narloch, V. F. (2021). Ethical and legal issues in psychedelic harm reduction and integration therapy. *Harm Reduction Journal*, *18*(1), 40. https://doi.org/10.1186/s12954-021-00489-1

Prasko, J., Ociskova, M., Vanek, J., Burkauskas, J., Slepecky, M., Bite, I., Krone, I., Sollar, T., & Juskiene, A. (2022). Managing transference and countertransference in cognitive behavioral supervision: Theoretical framework and clinical application. *Psychology Research and Behavior Management*, *15*, 2129–2155. https://doi.org/10.2147/PRBM.S369294

Prescott, D. S., Maeschalck, C. L., & Miller, S. D. (Eds.). (2017). *Feedback-informed treatment in clinical practice: Reaching for excellence*. American Psychological Association. https://doi.org/10.1037/0000039-000

Rea, K., & Wallace, B. (2021). Enhancing equity-oriented care in psychedelic medicine: Utilizing the EQUIP framework. *International Journal on Drug Policy*, *98*, Article 103429. https://doi.org/10.1016/j.drugpo.2021.103429

Richards, B. (2015). *Sacred knowledge: Psychedelics and religious experiences*. Columbia University Press. https://doi.org/10.7312/columbia/9780231174060.001.0001

Rochester, J., Vallely, A., Grof, P., Williams, M., Chang, H., & Caldwell, K. (2022). Entheogens and psychedelics in Canada: Proposal for a new paradigm. *Canadian Psychology*, *63*(3), 413–430. https://doi.org/10.1037/cap0000285

Roseman, L., Nutt, D. J., & Carhart-Harris, R. L. (2018). Quality of acute psychedelic experience predicts therapeutic efficacy of psilocybin for treatment-resistant depression. *Frontiers in Pharmacology*, *8*, Article 974. https://doi.org/10.3389/fphar.2017.00974

Rosenberg, M. B. (2015). *Nonviolent communication: A language of life* (3rd ed.). PuddleDancer.

Rousmaniere, T. (2016). *Deliberate practice for psychotherapists: A guide to improving clinical effectiveness*. Routledge. https://doi.org/10.4324/9781315472256

Rousmaniere, T. (2019). *Mastering the inner skills of psychotherapy: A deliberate practice manual*. Gold Lantern Books.

Rousmaniere, T., Goodyear, R., Miller, S. D., & Wampold, B. E. (Eds.). (2017). *The cycle of excellence: Using deliberate practice to improve supervision and training*. John Wiley & Sons. https://doi.org/10.1002/9781119165590

Rousseau, D. (2015). General systems theory: Its present and potential. *Systems Research and Behavioral Science*, *32*(5), 522–533. https://doi.org/10.1002/sres.2354

Rush, B., Marcus, O., Shore, R., Cunningham, L., Thompson, N., & Rideout, K. (2022). *Psychedelic medicine: A rapid review of therapeutic applications and implications for future research*. Homewood Research Institute. https://hriresearch.com/research/exploratory-research/research-reports/

Ryan, W., & Bennett, R. (2020). Ethical guidelines for ketamine clinicians. *The Journal of Psychedelic Psychiatry*, *2*(4), 19–23.

Safran, J. D. (2012). *Psychoanalysis and psychoanalytic therapies*. American Psychological Association.

Safran, J. D., & Muran, J. C. (2000). *Negotiating the therapeutic alliance: A relational treatment guide*. Guilford Press.

Schenberg, E. E. (2018). Psychedelic-assisted psychotherapy: A paradigm shift in psychiatric research and development. *Frontiers in Pharmacology*, *9*, Article 733. https://doi.org/10.3389/fphar.2018.00733

Schlag, A. K., Aday, J., Salam, I., Neill, J. C., & Nutt, D. J. (2022). Adverse effects of psychedelics: From anecdotes and misinformation to systematic science. *Journal of Psychopharmacology*, *36*(3), 258–272. https://doi.org/10.1177/02698811211069100

Schultz, R. E., Hoffman, A., & Rätsch, C. (2011). *Plants of the gods: Their sacred, healing, and hallucinogenic powers*. Healing Arts Press.

Schwartz, R. C., & Sweezy, M. (2019). *Internal family systems therapy*. Guilford Press.

Shapiro, A. K., & Shapiro, E. S. (1997). *The powerful placebo: From ancient priest to modern medicine*. Johns Hopkins University Press. https://doi.org/10.1353/book.3471

Shulgin, A. (2019). *The shadow: Transcription of a talk by Ann Shulgin at the 2019 Women's Congress*. https://visionarycongress.org/articles/wvc-articles/the-shadow-transcription-of-a-talk-by-ann-shulgin-at-the-2019-womens-congress-r6/

Shulgin, A., & Shulgin, A. (1990). *PIHKAL: A chemical love story*. Transform Press.

Shulgin, A., & Shulgin, A. (2002). *TIHKAL: The continuation*. Transform Press.

Sloshower, J., Guss, J., Krause, R., Wallace, R., Williams, M., Reed, S., & Skinta, M. (2020). Psilocybin-assisted therapy of major depressive disorder using acceptance and commitment therapy as a therapeutic frame. *Journal of Contextual Behavioral Science, 15*, 12–19. https://doi.org/10.31234/osf.io/u6v9y

Smith, D. T., Faber, S. C., Buchanan, N. T., Foster, D., & Green, L. (2022). The need for psychedelic-assisted therapy in the Black community and the burdens of its provision. *Frontiers in Psychiatry, 12*, Article 774736. https://doi.org/10.3389/fpsyt.2021.774736

Smith, H. (1964). Do drugs have religious import? *The Journal of Philosophy, 61*(18), 517–530. https://doi.org/10.2307/2023494

Squire, L. R. (2004). Memory systems of the brain: A brief history and current perspective. *Neurobiology of Learning and Memory, 82*(3), 171–177. https://doi.org/10.1016/j.nlm.2004.06.005

Statistics Canada. (2017, January 25). Immigration and diversity: Population projections for Canada and its regions, 2011 to 2036. Minister of Industry (Catalogue no. 91-551-X). https://www150.statcan.gc.ca/n1/en/pub/91-551-x/91-551-x2017001-eng.pdf?st=6Tuw3nWi

Stiles, W. B., Honos-Webb, L., & Surko, M. (1998). Responsiveness in psychotherapy. *Clinical Psychology: Science and Practice, 5*(4), 439–458. https://doi.org/10.1111/j.1468-2850.1998.tb00166.x

Stiles, W. B., & Horvath, A. O. (2017). Appropriate responsiveness as a contribution to therapist effects. In L. G. Castonguay & C. E. Hill (Eds.), *How and why are some therapists better than others? Understanding therapist effects* (pp. 71–84). American Psychological Association. https://doi.org/10.1037/0000034-005

Stolaroff, M. J. (1994). *Thanatos to Eros: 35 years of psychedelic exploration ethnomedicine and the study of consciousness*. Thaneros Press.

Stolaroff, M. J. (2020). *The secret chief revealed*. Albatross.

Strauss, D., de la Salle, S., Sloshower, J., & Williams, M. T. (2021). Research abuses against people of colour in psychedelic research. *Journal of Medical Ethics*. Advance online publication. https://doi.org/10.1136/medethics-2021-107262

Sue, D. W., & Sue, D. (2017). *Counseling the culturally diverse: Theory and practice*. John Wiley & Sons.

Suszek, H., Wegner, E., & Maliszewski, N. (2015). Transference and its usefulness in psychotherapy in the light of empirical evidence. *Annals of Psychology, 18*, 345–380. https://doi.org/10.18290/rpsych.2015.18.3-4en

Swift, J. K., & Greenberg, R. P. (2015). Foster the therapeutic alliance. In J. K. Swift & R. P. Greenberg (Eds.), *Premature termination in psychotherapy: Strategies for engaging clients and improving outcomes* (pp. 137–147). American Psychological Association. https://doi.org/10.1037/14469-010

Talia, A., Muzi, L., Lingiardi, V., & Taubner, S. (2020). How to be a secure base: Therapists' attachment representations and their link to attunement in psychotherapy. *Attachment & Human Development, 22*(2), 189–206. https://doi.org/10.1080/14616734.2018.1534247

Tapia, H. R. C., Guzmán, M. A. G., & Ortiz, S. A. C. (2021). Ayahuasca-induced psychosis: A case report. *Revista Colombiana de Psiquiatria*. Advance online publication. https://doi.org/10.1016/j.rcp.2020.11.014

Taylor, J. M., & Neimeyer, G. J. (2017). Lifelong professional improvement: The evolution of continuing education. In T. G. Rousmaniere, R. Goodyear, S. D. Miller, & B. Wampold (Eds.), *The cycle of excellence: Using deliberate practice to improve supervision and training* (pp. 219–248). Wiley-Blackwell.

Teixeira, P. J., Johnson, M. W., Timmermann, C., Watts, R., Erritzoe, D., Douglass, H., Kettner, H., & Carhart-Harris, R. L. (2022). *Psychedelics and health behaviour change*. Sage Publications. https://doi.org/10.1177/02698811211008554

Tracey, T. J. G., Wampold, B. E., Goodyear, R. K., & Lichtenberg, J. W. (2015). Improving expertise in psychotherapy. *Psychotherapy Bulletin, 50*(1), 7–13.

U.S. Census Bureau. (2014). *Non-Hispanic Whites may no longer comprise over 50 percent of the U.S. population by 2044*. https://www.census.gov/content/dam/Census/newsroom/releases/2015/cb15-tps16_graphic.pdf

U.S. Drug Enforcement Administration. (n.d.). *Drug scheduling*. https://www.dea.gov/drug-information/drug-scheduling

U.S. Food and Drug Administration. (n.d.). *Breakthrough therapies*. https://www.fda.gov/patients/fast-track-breakthrough-therapy-accelerated-approval-priority-review/breakthrough-therapy

Vaid, G., & Walker, B. (2022). Psychedelic psychotherapy: Building wholeness through connection. *Global Advances in Health and Medicine, 11*, Article 2164957X221081113. https://doi.org/10.1177/2164957X221081113

van der Kolk, B. (2015). *The body keeps the score: Mind, brain and body in the transformation of trauma*. Penguin Random House.

Vollenweider, F. X., & Kometer, M. (2010). The neurobiology of psychedelic drugs: Implications for the treatment of mood disorders. *Nature Reviews: Neuroscience, 11*(9), 642–651. https://doi.org/10.1038/nrn2884

Walser, R. D., Coulter, C., Hayes, S. C., & O'Connell, M. (2019). *The heart of ACT: Developing a flexible, process-based, and client-centered practice using acceptance and commitment therapy*. Context Press.

Walsh, Z., & Thiessen, M. S. (2018). Psychedelics and the new behaviourism: Considering the integration of third-wave behaviour therapies with psychedelic-assisted therapy. *International Review of Psychiatry, 30*(4), 343–349. https://doi.org/10.1080/09540261.2018.1474088

Wass, R., & Golding, C. (2014). Sharpening a tool for teaching: The zone of proximal development. *Teaching in Higher Education, 19*(6), 671–684. https://doi.org/10.1080/13562517.2014.901958

Watts, R., & Luoma, J. B. (2020). The use of the psychological flexibility model to support psychedelic assisted therapy. *Journal of Contextual Behavioral Science, 15*, 92–102. https://doi.org/10.1016/j.jcbs.2019.12.004

Weingarten, K. (2003). *Compassionate witnessing and the transformation of societal violence: How individuals can make a difference*. https://www.humiliationstudies.org/documents/WeingartenCompassionateWitnessing.pdf

Whitfield, H. J. (2021). A spectrum of selves reinforced in multilevel coherence: A contextual behavioural response to the challenges of psychedelic-assisted therapy development. *Frontiers in Psychiatry, 12*, Article 727572. https://doi.org/10.3389/fpsyt.2021.727572 [Erratum in *Frontiers in Psychiatry*, 2021, *12*, Article 832766]

Wießner, I., Falchi, M., Palhano-Fontes, F., Feilding, A., Ribeiro, S., & Tófoli, L. F. (2023). LSD, madness and healing: Mystical experiences as possible link between psychosis model and therapy model. *Psychological Medicine, 53*(4), 1151–1165. https://doi.org/10.1017/S0033291721002531

Williams, M. L., Korevaar, D., Harvey, R., Fitzgerald, P. B., Liknaitzky, P., O'Carroll, S., Puspanathan, P., Ross, M., Strauss, N., & Bennett-Levy, J. (2021). Translating psychedelic therapies from clinical trials to community clinics: Building bridges and addressing potential challenges ahead. *Frontiers in Psychiatry, 12*, Article 737738. https://doi.org/10.3389/fpsyt.2021.737738

Williams, M. T. (2020). *Managing microaggressions: Addressing everyday racism in therapeutic spaces*. Oxford University Press. https://doi.org/10.1093/med-psych/9780190875237.001.0001

Williams, M. T., Chapman, L. K., Wong, J., & Turkheimer, E. (2012, August 30). The role of ethnic identity in symptoms of anxiety and depression in African Americans. *Psychiatry Research, 199*(1), 31–36. https://doi.org/10.1016/j.psychres.2012.03.049

Williams, M. T., Duque, G., Wetterneck, C. T., Chapman, L. K., & DeLapp, R. C. T. (2018, April). Ethnic identity and regional differences in mental health in a national sample of African American young adults. *Journal of Racial and Ethnic Health Disparities, 5*(2), 312–321. https://doi.org/10.1007/s40615-017-0372-y

Williams, M. T., Reed, S., & Aggarwal, R. (2020). Culturally informed research design issues in a study for MDMA-assisted psychotherapy for posttraumatic stress disorder. *Journal of Psychedelic Studies*, 4(1), 40–50. https://doi.org/10.1556/2054.2019.016

Williams, M. T., Reed, S., & George, J. (2021). Culture and psychedelic psychotherapy: Ethnic and racial themes from three Black women therapists. *Journal of Psychedelic Studies*, 4(3), 125–138. https://doi.org/10.1556/2054.2020.00137

Winkler, P., & Csémy, L. (2014). Self-experimentations with psychedelics among mental health professionals: LSD in the former Czechoslovakia. *Journal of Psychoactive Drugs*, 46(1), 11–19. https://doi.org/10.1080/02791072.2013.873158

Winkler, P., Gorman, I., & Kocárová, R. (2016). Use of LSD by mental health professionals. *Neuropathology of Drug Addictions and Substance Misuse*, 2, 773–781. https://doi.org/10.1016/B978-0-12-800212-4.00072-8

Wolff, M., Evens, R., Mertens, L. J., Koslowski, M., Betzler, F., Gründer, G., & Jungaberle, H. (2020). Learning to let go: A cognitive-behavioral model of how psychedelic therapy promotes acceptance. *Frontiers in Psychiatry*, 11, 5. https://doi.org/10.3389/fpsyt.2020.00005

Zaretskii, V. (2009). The zone of proximal development: What Vygotsky did not have time to write. *Journal of Russian & East European Psychology*, 47(6), 70–93. https://doi.org/10.2753/RPO1061-0405470604

Zarley, B. D. (2019, October 12). Take a trip to Johns Hopkins' new psychedelic research center. *Freethink*. https://www.freethink.com/health/studying-psychedelic-research-johns-hopkins

Index

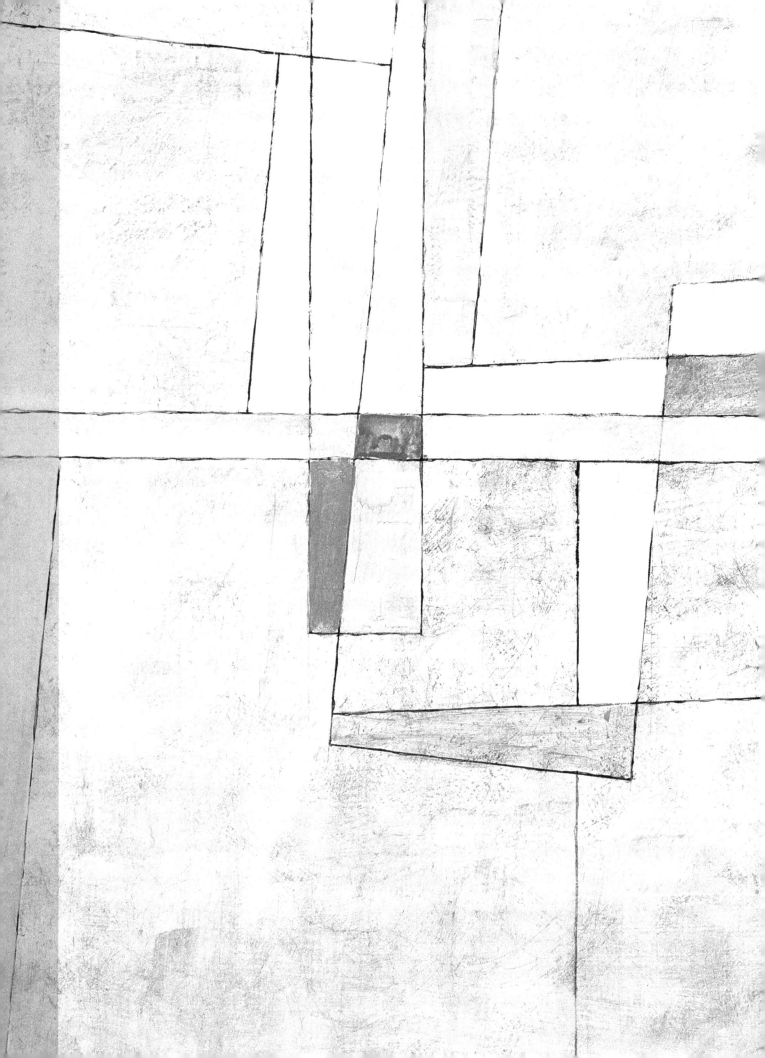

About the Authors

Shannon Dames, RN, MPH, EdD, serves as the chair of the Psychedelic-Assisted Therapy Programming at Vancouver Island University, in Nanaimo, British Columbia. She has served as a nurse for 2 decades. She is a published author with expertise in nursing practice, resilience development, and psychedelic-assisted therapy research and education. Dr. Dames works across agencies and disciplines to develop collaborative service delivery, education, and research in psychedelic medicine. Her current work focuses on the development of equity and culturally informed service delivery, research, and education infrastructure in the field of psychedelic-assisted therapy. Her work acknowledges multiple ways of knowing, with a specific interest in collaborating to understand how Western and Indigenous ways of knowing might be shared for the healing benefit of all.

Andrew Penn, MS, PMHNP, is a clinical professor of nursing at the University of California–San Francisco (UCSF), where he teaches psychopharmacology and clinical psychiatry. Additionally, he is an attending nurse practitioner at the San Francisco Veterans Administration Hospital and a researcher on psychedelic therapy studies at the Translational Psychedelic Research Program (TrPR lab) at UCSF. He has taught around the world, including South by Southwest, Aspen Health Ideas Festival, TEDx, and the Singapore Ministry of Health. As a cofounder of the Organization of Psychedelic and Entheogenic Nurses (https://www.OPENurses.org), he has advocated for and written about the perspective of nursing in psychedelic therapy in the *American Journal of Nursing* and the *Journal of Humanistic Psychology*. He can be found at https://www.andrewpennnp.com.

Monnica Williams, PhD, is a board-certified, licensed clinical psychologist, specializing in cognitive behavior therapies. She is a full tenured professor in the School of Psychology at the University of Ottawa, Canada Research Chair in Mental Health Disparities, and director of the Laboratory for Culture and Mental Health Disparities. She is the clinical director of the Behavioral Wellness Clinic in Connecticut and Behavioural Wellness Clinic in Ottawa. She has also founded outpatient clinics in Kentucky, Virginia, and Pennsylvania. Dr. Williams started her career as an assistant professor at the University of Pennsylvania School of Medicine in the Department of Psychiatry (2007–2011), where she worked with Dr. Edna Foa, an international authority on obsessive–compulsive disorder and posttraumatic stress disorder. She was also director of the Center for Mental Health Disparities at the University of Louisville in Psychological and Brain Sciences (2011–2016). At the University of Connecticut (2016–2019), she had appointments in psychological science and psychiatry.

Joseph A. Zamaria, PsyD, ABPP, is a licensed and board-certified clinical psychologist and an associate clinical professor of psychiatry and behavioral sciences at the University of California–San Francisco (UCSF) School of Medicine, where he is the associate program director for psychotherapy for the UCSF psychiatry residency and an attending psychologist in UCSF's outpatient psychiatry clinics. At UCSF, Dr. Zamaria has worked for years as a therapist and researcher in clinical trials of psychedelic-assisted therapy to treat a range of conditions. Additionally, he is on the faculty at the University of California–Berkeley within the Berkeley Center for the Science of Psychedelics, where he directs the psychotherapy and clinical science curricula.

Tony Rousmaniere, PsyD, is cofounder and program director of Sentio University and the Sentio Counseling Center, Los Angeles, California. He provides workshops, webinars, and advanced clinical training and supervision to clinicians around the world. Dr. Rousmaniere is the author or coeditor of more than a dozen books on deliberate practice and psychotherapy training. In 2017, he published the widely cited article "What Your Therapist Doesn't Know" in *The Atlantic*. He supports the open-data movement and publishes his aggregated clinical outcome data, in deidentified form, on his website (https://drtonyr.com). Dr. Rousmaniere is president of Division 29 of the American Psychological Association (Society for the Advancement of Psychotherapy).

Alexandre Vaz, PhD, is cofounder and chief academic officer of Sentio University and the Sentio Counseling Center, Los Angeles, California. He provides workshops, webinars, and advanced clinical training and supervision to clinicians around the world. Dr. Vaz is the author or coeditor of more than a dozen books on deliberate practice and psychotherapy training. He has held multiple committee roles for the Society for the Exploration of Psychotherapy Integration and the Society for Psychotherapy Research. Dr. Vaz is founder and host of "Psychotherapy Expert Talks," an acclaimed interview series with distinguished psychotherapists and therapy researchers.